Advance Praise for *Origi*

"For peace and harmony to prevail, the truth must be told. We are instructed never to take hope from the people."

> **—OREN LYONS**
> Faithkeeper of the Turtle Clan of the Onondaga Nation
> Author of *Exiled in the Land of the Free: Democracy, Indian Nations, and the US Constitution*

"Parry's richly-textured book holds out hope and guidance for this moment of political conflict over diversity amid fear for the continuation of life on the planet. Inviting us to see how this challenge is the stimulus to transform the conflict into unity of purpose, the author provides us with a roadmap for how to do it through a new worldview that reestablishes an Indigenous connection with the natural world. This worldview privileges place over time, relationship over product, and revalues the feminine, enabling us to rebalance culturally and ensure the survival of life on the planet."

> **—SALLY ROESCH WAGNER**
> Founding director of the Matilda Joslyn Gage Foundation
> Author of *Sisters in Spirit: Haudenosaunee Influence on Early American Feminists* and *The Women's Suffrage Movement*

"Thank you, thank you, Niawen (in Mohawk), K'olabal (in Maya Tzotzil), muchas gracias, merci beaucoup, to you. If all 'white' people held such a deep consciousness for Natives as you do, the world would already be truly blessed and sacred. There is no way one can stay neutral when reading you, I'm crying, I'm touched, shaking and totally stirred up!!! This is all so good in spirit."

> **—OHKI SIMINE FOREST** (Canadian Mohawk)
> Author of *Dreaming the Council Ways*, is a vision-holder and spiritual teacher

"Some people are aware of the impact Native cultures had on the development of the US. The vast majority are not. *Original Politics* finds a unique way of telling the true story."

— HARLAN MCKOSATO (Sac and Fox Nation)
Former long-time host of the nationally syndicated radio show
Native America Calling

"In a fractured time when a rude politics of nationalism rides in the high saddle as the climate crisis and many other environmental problems demand effective international co-operation, the world *needs* Glenn Aparicio Parry's *Original Politics: Making America Sacred Again*. Engagingly written, mixing the best of the past and present, the indigenous and immigrant, appreciating everyone's beauty: that is how we forge a sustainable future. Parry traces a path. Life on Earth will be better if everyone— *everyone*, regardless of race, religion, and class—re-learns what many indigenous ancestors call "the original instructions." Read this book, enjoy it, and pass the word: we cooperate, or we face a hot, miserable future world squabbling over toxic crumbs."

— BRUCE E. JOHANSEN
Author of *Forgotten Founders: How the American Indian Helped Shape Democracy* and *The Iroquois: The History and Culture of Native Americans*

"In a brilliant historical retelling, *Original Politics* makes clear that America's sacred legacy—while appearing to have fallen in the ditch of a crude and phony populism—is destined to be a thriving pluralistic democracy and a sanctuary of ecological values."

— JAMES O'DEA
Former president of The Institute of Noetic Sciences,
author of *Cultivating Peace* and *The Conscious Activist*

"*Original Politics: Making America Sacred Again* is an important and timely book for helping the United States move beyond its current crisis. Parry's writing flows beautifully and thoughtfully, as he shows how returning to the nation's mix of Native and European roots can effectively meet its current problems and heal its divisions."

— STEPHEN SACHS
Author of *Honoring the Circle: Ongoing Learning from American Indians on Politics and Society*, with Bruce Johansen, Betty Booth Donohue, Donald Grinde, et al.

"*Original Politics: Making America Sacred Again* points the way for the nation to recover its spiritual heritage by summarizing the Indigenous precepts informing the western hemisphere at Contact. I highly recommend this book to persons desiring a synopsis of Native epistemology in order to rediscover the sacred nature of the earth and its peoples. *Original Politics* is a timely and thoughtful approach to solving America's political and social problems."

—BETTY BOOTH DONOHUE (Cherokee Nation)
Author of *Bradford's Indian Book*

"The arrival of *Original Politics* into our current tormented and divisive U.S. political field is an exceptional gift. Glenn Aparicio Parry offers us a way through the maze, untangling the tight knots of dread, fear and outrage along the way by illuminating the larger and deeper vision of America's political life in the context of its destiny to embody 'unity within diversity.'

In this luminous work, even in the midst of such brutal political dismemberment, we are encouraged, through Parry's measured, insightful and practical guidance, to hold faith towards 'making American sacred again.' This is a book you will read in one sitting. Its unveiling of the deeper meaning of America's political journey, while sobering, is also completely galvanizing, educational, and heartening. I encourage you to get a copy without delay."

—THANISSARA MARY WEINBERG
Author of *Time to Stand Up: A Buddhist Manifesto for Our Times*,
North Atlantic Books

"In *Original Politics,* Parry draws on his lifetime of work in association with Native scholars and teachers as the lens through which he considers both the current polarized and dysfunctional American political situation and the coming global environmental catastrophe. Parry gently suggests that our public business, our politics, can only change when we return to the spiritual, caring values that characterize the way Native people see their purpose in life regarding nature: as guardians and caretakers, not as masters, users or exploiters. These concepts were inherent in the principles the founding fathers appropriated from Native American tribes whom they lived and worked with . . . principles from which we have allowed ourselves to stray from at our peril."

—SENATOR GERALD P. "JERRY" ORTIZ Y PINO
New Mexico Legislature

"Parry addresses the topic most dear to my heart— the future that we can and must build, a future that heals our brokenness. Never before have I read a history of America that linked Europeans and indigenous Americans except as mortal enemies. The soul of the book is contained in Ramana Maharshi's response to the question how should we treat others? "There are no others." These are life-changing words! I feel I'll have to sit with them in meditation every day from now on."

—ROBERT C. KOEHLER
Award-winning Chicago "peace journalist"
Author of *Courage Grows Strong at the Wound*

"Aparicio Parry takes us on an amazing reflective journey from our founding to our present-day politics, recognizing the contributions of the original peoples of our land to our constitution and founding principles. He goes on to analyze our current age of chaos through a brilliant spiritual frame that explains the unitive and divisive forces at play and which increases our appreciation for the process that we are in and must go through. His brilliant and insightful connections across centuries entertain and delight us. While he provides reason to be worried, he leaves us hopeful and more prepared to navigate our future, restoring faith in the transformation that is unfolding."

—MINO AKHTAR
Community organizer and peace activist
Author of the forthcoming *Becoming Muslim in America*

ORIGINAL
POLITICS

ORIGINAL POLITICS:

Making America Sacred Again

GLENN APARICIO PARRY

SelectBooks, Inc.
New York

This edition published by SelectBooks, Inc.
For information address SelectBooks, Inc., New York, New York.

First Edition
ISBN 978-1-59079-503-3

Library of Congress Cataloging-in-Publication Data

Names: Parry, Glenn Aparicio, 1955- author.
Title: Original politics : making America sacred again / Glenn Aparicio Parry.
Description: First edition. | New York : SelectBooks, 2020. | Includes bibliographical references and index. | Summary: "Author seeks to heal America's political divisions and threats to democratic values; he advocates piecing together fragments of our history-including the influence on our founding fathers of Native American beliefs in natural rights, egalitarian justice, and mankind's deep connection to nature, thus revealing a sacred purpose: to bring all peoples and the living natural world together"-- Provided by publisher.
Identifiers: LCCN 2019056485 (print) | LCCN 2019056486 (ebook) | ISBN 9781590795033 (paperback) | ISBN 9781590795026 (ebook)
Subjects: LCSH: Political culture--United States. | Democracy--United States. | Natural law--United States. | Natural theology. | Indian philosophy--North America. | Founding Fathers of the United States. | United States--Politics and government--Philosophy.
Classification: LCC JK1726 .P358 2020 (print) | LCC JK1726 (ebook) | DDC 306.20973--dc23
LC record available at https://lccn.loc.gov/2019056485
LC ebook record available at https://lccn.loc.gov/2019056486

Cover painting by Dyanne Strongbow
Book design by Janice Benight

Manufactured in the United States of America
10 9 8 7 6 5 4 3 2 1

Information about the cover painting

"Making America Sacred Again"

by Dyanne Strongbow

◆

The cover art on the front cover includes many sacred symbols. The bald eagle is a symbol of the United States, and also considered to be a sacred messenger to Creator among many Native American tribes; the white buffalo is a sacred Native American symbol of hope, whose birth is considered a harbinger of better times to come; the snake eating its own tail (ouroboros) is an ancient symbol sacred to many cultures, believed to have originally come from Egypt but also found in Navajo sand paintings in the Southwest. The ouroboros is associated with the Mother Goddess, womb, infinity, cosmic harmony, and the cycle of birth and death.

The particular wampum belt depicted on the back cover is Strongbow's artistic recreation of part of the largest known wampum belt in existence, the original being over six feet long. The Iroquois (Haudenosaunee) Confederacy gave this belt to George Washington in 1794 in commemoration of the Canandaigua Treaty between the Six Nations of the Iroquois and the United States. Wampum bead belts are traditionally used to narrate Iroquois history. The original George Washington belt depicts fifteen figures holding hands. The house in the center symbolizes the Haudenosaunee people who call themselves the People of the Long House. The two hands on opposite sides of the House depict the Mohawk Nation (Keepers of the Eastern door) and the Seneca Nation (Keepers of the Western door). They hold hands with the other thirteen figures, who represent the 13 colonies being joined together as one nation, in peace, unity, and harmony with each other and with the Haudenosaunee.[1]

To the ancestors who loved this continent we call America,
originally known as Turtle Island, and to the
next seven generations

Contents

PART FOUR

Return to Wholeness 235

Preface

As I was contemplating writing this book during the heat of the 2016 US election campaign, I embarked upon a solo cross-country train trip. I had been invited to give a presentation at a conference in Illinois called "Honoring the Ancestors of Ancient America"—a gathering that featured Native American wisdom holders and archaeologists. For some reason the sponsors chose me, even though I have no Native American blood, nor am I an archaeologist. Perhaps, I hoped, they considered me an archaeologist of the mind, as I am intensely interested in tracing our thinking throughout the ages. In any case, I was delighted to participate.

It had been years since I had last traveled by train in America, although I once did so frequently. I had forgotten how charming it could be—and how leisurely. If you are in a rush, Amtrak is not the way to go. If time is on your side, you can enjoy the ride. I loved that I had plenty of time to think, read, or just gaze out the window.

After a while, the pace was so slow I began to feel I was time traveling. I imagined I was Abraham Lincoln making his way to Washington for the first time. It took just as long, and must have been exciting to him. Our route passed through the margins of America rarely seen—from one sleepy town to another—traversing wide-open spaces, chugging up a few mountain passes, and dropping into canyons and river marshlands. I drank it all in while contemplating what memories the land might hold.

My favorite part was mealtime, not because of the railroad food, that is hardly inspired, but because of the interesting people I invariably met. You see, Amtrak required a reservation to dine, but because I was traveling alone they would randomly assign me to join other folks.

In several cases, I was assigned to join an entire group of strangers who were also traveling alone—which made for deliciously odd groupings—a true cross section of America.

It was during one of these random groupings that my desire to write this book was confirmed. I was paired with three other passengers who could not have been more different from each other in their political outlook. One, whose name may have been James, was a gay, African American poet from Albuquerque who was so far to the left on the political spectrum that he considered Sanders too far to the right, even though he supported him. Another was a young, White businessman from Kansas who proudly supported Trump (I think his name was Ernie). The third (I'll call him Red Hawk) was a Native American media personality from Oklahoma who didn't like any of the candidates. I was the only person with a somewhat favorable opinion of Hillary Clinton, but I decided to hold my cards close to the vest and ask questions instead.

I could not believe my good fortune! Here I was, contemplating writing a book about our divided nation, and I had just been gifted with my own little focus group—magically assembled by Amtrak. A gathering like this wouldn't happen in the outside world because people have learned to avoid political confrontations. We* seemingly use a secret code to quickly determine another's political beliefs—and if the stranger's ideas are opposed to ours, we quickly part company. This situation would be different, however, because we all had to eat. I immediately recognized it as a golden opportunity and said a silent prayer of gratitude. My next thought was, "Don't blow it. Ask the right questions. Keep the conversation civil."

I have experience in leading dialogue circles and knew I needed a dialogue question to start the conversation—something that spoke to the big picture. Suddenly a question popped into my mind. "What is the sacred purpose of America?" I asked, and then added, "And why do you think your candidate will fulfill it?" Not surprisingly, Ernie, the Trump supporter, jumped in first, and I braced myself for a stump speech about "making America great again." Instead, I was

---

* When I use the general "we" in this book, it typically refers to we of mainstream Western cultures, unless otherwise specified. When I refer to We the People, it refers to the people of the United States.

pleasantly surprised when he laid out a reasonably intelligent argument: The status quo of politics had become so corrupt that it was now necessary to take a sledge hammer to break it up—and Trump is just the guy to do it. We need to reset, he claimed. "Without Trump, America had lost its purpose. With Trump, we will regain it." I was not even remotely a Trump supporter; in fact, I considered him extremely dangerous. But amazingly I had no quarrel with what I was hearing.

James, the Bernie supporter, was having a harder time. He finally interrupted in exasperation, accusing Trump of being a racist and of dividing the nation. "Do you think Trump really cares about a guy like me—a gay, Black man? No, he doesn't, and he doesn't care about you either, Ernie. He's just a con man; get over it. He only cares about himself and how he can make himself and his family richer." I had no quarrel with anything James said either. And the fact that Ernie listened in silence, rather than escalating the conflict, pleased me.

It was Ernie who then skillfully diverted the conversation to talk about his hometown, Lawrence, Kansas. (We had just made a stop at the Lawrence, KS station). He had special affection for Lawrence, he said, even as he had moved to Wichita a decade ago to start his own manufacturing business. Wichita, he said, had a more diverse population; Lawrence was almost entirely White. He then pivoted to defending Trump against charges of racism, claiming he would do as much for the inner cities as the heartland—and that he would get the working class back to work. James was skeptical, again doubting that Trump cared about the middle class, and predicting that he would just use the office to enrich himself. He also predicted that Trump would start a war to boost the economy, touching on my greatest fear. They went back and forth for quite some time while Red Hawk and I remained silent.

And then I asked another question. "What is the difference between Trump and Bernie? They both want to cut out trade deals and put American workers first. They both think the system is rigged."

Ernie again took the bait. He had some sympathy for Sanders but didn't think he was strong enough to break up the system. "Sanders may be an Independent, but he is still a politician—all talk, no action," he said, echoing one of Trump's more common refrains. It was then that the most curious thing happened. The more James and Ernie talked, the more they seemed to agree. I found myself agreeing with both of them part of the time, and I was pleased that the conversation remained civil. Then after a while they were agreeing so much I found it oddly disconcerting. It was at that point that I decided to weigh in on the trade issue, telling them I found both Sanders and Trump too simplistic on trade. "They mistakenly blame trade deals for all our problems," I asserted, "when the main reason for the loss of manufacturing jobs is automation." I asked Ernie if he would refuse to automate if it would increase his business's productivity and profit. My question gave him pause. He then claimed that he would retain and retrain his workers. I wondered if he was telling the truth.

Red Hawk had remained silent this whole time—and I sensed he had something to say. I did not want to put him on the spot, and I didn't have to, for just at that moment he took the floor. He spoke deliberately, with authority and passion. I will do my best to recreate what he said:

> What none of you seem to realize is the extent that Native America[*] has made this country—*is* this country. This country is built upon this land of my ancestors, the blood, sweat, and tears of my Native brothers and sisters. It is from the living philosophy of Native America, not from books, that your founding fathers learned about liberty and justice. They saw the way we lived, took our ideas as their own—at least the ones that served them—and gave us no credit. And then they moved us out of the way, or killed us.
>
> They thought they killed us all off, but we are still here. And now, you need us again because you have lost your way. You have become lost in greed. You talk about money too much. The economy, like nature, goes in cycles—summer and winter, boom and bust; and throughout, the water, the soil,

---

[*] The term my train companion used, "Native America," refers to both the original peoples—and the place—of the American continent. I frequently use the same term in *Original Politics*.

the light, and the air are being poisoned by greed, by fracking, by the pipelines that transport the oil. This is what Standing Rock[2] is all about. It is about remembering that we are the water, the earth, the air and the light. Your politicians have forgotten this. They are too selfish, as are the voters.

The true spirit of America is in the land. It is in each breath we take, which is only the recycled breath of our ancestors. We need to remember to live in the right way, by the original instructions Creator taught us. My people have forgotten these instructions, too. We all need to awaken from our sleep and stop dreaming—that's all the American dream is, you know—a dream. We need to 'Just do it,' you know, like Nike. (And then he laughed).

I was blown away. James and Ernie went silent, seemingly also in appreciation. Ernie eventually asked a few follow-up questions and was careful to be polite. Amazingly, everyone was getting along.

Soon our dinner was over, but I knew my writing was about to begin. I needed to explore my own dialogue question—to discover the sacred purpose of America for myself. I yearned to find out more about how Native America may have influenced the founding of this nation and if it is still affecting us now. I felt a calling to reignite the sacred flame of America's purpose—and to bring understanding and healing between diverse peoples. I had begun the path to a more sacred, original politics. I had already started this book.

Introduction

Original Politics emerged because I realized that some original thinking about American politics was necessary at this time. The full title *Original Politics: Making America Sacred Again*, requires some further explanation, however. As I explained in my previous book, *Original Thinking*, the meaning of the word "original" has shifted over time. Whereas it once meant *origin*, as in the *place of origin*, or source, and still retains this meaning, it has increasingly come to represent something brand new—something inventive that has never been said or done before (particularly in Western culture).

The changing meaning of "original" represented a shift in emphasis from *place* to *time*—more specifically from the place where life *revolved around* the cycles of nature to the beginning of *linear time*. This was a significant development. It contributed to the Western predilection for novelty and progress at the expense of tradition and a sense of place. Yet because the word original can mean new but at the same time retains a connection to origin, as in an ancient or old source, what is original can be both old and new. Therefore, my intent in *Original Politics* is to bring a fresh, hopefully timeless perspective to American history.

Moreover, when I say *Making America Sacred Again*, I am referring both to the nation and the place, the land of our ancestors. As William Faulkner famously said: "The past is not dead. It isn't even past."[3] All the hopes, dreams, and aspirations of our ancestors—as well as the broken promises and treaties—remain in this sacred ground. That is why I dedicate this book to the ancestors of this land. I also dedicate this book to the next seven generations because the tradition of making decisions based on what benefits distant generations—a practice prevalent in Native America—is important.[4] We have a responsibility to leave a sacred America to coming generations.

The bringing together of politics and the sacred also requires explanation, for these are not ordinarily considered together. The sacred is associated with religion. Politics is secular. This is particularly true in America, where there is separation of church and state. Moreover, nearly everyone I know believes politics is innately corrupt. I do not, despite the seemingly unprecedented level of political corruption today. What gives me hope? I address these questions over the course of the book, but the short answer is this: Politics and America can be made sacred again because they were originally sacred. Both the land and the way people interacted with each other were once considered sacred.

There was once a time when human action was viewed differently, not as separate from nature, but as an integral part of our connection to the whole. On this continent of America, and all over the world, ancient peoples believed they had a responsibility to consider their actions in light of future generations and all of nature—and if they erred, to conduct ceremonies that sought to rebalance the place of humans in the greater whole. These ancient peoples did not assume they knew the answers. They referred to the whole as a Great Mystery. They believed that humans had an integral, if relative, place in the world and that we were the microcosm of the macrocosm. They knew their actions mattered, not only for other humans—but for everything.

Then something changed, particularly in the West, that shifted our view of what it meant to be human. We repositioned our place in the world. Rather than focusing on our connectedness with the rest of creation, we focused on what made us unique and different—and we began to define humanity by those differences. In so doing, we changed the role of human action; we began to envision our actions in terms of human purposes only. We increasingly depended upon other humans for our survival and began to gather in cities. As a result, by the time of Aristotle, Western peoples had redefined politics as human and urban-centered. That is why the word politics comes from the Greek *polis,* as in metropolis. Curiously, although the founding fathers of America tried to balance power between rural and urban communities through the electoral college and other measures, we are still sorting through this divide all these years later.

Living in Interesting Times

Americans are now living through the proverbial "interesting times"— times of danger and uncertainty when there is also opportunity for substantive change. Our government and institutions are in jeopardy of being overturned, but they are also being revealed for what they truly are. The political landscape is as polarized as at any time since the Civil War era and the number of hate crimes have risen. At the same time, there are emergent trends that give us hope, such as more women than ever running for office and winning.

The recent election of two Native American congresswomen, New Mexican Representative Deb Haaland (of the Laguna Pueblo tribe) and Kansas Representative Sharice Davids (of the Ho-Chunk Nation), is significant because Native American politics—practiced by both men's and women's councils—were highly influential in the founding of the United States. It is also significant how many women of all walks of life were recently elected. We could be at a turning point where previously repressed voices begin to speak out and move American society toward a greater balance.

It is with this end in mind that *Original Politics* was written—for the purpose of helping to create a whole and sacred America. To do that, it is necessary to piece together the forgotten fragments of history that are currently keeping the country divided. The most significant forgotten piece is the profound effect Native America had on the founding values of this nation.

Native American influence on the creation of the United States is the foundational theme of the book. I chronicle how the best aspects of the founding vision of America were inspired, or directly appropriated, from living Native American cultural concepts of natural rights, liberty, and egalitarian justice. I further trace the influence of

Native America not only on the founding fathers, but on the 'founding mothers' of the 19th century women's movement, as well as the 19th century abolitionist movement, and even upon modern ecological movements.

While I am not an historian by trade, I found it imperative to study the roots of the nation to understand how and why we got to where we are now. An historical perspective was essential in searching for the sacred purpose of America. History is not only about things dead and buried. History is alive in the present. That is why I offer a nonlinear account, pausing from time to time to consider how the past becomes manifest in the present and how it may foretell our future.

History also provides a larger context wherein the polarization and fragmentation that seems to riddle modern politics is no longer seen as fixed or permanent; nor is it as hopelessly antagonistic. Instead, current difficulties are reframed as part of a natural and inevitable stage in an unfolding, universal process. This does not mean that an eventual resolution is foreordained or inevitable; we still must do the work to negotiate our differences and heal.

Ultimately, human history is a subset of larger natural forces that govern not only humanity but the whole planet and cosmos. The fact that human political action is nested in the natural world is an important concept of original politics. Bearing this in mind, we can proceed from a place that is grounded in living natural processes rather than mere human enterprise. This strengthens our patience and resolve, and in the end we may see our nation and ourselves more clearly.

In sum, all of us—politicians and private citizens alike—are participants in the dance of life, a sacred and mysterious unfolding of nature that is inexorable and powerful beyond anything human beings can master or even imagine. If we oppose this force, we will be engulfed by it, much like a tidal wave engulfs the shore. Wise human beings and statespersons align themselves with the will of Nature. They recognize that the source of power begins not within themselves but in nature, and that our task is to be a conduit of that power, not to overcome it. This is what is meant by making America sacred again.

The Four Parts of the Book

The book unfolds in a circle of four interrelated parts mirroring how nature unfolds in iterative cycles (seen in the following diagram). The parts are aligned with the unfolding of creation described in the ancient Chinese text, *The Tao Te Ching*. The Tao is the One Absolute Principle underlying all creation, but this unitive consciousness cannot be sustained. The *One* becomes the *Two* (principle of complementarity); the two then becomes the *Many Things* (a fragmented, fractured reality); but it is the One (the Tao) that drives the whole process, and the urge to return to wholeness remains throughout. Thus the four parts of *Original Politics* are Part One: Unitive Consciousness, Part II: Dance of the Opposites, Part III: Maximum Diversity, and Part IV: Return to Wholeness.

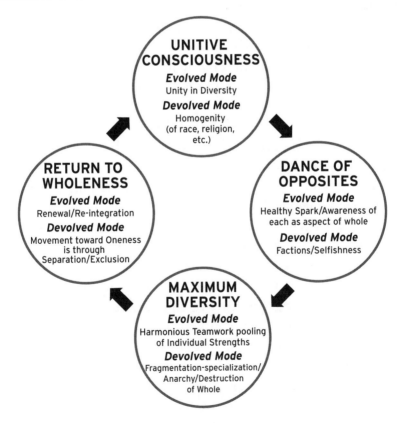

Part I: Unitive Consciousness addresses our nation's founding and unique identity that we established at the outset. This identity was forged from significant, if largely unacknowledged, contact with Native Americans.

Part II: Dance of the Opposites chronicles the emergence of differing philosophies in the 19th century that gave birth to the Democratic and Republican parties—and also the civil rights movement—coming to a head during the Civil War (duality consciousness/dance of opposites) that is markedly similar to today.

Part III: Maximum Diversity discusses the political climate of the past century culminating in the 2016 election that was seen as apocalyptic by both sides, and the Trump presidency that has disrupted the status quo of the world order and of America's institutions and political parties.

Part IV: Return to Wholeness describes an imagined future reclamation, a reconciliation of opposites heralding a movement toward greater wholeness and healing through respectful dialogue and love of unity in diversity within nature and within ourselves.

EVOLUTION AND DEVOLUTION

It is important to note that each phase of the cycle has an evolved and devolved mode. In calling one mode evolved and the other devolved, I run the risk of being misunderstood as making value judgments when what I am intending is more observation than judgment. The devolved mode is necessary at some point to move from one stage to the other, for a system must degrade and break down (principle of entropy) before something new can be created.

In Part I, Unitive Consciousness, the evolved mode seeks unity in diversity, recognizing that there are many aspects of one whole, as in the many rays of the sun; the devolved mode, while still unitive, seeks an undifferentiated oneness, as in totalitarianism or monarchy based on homogeneity of race or religion. During the founding of the United States both evolved and devolved modes of unitive consciousness were present and in conflict with one another—something that was true in the fighting of the Revolutionary War—and, in a certain sense, this dynamic has never really gone away.

In Part II, Dance of the Opposites, the evolved mode is the recognition and acceptance of the integrity of the difference between the political parties; the devolved mode is the hardening of divisive factions between the parties that led to the Civil War. We are experiencing a similar divisiveness today, only with a greater degree of complexity. The overall arc of American history has been in the direction of unity in diversity (as evidenced by increasing inclusivity of women and people of color), although there have been periodic calls to return to a simpler era when the United States was less diverse.

Part III is where we are today and, more specifically, we are now in the devolved mode of Maximum Diversity. The populist campaign of Donald Trump and its slogan "Make America Great Again" implied a return to a simpler era of less diversity. While this did not mark the beginning of a devolved mode of Maximum Diversity, it ushered in its acceleration. Today, the country is nearly as divided as at any time in our nation's history, and our values and institutions are being challenged, if not upended, on a daily basis. The Trump presidency has arguably been an attack on our republic, moving us precariously close to an authoritarian state.

At the same time, the disruptive force of the Trump administration presents an opportunity. It may serve as a catalyst in speeding things up, uncovering the shadow side of America that has previously remained concealed. The manifestation of the national shadow enables us to see what needs to change. In the best-case scenario, the Trump presidency will turn out to be an apocalypse only in the original sense of the word—an unveiling or revelation of what was already there, but hidden. It is in this way that the greatest crises we face often serve to accelerate healing, albeit after the initial disruption, and are therefore blessings in disguise. Sometimes things need to get worse before they get better.

In Part IV, Return to Wholeness, I envision a better world. However, I do not jump to specifying exactly how to rearrange the world order. It is premature, and perhaps foolhardy, to try to impose order in the midst of chaos. Instead, I discuss how to dance with chaos, adopting a flexible stance more than a strategy. I then offer baby steps we can take to move us toward greater wholeness. These baby steps do not require a restructuring of our current worldview.

In the final three chapters, I introduce a radically different worldview, one more in accord with the ancient view of original politics, but also directed at the challenges of today, including climate change. To make deep structural change, a new worldview is required.

Part IV is, for me, the most heartfelt, and in some ways the most important part of the book. For some people, it may require a shift from head to heart to understand my viewpoint. It is with all my heart that I envision a world in which humankind reestablishes an intimate connection with the natural world. It is with all my heart that I wish We, the people, will remember how to love Mother Nature, for it is love of biodiversity, I contend, that will lead to love of each other.

Note to the Reader

I occasionally refer to Indigenous peoples of the North American continent as "Indian," particularly in the beginning of the book (mostly when I am looking through the eyes of Europeans who referred to Native Americans as Indians when not referring to them as "savages"). The word "Indian" was once synonymous with the word "American," but of course the meaning of the word has changed. Later on in this book, I mostly use "Natives," "Native Americans," "American Indians," or "Indigenous peoples." Similarly, I sometimes refer to the "Haudenosaunee" (People of the Long House) as *Iroquois* or use parentheses to help clarify their relative equivalence, particularly in the beginning of the book. I use *Haudenosaunee* more as the book progresses because it is a more respectful term, although at this time "Iroquois" is still more widely used. My main goal is communication, but I recognize that some people have problems and disagreements with the use of many of these terms.

PART ONE

UNITIVE CONSCIOUSNESS

"Everything the Power of the World
does is done in a circle."[5]

—BLACK ELK

"If I seem to take part in politics,
it is only because politics encircles us today
like the coil of a snake from which one cannot
get out, no matter how much one tries.
I wish therefore to wrestle with the snake."[6]

—MAHATMA GANDHI

"When you say 'Indian government' to the
Iroquois . . . we think about the Creator's
law, not parliamentary procedure."[7]

—TOM PORTER

The Peacemaker and the Tree of Peace:
An Iroquois (Haudenosaunee) Story

A very long time ago, the people had forgotten how to be thankful or to remember the blessings of life they received from Creator. A feeling of deep discontent set in upon the people, as bloody wars were raging in every village among the 5 nations of the Iroquois (Haudenosaunee).

Amidst this chaos, Creator sent a messenger of peace to be born amongst the people. The traditional Haudenosaunee people consider his name too sacred to be spoken, so they refer to him simply as the *Peacemaker*. His mission was to restore love, peace, and harmony back to the people. He did this by proposing a set of laws in which the people of the Nations could live in unity and peace, called the Great Law of Peace.

The Peacemaker set out to spread peace and unity throughout Haudenosaunee territory. The first person to accept the words of the Great Law of Peace was a woman named Jikonsahseh. She was a pivotal figure, as her home was already a neutral zone for anyone passing through, including war parties, who would lay down their weapons outside of her dwelling. There, she fed them and offered them rest and safety.

When the Peacemaker spoke to Jikonsahseh, she broke down in tears over the beauty of his message and swore to follow it for the rest of her days. The Peacemaker told her then that she would be the spiritual Clan Mother, representing the leadership for all the women, and that she would always be remembered for her role.

Then, the Peacemaker came to the house of an Onondaga leader named Hayo'wetha (Hiawatha). Hiawatha believed in the message of peace and wanted the Haudenosaunee people to live in a united way. His wife and daughters had been killed by an evil Onondaga leader called Tadadaho during the violent times. The Peacemaker helped Hiawatha mourn his loss and eased his pain. Hiawatha then agreed to accompany the Peacemaker on his mission to unite the people.

The Peacemaker used arrows to demonstrate the strength of unity. First, he took a single arrow and broke it in half. Then, he took five arrows and tied them together. The group of five arrows could not be broken. "A single arrow is weak and can be broken. A bundle of arrows tied together cannot be broken. This represents the strength of having a Confederacy. It is strong and cannot be broken." The Mohawk, Oneida, Cayuga, Seneca, and Onondaga accepted the message of peace.

But the evil Tadadaho continued to resist, hating the message of peace. Tadadaho was feared by all. His body was crooked and his hair was full of snakes, symbolizing his twisted mind. But the Peacemaker was unafraid. He promised Tadadaho that if he accepted the message of peace, Onondaga would be the capital of the Grand Council. Tadadaho finally succumbed. The messengers of peace than combed the snakes from his hair. The name Hiawatha means "he who combs," indicating his integral role in convincing Tadadaho to accept the Great Law of Peace.

The Five Nations became known as the Haudenosaunee (Iroquois) Confederacy.

The people gathered to celebrate. The Peacemaker then looked around for an enduring symbol. He saw a very tall, evergreen tree and explained that the evergreen tree represented the solidity of the united nations, as it stays green, even with the change of the seasons. He then partially uprooted the tree to create a cavity. He instructed the men to cast down their weapons of war into the cavity, and to bury their greed, hatred, and jealousy there. The tree was then replanted and the Peacemaker said," Here we bury all weapons of strife. We bury them from sight forever, and plant again this tree. Thus, shall Great Peace be established and hostilities cease between the Five Nations."

The roots that spread out from the tree are called the Great White Roots of Peace, and they spread in the four directions: one to the

North; one to the South; one to the East; and one to the West. On top of this Great Tree was placed an Eagle.

The Peacemaker then asked Jikonsahseh to help each nation select the men who would serve on the Grand Council of fifty members[8] that would make the decisions for the Confederacy based on the Great Law of Peace. Important decisions would all be made on the basis of consensus. And that is how the Great Law of Peace became one of the earliest examples of a formal democratic governance, later to influence the founding fathers of the United States.[9]

CHAPTER ONE

Original Unitive Consciousness

The Mayflower Pilgrims believed they were fleeing a world of religious persecution to reach salvation on a distant shore—a new Jerusalem, a promised land of purity and abundance. The settlers may have made their exodus from Europe, but they did not leave their European values behind. They not only brought their religious beliefs to their new homeland; they arrived with their secular ones as well, including the Enlightenment mentality that rational thought can overcome nature. In the New World they soon lived side-by-side with Native Americans who lived in relative harmony with the land and in far more egalitarian societies than they were accustomed to.

In this way, long before the then Euro-Americans began to formulate their concept of a new political nation, the settlers had an opportunity to live on this continent and to observe and interact with Native Americans. They lived alongside Native Americans for a century and a half as they formed their ideas of community and government. Yet few historians consider the impact this cultural exchange had on the founding of the nation. In truth, the influence of Native America—both the place and the original peoples of this continent—contributed mightily to the formation of the United States. The encounter between Native Americans and Euro-Americans was never a smooth or easy process, but it was out of this awkward collision of these different concepts of the world that the nation of America was born.

The unusual circumstances of our nation's birth do not diminish the historic significance of the United States. The founding of our representational republic was unique and important because it represented a radical departure from the monarchies that dominated Europe at that time. However, as novel as the American experiment was, relative to Europe, it was not new on the American continent (where egalitarian democracy and personal liberty were the norm among Native American societies). The notion that the founding fathers came up with the idea for America on their own is, in my view, mistaken, as is the belief that they simply resurrected ancient Greek democratic ideals. It makes more sense that they designed their new society in large part upon the living example of Native America's values and ideas. There is ample evidence to support this conclusion, as I demonstrate in due course.

From the beginning, the meeting between European settlers and Native Americans was jagged—not just a clash of worldviews, but of origin stories, each culture emphasizing different values. The European narrative was essentially a reenactment of the Exodus story from the Bible; the journey of the colonists can be likened to that of Moses leading his people forth from Egypt in search of the proverbial promised land of milk and honey. Like the biblical story, the journey of the settlers was arduous as they traveled from distant shore to distant shore, intent upon forging a new society in a new world.

Indigenous origin stories, on the other hand, told of peoples being grounded in a sense of place. Their stories spoke of the people evolving from the land, often emerging from deep within the earth—from other worlds or dimensions—to inhabit the surface of the land they loved. The Indigenous North Americans were connected to the earth, much like an umbilical cord connects one to one's mother. They were physically, emotionally, and spiritually tied to the land they occupied.

In short, there was a stark difference between these narratives. One was about intimate, familial connection to place; the other was about the hero's journey away from one's place of origin to start anew in a foreign land.

The gulf between these two kinds of stories may seem impassable, but it was out of this dramatic (and sometimes violent) cross-fertilization of worldviews that America's character and destiny was formed.

How this happened, and who or what provided the bridge between the worlds, provides the foundation of this book. I also investigate how this historical influence continues to reverberate in present-day America and how that initial spark has evolved and devolved. It is during periods of devolution, such as now—when the psychological shadow of unresolved conflicts returns and triggers a national identity crisis—that there is an opportunity to make deep substantive changes. Devolution may even promote healing, for healing comes through awareness and transformation of shadow elements into a higher-level of integration.

WHAT REALLY HAPPENED DURING THE FIRST CONTACT BETWEEN INDIGENOUS NORTH AMERICANS AND EUROPEANS?

There are many stories of how Native Americans experienced the arrival of the first Europeans at the time of Columbus. According to one popular account, the Natives first thought the ships were floating islands; the mast was thought to be a tree, and the sails were taken to be white clouds. It goes on to say that the Natives eagerly rowed their canoes out to these "islands" to pick strawberries.[10] The only problem with this narrative (and others like it) is that it is almost certainly untrue. These accounts were the fanciful musings of Europeans, not the first-hand accounts of Native peoples.

A more reliable indicator of how Native Americans experienced the arrival of Europeans can be found in their traditional oral histories. These oral accounts are remarkably consistent over time, according to the late Native American author, scholar, and activist Vine Deloria, Jr., and thus he asserted that they can serve as sources of the historical facts, while also providing insight into the Indigenous mind.[11] Many of these histories describe encounters with outsiders, whom they often referred to as "cannibal giants." These "cannibals" were sometimes real flesh-eaters, but that is not my primary concern here. Native oral tradition speaks of invaders as "cannibals" in large part because of their insatiable appetite to subsume Native culture.

Columbus himself was spoken of in this manner by Native American author Jack D. Forbes in his book *Columbus and Other Cannibals*.

The interesting thing about these stories is that the invaders were rarely met with hostility; in fact, in most accounts, they were greeted with hospitality. The tribe "killed the strangers with kindness," which is to say that in many of these narratives the invading "cannibals" were at least partially changed by the encounter, and as a result became less of a threat. This oral tradition cannot be dismissed as fictional stories. It became a working strategy among Native American tribes, who sought to transform the behavior of foreign invaders by "indigenizing" their worldview. I return to this point later.

The written stories of first contacts from the European perspective confirm that the people they referred to as "Indians" welcomed them with various gifts and kindnesses. Columbus, who described the Taino of the Caribbean as a "loving people without covertness," went on to say that they came to his ships "loaded with balls of cotton, parrots, javelins, and other things too numerous to mention; these they exchanged for whatever we chose to give them." But he also saw the Taino as a people he could easily overpower, boasting "I could conquer the whole of them with fifty men, and govern them as I pleased."[12]

Columbus was wrong in this last assertion. Native peoples never gave up their lands easily or willingly. I imagine the Indians also made some incorrect assumptions about the Europeans, for upon first contact, it makes sense that neither side would have seen the other clearly. In all likelihood, both saw a people wholly different from themselves—an archetypal Other. Everything about their counterpart would have appeared different and strange—not just their skin color, but their clothing, customs, attitudes, values, and expressions of spirituality. I doubt that either side correctly identified exactly *why* the other people made them so uncomfortable—but I believe the root of their discontent may have come from something they had already rejected in themselves, something they then projected upon the other. I will return to this subject shortly and throughout this book, since it is central to healing through a process of arriving at an understanding of the diverse points of view.

In any case, whatever assumptions Indians may have made about the European settlers cannot be known with certainty because of a lack of written accounts, unlike many of the assumptions European settlers made about the Indians, which are easy to verify but were often incorrect. The core assumption made by the Europeans was that they were meeting a society less advanced than their own—i.e., primitive or savage (even as the Indians were later romanticized as "noble savages.") The assumption of primitiveness was partly based on religion since many Europeans were convinced that those who had accepted Jesus Christ as their savior were superior. A corollary assumption was that Europeans were more advanced because they had superior science and technology. This last assumption was perhaps the most pervasive and intractable, and almost universally believed today. Some of my readers may now be asking: "Isn't it obvious that Europeans had superior technology? What's wrong with that assumption?"

Well, it depends upon what kind of science and technology we measure. If the standard is force, computed in terms of the number of horses, cattle, guns, gunpowder, cannon fire, mills, and forges, then, yes, the colonists held the edge. But if the metric is ecological knowledge—deep, intimate knowledge concerning such things as animal tracking and migration patterns; the harvesting of berries, seeds, and nuts; herbal medicines; what crops to grow, and where and when; and weather patterns, water sources, and terrain (woods, mountains, or canyons)—then the Indians had the superior technology.

DIFFERENCES IN WORLDVIEW OF THE NATIVES AND SETTLERS

The differences in technology were a direct reflection of differences in how the cultures perceived their world. European technology was better suited to willfully *remaking* the land; Native technology was better suited to *working with* the existing (dynamic) balance of relationships and alliances held within the land.

This goes to the heart of a difference in worldviews about what it means to be human. The Western worldview at the time was moving in the direction of a newly emergent philosophy, one that increasingly viewed self and humanity as separate and transcendent from nature. This separation had begun in earnest six hundred years before during the Renaissance, and by the time of the 18th century Enlightenment, it had developed into a powerful new science that required an objective perspective from which to study, predict, and ultimately control the natural world. In time, the extraordinary successes of modern science fueled a growing belief that humanity would eventually master the natural world. But in our zest for scientific innovation, we (in the West) ignored the shadow side of progress—a widening divide between man and nature.

The scientific worldview was not just different from that of American Indians; it was a departure from the perennial wisdom of our Western forebears who had long believed that humans and Nature were one—that man was the microcosm of the macrocosm. It was this aspect of themselves that the colonists had rejected before setting sail—only to find it again in the Indians they met on the American continent. Hence it should come as no surprise that they would perceive the Natives as less developed.

HOW DID NATIVE AMERICANS ARRIVE AT THEIR VIEWPOINTS OF THE WORLD?

This question was rarely asked by the colonists, apart from certain people who had significant dealings with Native Americans and took genuine interest in the whole of their culture, such as Roger Williams and Ben Franklin, two influential people I examine more closely in subsequent chapters. Most colonists never considered asking this, for they assumed that the Indian worldview was backward, a vestige of another time—reminiscent of their own Garden of Eden story—and not a conscious choice.

When people imply that Indigenous peoples have lived in exactly the same manner for eons, this is a naïve view tinged with racism. Such a view emerges from the Western notion of linear progression that conveniently sees the West on the forefront of progress and non-Western peoples as stuck in their ways or trailing behind. But this is simply not true. Native peoples have evolved and changed, like all peoples, over time. While Native people themselves might say they have been following *original instructions* (given to them by Creator) since time immemorial, that is because the experience of receiving original instructions is inherently renewing. The instructions change with the times. The word "original" provides a clue here because it can mean old and/or new. For Indigenous people, ceremonies and songs are their means of *renewal*. The ceremonies are a direct reconnection with Spirit. They literally *inspire* (reconnect with the sacred breath of Spirit) and this is the means of their renewal.

It is also true that Native peoples have not always followed their original instructions. Being human, at some point in their histories they undoubtedly lapsed. This narrative is supported by the Haudenosaunee (Iroquois) story of the Peacemaker, also known as Deganawida, that begins part one. Peacemaker was born at a time when the people had begun to selfishly take from Mother Nature without regard to her replenishment, and a course correction was desperately needed. Peacemaker traveled amongst the people teaching another way. This way, now known as the *Law of Peace*, was foundational to the enduring Iroquois Confederacy and greatly influenced the founding of the United States.

If all Indigenous peoples made a similar course correction, it would flip the usual script; it would mean that Native Americans, not Europeans, were the more advanced civilization because Natives had already discovered what Western peoples are only discovering today or perhaps just remembering—that Nature cannot be overcome— and any attempt to do so is not only futile; it is suicidal. Imagine for a moment that the latter narrative is correct—that Native peoples rejected the notion of pillaging from nature because they knew the result. What, then, would native peoples from Northeastern America have felt upon first encountering the Europeans? They would have felt some sense of responsibility for their younger brothers who had not yet realized the crucial importance of living in harmony with the rest of creation.[13]

In any case, Europeans and Indians had a remarkably different sense of self and society upon first contact. The European mind considered each individual self to be an autonomous being and society to be the sum of self-interested individuals held together by the rule of law. In this worldview, there is always a dynamic tension between the individual and society, and the social contract theories of Hobbes, Locke, and Rousseau—so integral to modern politics—attempted to articulate (and attenuate) this tension. There wasn't the same tension in Indigenous societies because the Indigenous sense of self was essentially non-egoic, derived from the web of relationships in which the person was embedded. "Tribal man is hardly a personal self," according to Vine Deloria Jr., who added, "He does not so much live in a tribe—the tribe lives in him."[14]

Indigenous views of the sacred elements—light, air, water, and earth—are based in the same sense of relationship. While there is an overlap between Western concepts of God/Holy Spirit and Great Spirit (translated in Cherokee as "One that Thinks, Breathes, Creates"),[15] Indigenous people would generally disagree with the Western scientific notion of the elements as merely the constituents or building blocks of life. Grandfather Leon Secatero, the late Head Man of the Canoncito Band of Navajo, said, "The elements [themselves] are the creators."[16] Grandfather Leon considered the elements alive, whether they were inside or outside of us; no distinction was necessary. For the Navajo, the air we breathe in is the One Living Air—or *nilch'i*, whether it exists outside the body or as a breath within the body, for all processes on Earth and throughout the cosmos.[17]

Most moderns dismiss the idea of living air, labeling this thinking as mere animism, but it is worth noting that a similar way of thinking once prevailed throughout the world. In India the living air has traditionally been known as *prana*; the ancient Greeks knew the breath as *pneuma*; the Romans called it *spiritus*; the Jews named it *ruach*. In the Bible it is the *ruach*—the living, breathing, heart of God— that first animates the world. "The Ruach of God was hovering over the surface of the waters."

THE RENAISSANCE WORLDVIEW

It is important to remember that the 18th century Enlightenment was preceded by a period now known as the European Renaissance (roughly the 15th–17th centuries) and that the Renaissance began as a movement that looked back to the ancient wisdom of Greco-Roman times.[19] The symbol of the Renaissance was *Janus*, the Roman god of doorways and transitions who looked both backward and forward (from which we derive the name January, our first month of the year).

In the early Renaissance period, the ancient idea of man as microcosm of the macrocosm was still very much intact. Leonardo da Vinci was following the wisdom of the ancients when he astutely observed that the elements work in similar ways regardless of whether they are inside or outside the human body. In his notebooks, da Vinci helped to preserve this perennial wisdom:

> Man has been called by the ancients a lessor world, and indeed the term is rightly applied, seeing that if man is compounded of earth, water, air and fire, this body of the earth is the same: and as man has within himself bones as a stay and framework for the flesh, so the world has the rocks which are the supports of the earth; as man has within him a pool of blood wherein the lungs as he breathes expand and contract, so the body of the earth has its ocean, which also rises and falls every six hours with the breathing of the world as from the said pool of blood proceed the veins which spread their branches through the human body, in just the same manner the ocean fills the body of the earth with an infinite number of veins of water.[20]

This view expressed by da Vinci is in remarkable consonance with that of Native American peoples (both ancient and modern) who have always prayed to the elements because they understood our radical interconnection with light, air, water, and earth. After all, we cannot live without the warmth of the sun—nor could the trees, plants, and other animals. The trees give out the breath of life (oxygen) we humans need to live—and we (humans and other animals) give back to the trees what they need to live (CO_2). All life on Earth is dependent upon the elements, and we humans are as dependent as any other creature. We are not only the microcosm of the macrocosm; we are radically related and intertwined with all that lives on Earth. This is no doubt why Native peoples commonly speak of our relationship with the elements and all life on Earth in kinship terms, referring to them as "all my relations" who are bound together in a *Sacred Hoop* (circle of life) interconnection. Imagine the implications of such a worldview on how we might revision politics. Rather than human affairs being conducted independent from the rest of nature, we would make decisions based upon the impact on the entire planet. This would require us to restore the ancient Western view (or the Native view, ancient or modern) of what it means to be human.

Is TIME A CIRCLE OR A LINE?

The human conception of time used to be simple. Time *was nature*—wholly dependent upon the natural rhythms of a particular place. We did our best to synchronize with the seasons, with the migration of animals and the arrival of berries, seeds, and nuts because our lives depended upon doing this. For millennia, time was seen as a series of iterative cycles, even in the West; for both Plato and Aristotle, time unfolded in the energy of a circle. The circle has always represented the whole. But Western consciousness reoriented its view of time and in doing so exchanged the circle for the line. This evolution happened gradually, over millennia, until the Renaissance. Then came the tipping point, the moment when we suddenly shifted our orientation. The catalyzing event was the discovery and subsequent deployment of linear perspective in art. Once we began to view linear perspective and linear time as *real*, everything changed—not just in art, but in science, consciousness, and politics. That was because it literally changed our worldview from an immersion in one's environment to an objective distance from it, as seen in the following two illustrations of the city of Florence, Italy.

A clarified rendition line drawing depicting Florence, Italy in Pre-perspective terms, based on a fresco in the Loggia del Bigallo, Florence, c. 1350.

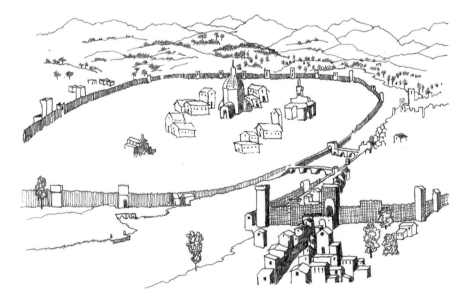

A clarified rendition line drawing depicting Florence, Italy, Post-perspective, after a painting now in the Museo Firenze, Florence, c. 1480.

The principal positive outcome in adopting linear perspective was that it allowed the scientific observer to remain detached, enabling more objective analysis and precise measurement of nature. However, as the American author Paula Underwood was fond of saying, "That which enables, disables also."[21] The Western adoption of a linear perspective did much to disable the ancient worldview of what it meant to be human in relation to nature and with sometimes devastating consequences.

The shift in perspective happened during Leonardo da Vinci's lifetime. The young Leonardo believed that "the natures" projected their energy upon a passive, receptive eye, for all of nature was understood to be animate and alive. But by the end of his lifetime, as he and many others adopted a linear perspective, energy had been redirected away from living nature and into our own head—and consequently, if perhaps accidentally—deadening the world around us. Energy now flowed in one direction: from our eye out onto the landscape. This is how the eye of perspective eventually gave birth to the "I"—the ego— of the 18th century. Humanity became reimagined as the center of consciousness, and all other creatures became marginalized. While we sometimes accorded other creatures a lesser consciousness, we often did so begrudgingly.

Perhaps the most important shift was in our view of time because linear perspective contributed to, if not created, the switch from time as circle to time as a line. With linear perspective, objects in front of—and closest to—the viewer are thought of as occurring in the *near future*; and objects in front of—and furthest from—the viewer are considered as happening in the *distant future*. Linear perspective is thus a line of progression and the precursor of conceiving of time as a line. While the idea of linear time has been tacitly accepted by modern Western culture, it is not the only way we can, or should, think of time. As Einstein, the author of relativity theory, is purported to have said, "linear time is an illusion," although a "stubbornly persistent" one.[22]

There were ramifications to the Western adoption of linear time. It led the West away from thousands of years of tradition that emphasized the importance of people aligning with nature's rhythms. This created a new emphasis on human action independent from nature's cycles, which gave humankind a rational justification for sacrificing the ecology in favor of human linear progress.

THE WESTERN STORY OF LINEAR HUMAN PROGRESS

Once the West adopted linear perspective as real, it became our way of viewing the world. Our focus increasingly shifted to the future that now stretched out ahead of us. Whereas previously we considered it hubris for humans to know the future and went to oracles for such wisdom, we began to seek to predict and control future outcomes though scientific experimentation. Moreover, we convinced ourselves that we were always progressing since we were building upon a past body of knowledge. I am sure that idea seems like common sense to most of my readers, but it is really just an idea. Current knowledge is not always superior to previous knowledge. We just convince ourselves that this is so.

The story of linear human progress became the central organizing story of the Western world. Knowledge, once considered the province of nature, became usurped by the superiority of human knowledge. We learned less and less from lived experience in nature or from apprenticeships and more and more from information stored in books or the minds of teachers. Spontaneous inspiration from nature was discouraged as we increasingly relied on inert, stored knowledge. This affected everything we did, particularly in our orientation to science and knowledge. It even eventually affected our orientation to politics. By the time the United States was formed, Hamilton and Madison had come to view politics as a science. If other sciences could advance by building upon prior knowledge, so could politics, they reasoned. The cycles of nature and man became forgotten. Human linear progress became the central organizing principle.

To be clear, I am not saying the story of human linear progress is necessarily incorrect. I am simply saying that it is a story, a way of seeing and thinking about things that enables us to have certain perceptions while blinding ourselves to other levels of reality.

Ramifications of Linear versus Circular Time

The essential point about different worldviews is that they enable one way of seeing while disabling another. The benefit to seeing the world in a detached way is that it enables careful study; and the benefit to seeing the world in an immersive way is that it includes us as an integral part of that same world. There are obvious advantages to seeing time as a line (such as keeping of appointments); but there are also advantages to seeing time in iterative cycles (such as moving in rhythm with nature, which can be more relaxing, even healing). There are ramifications and consequences to either view.

It was only after linear perspective became known as realism that Newton formulated the concept of absolute time, which essentially said that time exists independently from space and can be measured in precise intervals. In effect, absolute time remade time from something real (nature's rhythms) into an abstraction, something that happens independent of humans. While we still acknowledge a sense of time within us—which we call circadian rhythms—in general, time is perceived as an abstraction outside our control, causing disruption, even anguish, for some people.

Ramifications of Linear versus Circular Thinking in Politics

There are important ramifications to circular or linear thinking in terms of the governance of a people or nation. A circular view sees all things and all viewpoints as related—as part of a larger whole of nature. Council government is itself conducted in a circle, a dialogue circle intended to mirror the circle of nature. The emphasis is on renewal and long-term sustainability for the benefit of future generations. Decisions are made carefully in council government, as they should be. But the downside to such a way of governance can be a decision-making process that is overly deliberate, unable to keep up with the times.

A linear view of time and history, on the other hand, leads to a different philosophy of governing. The theoretical advantage of linear political thinking is that it can lead to continual forward progress and rapid response, improvements to standard of living, technology, and so forth. But the disadvantages of linear thinking are manifold. Differing views are held in opposition; they are considered separate, rather than different aspects of one whole. This leads to win-lose, zero-sum thinking. Perhaps most importantly, perennial wisdom of the past tends to be ignored or dismissed. A linear progressive world-view can be insular and arrogant.

Much of modernity is the result of the Enlightenment worldview supplanting that of the early Renaissance (a worldview that used to acknowledge the importance of looking back to perennial wisdom) in favor of progress. To some degree, political liberalism has more readily adopted progressive causes, and conservatism pushes back against this forward inertia. There has always been a dance between conservatives and liberals—a dance between the poles (and the polls) that at various times seems to promote one or the other perspective as triumphant. But this is all a necessary part of the process, as I demonstrate in due course.

When conservatives put the brakes on too-rapid progress, that can be a good thing, particularly if conservatives are intervening to conserve something vital to our welfare, such as the environment—something that happened as recently as the 1970s under the Nixon administration establishment of the EPA and passage of the Clean Air and Water Acts. And while modern conservatism has seemingly forgotten its green roots, I predict this ecological ethic will resurface (as it already has in Europe) because it must return if humanity is to survive.

MAKING AMERICA SACRED

I have said that politics can help make America sacred again, but what does it mean to be sacred? The word sacred comes from the Latin *sacare,* which means "to devote" or "dedicate." When we do things in a sacred way, we invoke connection and relationship to others.[23] We invoke the whole. Making things sacred is literally a desire to make *holy,* for the modern English "holy" is related to wholeness and health. The word holy is derived from the Old English *halig,* the old Saxon *helag*, and the German *heilig* (all meaning whole), and also the Old English *hal* and German *heil* (for health).

The original politics of a sacred America, therefore, is meant to consecrate our actions in service of a greater good beyond the personal. It is a path of service dedicated to others—an open-hearted intention of acting with awareness of our integral connection to the whole. For the mystic, sacredness is an immediate awareness of our ever-present oneness with God or the Creator. But an experience of oneness—what I am calling *unitive consciousness*—is not relegated to mystics. It can be experienced as an inspiration, epiphany, or revelation in which Nature reveals herself to and through the human. As such, it can arise in anyone.

While this form of revelation of knowledge from nature became equated in the West with the miraculous, akin to Moses receiving his instructions from the burning bush, it was normal for Native Americans to perceive their thoughts as coming directly from the land. For Natives, all of nature spoke. It was not considered unusual to receive messages from animals, plants, or even a rock.

The original politics of Native America was therefore never a closed system. It did not set human affairs apart from nature or view humans as superior and transcendent from other creatures. It was a conscious attempt to harmoniously align human affairs with these larger forces. At its best, it was a politics of the heart that sought to sync the human heartbeat with the heartbeat of nature—a form of sacramental reciprocation or communion with the Great Mystery.

To a significant degree, Native Americans today still approach politics in a similar manner. This is not to say that Native peoples ever fully embodied what I am referring to as sacred or original politics. Tribes have had their own share of disharmony, their traditional enemies, wars, and so forth. At the same time, Native American worldviews have long included a concept of human action as nested in the natural world to a much greater degree than the European worldview, and this continues today. Native peoples of North America, then and now, have held closer to a unitive consciousness—an awareness of their place in the oneness of The Great Mystery—than have Euro-American peoples.

The story I am about to tell is one of the partnership between Native Americans and the European settlers that originally formed—and still informs—this nation called the United States. But the original partnership that gave rise to America was not between Native American and European. It was between the land and its original peoples. This sacred relationship of human and place—between human and humus (the living soil)—was developed long before the arrival of Europeans. Native Americans believed their *original instructions* came from their place of origin. It was out of this sacred relationship between land and the people that the conception of what it meant to be human was formed. It is the land herself who holds the memory of all that has happened here, and it is the land herself that holds the potential to give rise to a Turtle Island* Renaissance one day. That resurgence, like the European Renaissance before it, will look backward to go forward.

---

* Turtle Island is the original name for the American continent, now usually applied only to North America. The concept of Turtle Island is based on many creation myths of the Indigenous peoples who have lived here for millennia. There are also numerous cross-cultural stories of the entire Earth, and sometimes the cosmos, being supported on the back of a Great Turtle.

CHAPTER TWO

The Seeds of a Uniquely American Character

The First Contact at Plymouth Rock

When the Mayflower Pilgrims arrived in Plymouth in late autumn of 1620, they did not immediately encounter any Indians when they ventured ashore. The Wampanoag (a loose confederation of many tribes) were immediately aware of their presence but chose to watch them from a distance rather than initiate contact. It was apparent that these new arrivals were different from those who had come before, for this time the strangers brought women and children, an indication they were intent on staying rather than trading and returning like other exploratory parties of the past century. Significantly, even though the Pilgrims were clearly establishing a settlement of the Plymouth Plantation, the Wampanoag freely let them stay, viewing them as potential trading partners or allies in keeping with an already well-developed strategy of establishing peaceful coexistence with outsiders.[24] And so the Wampanoag continued to watch as the Pilgrims suffered through the winter months, with many becoming ill and half the community was lost to death. The Pilgrims persevered, however, and by the end of the first year they had managed to build eleven structures, four of which were designated for common use.[25]

The Pilgrims were also aware of the Indians who were observed to be watching them; but no significant contact was made until March 16th of 1621. On that historic day, a lone, tall Indian brave showed himself on top of a nearby hill and proceeded to confidently stride into the village armed only with a single bow and two arrows, one of which was headed and the other unheaded (most likely a representation of the possibilities of war and peace). The Indian brave was about to enter the rendezvous where the women and children were gathered when a group of men suddenly blocked his path. The Indian, unfazed, stopped and waved to the men, and made the now famous pronouncement, "Welcome, Englishmen!" Imagine the surprise and delight of the colonists—who had endured thousands of miles of an arduous journey away from their homeland and then a bitter, cold winter—to be greeted in their native language on the new continent. To the Pilgrims, who believed everything happened for a reason, this was nothing short of divine intervention. And it unquestionably eased tensions and distrust on both sides.[26]

The Indian brave was called Samoset by the Pilgrims (most likely a mishearing of his English given name, Somerset). During this auspicious first contact, Samoset proceeded to inform the Pilgrims of the history of the land in broken but understandable English; he went on to explain that most of the Native inhabitants of this area had recently perished in a great plague. Then he told them of Massasoit (also known as Ousamequin),[27] the grand sachem (intertribal chief) of all the Wampanoag, and he also mentioned his friend, Tisquantum, who spoke better English than he did.

Although it was Samoset who was chosen to make the first contact with the colonists, it was Tisquantum (known to the colonists as Squanto) whom the Wampanoag chose to be their principal cultural ambassador. Tisquantum spoke English because of his remarkable history. Having been earlier kidnapped by British explorer George Weymouth in 1605 and taken back to Europe, Tisquantum lived in England for a long period of time, from six years to more than a decade, after which he was sold into slavery to the Spanish. He eventually managed to escape and return to America about a decade and a half after his initial capture.[28]

It is well known that Squanto was an interpreter and cultural ambassador. In truth he was more than that. He was purposely selected by the Indians to live amongst the settlers, not merely to make them feel welcome, but as part of a strategy to "indianize" them. This strategy was in keeping with the traditional stories of how to transform so-called cannibals (or rogue foreigners) discussed in chapter one. The approach was initially quite successful, certainly far more successful than the reciprocal strategy of trying to "civilize" and assimilate the Indians. The proof of this is how few Indians voluntarily chose to give up their ways, while a much larger contingent of Europeans chose to intermarry and live amongst the Indians. (This was a trend that continued well into the 18th century. Ben Franklin noticed it, commenting that "No European who has tasted Savage Life can afterwards bear to live in our societies.")[29] The indianization strategy only became unsustainable when the numbers of settlers increased beyond the capacity of the Indians to have an impact; but it worked for quite some time.[30]

There was, in fact, an initial fifty-five-year period of peaceful cultural exchange between the Mayflower Pilgrims and the Wampanoag tribes that continued throughout the lifetime of the grand sachem Massasoit.[31] The peace came early, with the signing of a treaty between Massasoit and the Plymouth colony, a treaty that was also a commitment to a military alliance, wherein they pledged to aid the other if any outside party unjustly warred against either.[32]

In time, Massasoit became highly respected, even beloved, by the colonists. When the sachem took ill, Governor Winslow took it upon himself to travel for miles through deep snow to deliver chicken broth to him, and Massasoit recovered. It was only when Massasoit died and his son Metacom took over as sachem that relations soured between the Indians and the Plymouth settlement, culminating in the brutal King Phillip's war of 1675. (Metacom was called King Phillip by the colonists).[33] This is not to imply that there was peace in all the land surrounding the Plymouth settlement during those first fifty-five years. Relations between the Pequot and the Plymouth Colony had deteriorated much earlier, culminating in the 1636 war between the Pequot and the Plymouth and Massachusetts Bay colonies and their allies, the Wampanoag and Narragansett, when the Pequot were nearly vanquished. It was the Pequot, ironically, that enacted a measure of revenge in the 1990s by opening a large and immediately successful casino in Connecticut (just 150 miles from New York City), something that irked Donald Trump when his Atlantic City casinos began faltering at that time.[34]

THANKSGIVING

Many of the early encounters between the Pilgrims and the Indians have been mired in controversy, but none more than Thanksgiving, which tends to provoke emotional responses in both Native and non-Native people, depending upon who is narrating the history. It may be that the controversies have served a positive purpose, for as people have revisited and debated our origins, a more complex, nuanced picture has begun to emerge. The narrative taught to school children has begun to shift away from a wholesale celebration of our immigrant past while whitewashing the sins of colonization toward a slightly better recognition of the Indigenous peoples who were already here when the Pilgrims arrived.[35]

Ever since President Lincoln established Thanksgiving as a national holiday, American elementary schools tended to portray the gathering as a formal English affair with a bunch of Pilgrims sitting around a table adorned with white tablecloth joined by only a few curious Natives. While that was a fictional portrayal, there is every reason to believe that some form of thanksgiving harvest ceremony did occur. The Plymouth museum lists fifty-three Pilgrims who were present at the first Thanksgiving.[36] From Governor Winslow's journal, we learned that the Pilgrims were joined by upwards of a hundred Native participants who brought plentiful wild game. It was also undoubtedly the case that this kind of gathering improved relations between the Pilgrims and the Natives. While they had already established a peace treaty with Massasoit, the Pilgrims had some amends to make from the first winter when they had managed to irritate the Indians by stealing a voluminous amount of buried corn seed from a place known today as Corn Hill. Other disputes arose over damage from livestock, selling of alcohol to Indians, and dishonest trading.

Overall, however, there was more than a half century of friendly intercultural exchange between Pilgrims and Indians that helped create the development of a distinctly American character on this soil. The blending of old and new worlds parted ways with the European class system, enabling hard working individuals to prosper through living off the land. While many Euro-Americans never approached the level of familiarity with the land that existed in Native American societies, the origin of this distinctly American character is, arguably, in the land herself. And the longer one stayed here, the more attuned one could potentially come to the frequencies of particular places.

THE MAYFLOWER COMPACT

Some researchers claim the Mayflower Pilgrims were the first Europeans to establish a democratic society in America. As evidence of this, they point to the Mayflower Compact, signed aboard their ship even before the Pilgrims came ashore.[37] But while the compact may represent an effort to establish a democracy of sorts, the social contract it outlined was, in my view, initially much more of a theocracy than a democracy, with the effort to separate church and state not beginning until a decade later with the arrival of Roger Williams and the establishment of the Massachusetts Bay Colony. For the Mayflower Pilgrims of the Plymouth colony, their worldview placed their Christian religion front and center above all else. The evidence for this is found in the first six lines of the Mayflower Compact. The phrase "civil body politic" does not appear until the seventh line. I italicized some of the phrases in the compact to indicate how much of it is about their religious faith:

> *In the name of God*, Amen. We, whose names are underwritten, the loyal subjects of our dread Sovereign Lord King James, *by the Grace of God*, of Great Britain, France, and Ireland, King, defender of the Faith, etc.
>
> Having undertaken, *for the Glory of God*, and *advancements of the Christian faith* and honor of our King and Country, a voyage to plant the first colony in the Northern parts

of Virginia, do by these presents, solemnly and mutually, *in the presence of* God, and one another, covenant and combine ourselves together into a civil body politic; for our better ordering, and preservation and furtherance of the ends afore-said; and by virtue hereof to enact, constitute, and frame, such just and equal laws, ordinances, acts, constitutions, and offices, from time to time, as shall be thought most meet and convenient for the general good of the colony; unto which we promise all due submission and obedience.

In witness whereof we have hereunto subscribed our names at Cape Cod the 11th of November, in the year of the reign of our Sovereign Lord King James, of England, France, and Ireland, the eighteenth, and of Scotland the fifty-fourth, 1620.[38]

ROGER WILLIAMS AND THE SEEDS OF A UNIQUELY AMERICAN CHARACTER

As significant a figure as Massasoit was in maintaining the peace between the Euro-Americans and the Natives, Roger Williams was an equally important counterpart. Although Williams did not arrive until 1631, and his initial friendships were with the Narragansett, he later established friendships with Massasoit and the Wampanoag. Williams became the strongest advocate of Native American sover-eignty and was the originator of the concept of separating church and state.

Williams was a unique character—an intellectually curious, Cambridge-educated Puritan preacher and theologian who, for personal and philosophical reasons, embraced diverse thinking and cultures. The 19th century historian Vernon Parrington made this claim: "Williams was the most provocative figure thrown upon the Massachusetts shores . . . the one original thinker amongst a number of capable social architects."[39]

Williams was an original thinker in many senses. He was creative, open-minded, and independent, yes; but he was truly *original* in the sense of developing a connection to the *origin*—meaning the place—of America. Williams developed a deep sense of place and love for his new continent because he listened to its native inhabitants, who in turn taught him to listen to the land.

It is important to realize that America was a place long before it was an idea for a political nation. As I expressed in *Original Thinking*, particular places give rise to particular ideas.[40] Williams was first in a lineage of like-minded American thinkers, a line that runs through Franklin, Jefferson, Thoreau, Emerson, James, and Pierce, among others; all were born and raised on this continent, and all were strongly influenced by Native America (its people and land). It is a mistake to imagine original thinkers standing alone, having no antecedents or connection to the history of the place they are living in. To some extent, every person is a product of their time, place, and culture; and every person is a combination of tradition and innovation. The French *milieu*, which literally translates as "middle place," implies this. Even the most significant persons straddle history; they are dependent upon their predecessors while influencing future generations to come.

Williams, for instance, was a protégé of Edward Coke, the English barrister who favored religious liberty and diversity. It was Coke who ruled against unfettered parliamentary power in the Bonham case of 1610—a case the American colonists made famous a century and a half later, using it as justification for their opposition to the British Stamp Act of 1765. It was their rallying cry of "no taxation without representation" that led the colonists in the direction of the American Revolution. This is only one important instance among many in which Williams is linked to the American Revolution.

Perhaps the thing that most distinguished Williams from his contemporaries—especially his religious brethren—was his open-hearted acceptance of the Native peoples of America. Nearly all his contemporaries took a condescending attitude toward "Indians" whom they viewed as arrested in their development, both technologically and spiritually—the latter belief based solely on their Christian faith in what they considered the one true God. Williams parted with such sanctimonious dogma. He also rejected the "Doctrine of Discovery" (a carryover from specific Roman Catholic papal bulls asserting any lands unoccupied by Christians were available to be discovered and seized) as absurd, because the lands were already occupied when the colonists arrived.

A century later, Franklin demonstrated a similar affinity for Native Americans, probably in part because Franklin was influenced by Williams. The connecting thread that unites Williams with the founding fathers is that they all valued what they learned from their encounters with Native Americans: lessons about personal liberty, natural rights, economic equality, and religious and political freedom.

The concept of inalienable (or natural) rights, so integral to the Declaration of Independence, was clearly derived from the value that Native America placed on life and liberty. Natives understood these natural rights of life and liberty to be original blessings given to them by Creator. Thus, it is a mistake, and perhaps a bit lazy, to trace the origin of the concept of natural rights to the British philosopher John Locke alone. While it is true that Locke was an influence on the founding fathers, he was, like many European social reformers of his day, greatly influenced by Native America.

Many simply have not accounted for how rapidly the knowledge of Indian societies traveled to Europe and back again. This process began almost immediately after the initial excursion of Columbus in the late 15th century. By 1516, Sir Thomas More was incorporating accounts of the first travelers to America in his landmark book *Utopia*, which envisioned a world of equality without money. The work criticized European society by using a fictitious Native American society that incorporated principles of democracy, but in a style closer to European ways—which may have accounted for why the book resonated with European political reformers. In any case, *Utopia* became vastly influential because it was translated into all the major European languages and has remained in print to this day.[41]

But *Utopia* was just the beginning. There was a continuous stream of narratives flowing back and forth. Some were first-hand accounts, and many were fanciful distortions written by people who never ventured across the ocean. There were critiques of European societies penned by individuals who, like More, used Indian characters or nations (real or fictitious) as foils.[42] As carriers of cultural exchange, Williams and Franklin were reliable sources, making multiple trips back to Europe. Williams made two round trip voyages, and Franklin four. Significantly, Franklin lived for nearly a decade in France toward the end of his life, and in doing so, did much to publicize the New World to Europeans.

For 16th and 17th century Europeans, the most striking aspect of Indian society was its social harmony based in personal liberty. The fact that Indians lived in harmonious, egalitarian societies with little to no concept of personal property was enormously appealing—as were the facts that they were not beholden to kings or monarchs and their political leaders acted democratically—in concert with the will of the community—lest they be removed.

It is very likely that Williams read More's *Utopia* and was influenced by the book before he ever set sail on his maiden voyage to America. But of course once he was in the New World, he could see this for himself. Significantly, Williams didn't simply observe the practices of Native Americans; he cultivated abiding friendships with them. To him, Indians were not heathens but people worthy of respect. His friendships were based in reciprocal generosity, in part because Williams was willing to learn Indian ways.

Both Williams and the founding fathers detected little crime or unhappiness in Indian communities that had few taboos and scant governmental oversight. Our founding fathers concluded that Indians lived in keeping with "natural law" (the laws of the natural world)—and this inspired Jefferson, Paine, and other founders to create a system of government that would mirror natural law, and thereby make government as unobtrusive as possible. The founders also sought to empower the people—but only to the degree they deemed appropriate. It is inaccurate to call the United States a democracy because what the founders created was a representational republic. This republic, however incomplete at the outset, was still a radical departure from the European monarchies that prevailed at that time, and a significant step toward liberty, justice, and natural rights of man.

Williams laid much of the groundwork for the future republic by incessantly arguing for religious and political freedom, as well as economic equality. He anticipated many of the arguments the founding fathers would later make, including the separation of church and state.

SEPARATION OF CHURCH AND STATE

More than a century before the founding fathers, Williams articulated a case for separation of church and state, which was mainly an argument for freedom to worship according to one's personal beliefs without interference from the government. While Williams' position was one of heart and conscience, he also realized that the only way to prevent religious wars was to promote religious tolerance, and so he did. Williams never assumed any right to impose his religion in place of someone else's, asserting that the "forcing of conscience is soul-rape."[43]

Williams' thoughts and actions were such a radical departure from his Puritan brethren that it resulted in his banishment from the Massachusetts Bay Colony in his first decade in America. A similar fate befell Anne Hutchinson, another outspoken advocate for separation of church and state. But Williams, because he had cultivated so many friendships with Native peoples, quickly negotiated a favorable arrangement to purchase land from the Narragansett Indians and proceeded to set up a new colony known as the Bay Rhode Island. The Indians were happy to accommodate Williams, setting aside a large area of land at a small price—so small in fact that Williams said later that Rhode Island was "purchased with love."[44] Hutchinson, who had been ostracized with no place to go, joined Williams in the Rhode Island Colony. Other religious groups, such as the Quakers, Baptists, and Jews found safe haven in the new colony.

Curiously, Williams attributed his inspiration for separation of church and state to the Indians. Williams asserted his belief that the

Indians would "never think of imposing personal religious values on civil society."[45] In crediting the Indians for the concept, I suppose that Williams was trying to protect them. It also could be that Williams simply misinterpreted a Native American distaste for telling others what to do, particularly in matters of the heart and spirit. Such an ethic is still commonplace in modern Native societies, where a common refrain when asking for advice or permission is, "It's up to you." While the freedom to make personal choices was (and still is) valued by Native America, this is a far cry from separating church and state. Personal choices are of immediate, real concern; whereas the separation of church and state is a choice between abstract values that holds little meaning to most Native peoples and would have meant even less in Williams' day.

Something akin to original politics was the norm in 18th-century Native American tribes. It is also true that Western societies once shared the same original understanding of politics but have been moving away from it for quite some time, ever since we passed the time of Socrates and Aristotle. The Pre-Socratics believed that man was the microcosm of the macrocosm—and that humanity ought to take its cues for action based on how all of nature, not just human society, was unfolding.

By the time of Aristotle, Western thought had increasingly separated human affairs from other realms, marginalizing or forgetting how we were embedded in the greater whole of nature. Aristotle's *Politics*, his seminal book on the subject, referred to politics with a human-centric, even urban focus.[46] It bears repeating that the word politics is derived from the *polis*—the city. (It does not derive from "many, blood sucking parasites"—despite what modern comedians may say). The exclusively human emphasis of modern politics precludes it from being sacred, in my estimation.

Original politics is sacred because it acknowledges a purpose that is larger than human, having the intent of benefiting all our relations with which we share the planet and cosmos. I suspect that Roger Williams, in his own way, desired a sacredness in his politics—and that his way of doing it was to respect the integrity of difference in personal relations. The desire on his part to maintain the peace is undoubtedly what led him to propose a separation of church and state.

LAND, LANGUAGE, AND WORLDVIEW

Upon Williams' arrival in Plymouth, he was pleasantly surprised by the warm hospitality he received from the Narragansett tribe, and he quickly became close friends with Miantonomi, Canonicus, and later with the Wampanoag sachem, Massasoit. He traveled throughout the forest with his new friends, immersing himself in the land, language, and culture. He quickly became conversant in many Native American languages. In fact, Williams eventually became so familiar with Native American languages that he wrote a book about it called *A Key Into the Language of America*[47] to explain how knowing the languages was the best means to understanding the continent. And indeed it was.

Williams' facility with indigenous American languages served to open a new worldview for him. This was because these languages are radically immersive, unlike English, which had already become a language of subject-object separation in Williams's day.

It is not a coincidence that the evolution of the English language toward subject-object division came about with the advent of linear perspective in art. Language, arts, and sciences all combine to create a cultural worldview. The language we speak does not determine our worldview, but it tends to limit the range of our perception.[48]

A good example of how language colors our perspective of the world can be found in the European approach to wild lands. These lands are known as *wilderness*, which implies a fear of the unknown because it is derived from the Old English *wilddēoren*, associated with wild and savage (or untamed) land. The typical Native American worldview, on the other hand, viewed nature as a place of wholeness and blessing rather than simply a wilderness to be tamed. The etymology of wilderness is also a key to why Europeans called Native Americans "savage," meaning wild and untamed. Thus, those who were comfortable with the wilderness of nature were somehow perceived as being not cultivated or refined in the development of their culture. But a lot has to do with the core perception of nature herself.

Native emphasis has always been on building relationships and alliances with other creatures in the natural world; whereas the European approach was about conquering or subduing nature to eradicate discomfort. The bulk of the colonists were most comfortable remaining in the settlements they established. Men like Williams, who developed real knowledge of the land by venturing out into it on a regular basis, were relatively rare.

THE PRINCIPLE OF WUNNAUMWÁUONCK

From Canonicus, Williams learned the important principle of *wunnaumwáuonck*, which has been defined as "faithfully aligning one's thoughts, words, and action." To this definition, I would suggest adding "with nature," as that would clearly have been the end goal of what thoughts, words, and actions needed to be aligned with. In any case, the principle of *wunnaumwáuonck* served to reinforce the friendship between Williams and Canonicus, and Williams went on to become an important conduit for the deeper meaning of Native culture. This went far beyond the mundane things that history books typically mention about Native American culture (that is, hunting and gathering, planting, fishing, and cooking). When Williams learned Native American languages, I can imagine that a whole new view of life was opened to him.

Williams already took a different approach to nature and to religion. He was more of a mystic than a theologian; he was inclined toward the spirit rather than the letter of religion. His recognition of the "indwelling God of Love in a world of material things" anticipated Emerson and the Concord school, as well as Unitarian, Unity, and other "new thought" movements of the twentieth century. However, Williams was not an ascetic who removed himself from society. He was closer to Gandhi, who seamlessly merged the spiritual and the political in his thinking. Harrington considered him as much of a political philosopher as a theologian—and found his political leanings to be a forerunner of Paine, but Williams also anticipated Burke and the French romantics such as Rousseau and Coleridge in his appetite for the real versus the abstract.

Williams's impact lasted far beyond many of his contemporaries, in part because Milton, the English poet and author of *Paradise Lost*, and Cromwell, the English military and political leader, both admired Williams. They in turn inspired Hobbes and Locke, who inspired Franklin, Paine, and many of the founding fathers of America.[50]

CHAPTER THREE

Native American Influence on the Founding of the United States

During King George's War of the 1740s (the third of four French and Indian wars), the British Crown sent emissaries such as Ben Franklin to negotiate a military alliance with the Iroquois, not knowing that this would give Franklin and other colonists a taste of what a free and egalitarian society could be. This taste of liberty, coupled with the Iroquois urging the colonists to unite amongst themselves, is what led to the American Revolution.[51]

Even before then, the colonists had already established an identity distinct from Europe, one that came directly from contact with the participatory democracy of Native American tribes. By 1740, New England towns were having town meetings.[52] In Franklin's Pennsylvania, William Penn and the Quakers maintained good relations with the Lenape (Delaware) Indians, leading to the creation of Tammany societies named after the Lenape Chief Tammany (also known as Tamanend). These Tammany societies sprang up across New England before the Revolutionary War, and the Tammany society of New York eventually became the political machine known as Tammany Hall.[53]

Native symbols and motifs were widespread across pre-Revolutionary America. But it was the real living example of egalitarian Native societies devoid of class conflict, not the symbols, that inspired Euro-Americans. The idea that every man could succeed was riveted in the American imagination. This does not mean that the colonists expected life to be easy in America; and, clearly, it wasn't. As challenging as it must have been, the colonists relished the opportunity to begin anew on a level-playing field.

Franklin wrote of the "happy mediocrity" that prevailed in America, "where the cultivator works for himself and supports his family in decent plenty," and contrasted this with the deplorable conditions in Europe of "poverty and misery; the few rich and haughty landlords, the multitude of poor, abject, rack-rented, tithe-paying tenants, and half-paid and half-starved laborers," concluding that there is evidence of a "great difference in our favor."[54] Jefferson similarly described the class structure of Europe as "wolves over sheep."[55] Jefferson, like Franklin, saw America as a land of equal opportunity, and he too was influenced by the example of egalitarian Native American societies.

Jefferson's contact with Natives began early because Jefferson's father, Peter Jefferson, was an avid naturalist and kept company with many Native elders. This included Ontassete, who Jefferson noted "was always a guest of my father on his journeys to and from Williamsburg." Thomas Jefferson later described Ontassete as "the great warrior and orator of the Cherokees."[56]

George Washington also had significant contact with Native Americans early in his life and wrote about it in his journals. Historians tend to ignore or minimize this, concentrating instead on Washington's military prowess and ascension to becoming America's first president after the signing of the US Constitution. But as a young man, Washington was a surveyor, and in that line of work he had ample opportunities to interact with Native Americans. In fact, he relied upon Indian scouts all his life for knowledge of the local topography.

As a member of the Virginia militia, Washington befriended two members of the Haudenosaunee Confederacy: Tanacharison (Half-King) of the Seneca and Monacatootha of the Oneida. Through these friendships, he was invited to attend council meetings where he obtained some insight into Native forms of philosophy and governance. Along with Franklin and Sir William Johnson (an influential Irish merchant), Washington was one of the key colonists who paved the way for a military alliance with the Iroquois against the French in the French and Indian Wars.

Washington managed to make a good impression despite being saddled with the Algonquin name *Conotocarious* (or "Town Destroyer)" that was given to his great-grandfather, John Washington, for his actions a century before. Perhaps in fulfillment of his name, Washington ended up destroying tribal villages during the Revolutionary War—but I am getting ahead of my story.[57]

Thomas Paine was another founding father who had significant contact with Native Americans. For Paine, these encounters were life-changing, infiltrating his philosophical outlook as expressed in *Common Sense*, the famous pamphlet that supported the American Revolution, and later in *The Natural Rights of Man*, written immediately after the French Revolution.

Paine was mentored by Franklin, who sponsored his relocation to America a few years before the American Revolution and introduced him to Native American leaders. But it was Franklin himself who was the greatest advocate for Native Americans, and he also had the most sustained period of diplomatic contact with them. This began as early as 1736 when Franklin, a printer, began publishing Indian treaties, something he continued doing until 1762. Franklin continued to publish Indian treaty accounts even after he was elected into the Pennsylvania Assembly, often taking the side of the Indians in writing his commentaries. His support of Indian causes was said to be the reason for his (eventual) defeat in the Pennsylvania assembly.[58]

In any case, it was not the assembly position that gave Franklin the greatest opportunity to interact with Native America; it was his appointment as Indian Commissioner of Pennsylvania that enabled Franklin to establish diplomatic ties with the Haudenosaunee and an abiding friendship with Chief Canassatego, sachem (Chief) of the Onondaga—a friendship that turned the tide of history. It was Canassatego who urged Franklin to unite the colonists as the Iroquois had done in their successful confederacy; and it was Canassatego himself who addressed a colonial assembly in Lancaster Pennsylvania on July 4, 1744, with the following potent words (which, not coincidentally, were published by Franklin):

> Our wise forefathers established Union and Amity between
> the Five Nations. This has made us formidable; this has given
> us great Weight and Authority with our neighboring Nations.
> We are a powerful Confederacy; *and by your observing the*
> *same methods our wise forefathers have taken,* you will
> acquire such Strength and power. Therefore, whatever befalls
> you, never fall out with one another. (italics are mine).[59]

To amplify his spoken message, legend has it that Chief Canassatego presented Franklin with the gift of a single arrow (in a manner reminiscent of what Peacemaker was said to have once done for the Iroquois). While Franklin was examining the arrow, the chief suddenly took back the arrow and broke it over his knee. Canassatego then reached behind him to pick up a sheaf of thirteen bundled arrows and attempted to break them across his knee. But this time the arrows would not break because they were joined as one. He then ceremoniously presented the bundle to Franklin, and the meaning was plain to all. Franklin never forgot the import of this symbolic gesture, and years later while serving as a committee member designing the Great Seal of the United States, he recommended that the symbol of the thirteen bundled arrows be carried in the talon of the eagle, which it is to this day.[60]

While Chief Canassatego died six years after the 1744 Lancaster conference, his words lived on, carried forward by Franklin. Then, just four years after Canassatego's death, Franklin reminded the colonists of the sachem's words at the Albany Conference of 1754. Curiously, while there was ample evidence that Franklin greatly respected Canassatego and the Iroquois, he relied on a racial slur when he said:

> It would be a strange thing if Six Nations of ignorant savages
> should be capable of forming such a union and be able to
> execute it in such a manner that it has subsisted for ages and
> appears indissoluble, and yet a like union should be impractical
> for ten or a dozen English colonies to whom it is more neces-
> sary and must be more advantageous, and who cannot be
> supposed to want an equal understanding of their interest.[61]

Because Franklin so respected Canassatego, I suspect he employed the words "ignorant savages" not from personal racial bias, but in an effort to reach the colonists at their level, attempting to shame them into action. It is also possible that Franklin internalized the systemic racism of his day while simultaneously respecting certain individual Native Americans he came to know. Either, or some combination of both, are possible. With the benefit of hindsight, we can see that racial and gender bias, discrimination, and genocide have always been a shadow element in the founding and evolution of a nation later described by Lincoln as a government "of the people, by the people, for the people."[62]

History has shown that racial prejudice runs deep in the human psyche. Native Americans themselves have not been immune to "othering" peoples different from their tribe; in fact, many Native American nations—Dinè (Navajo), Cherokee, and Haudenosaunee (Iroquois) among them—describe themselves in words that translate to "The People," which, if taken at face value, could imply that those not of the tribe are less than fully human. Native American tribes also were known to make slaves of those they conquered, although in most cases these slaves were given a path to later becoming part of the tribe. The tendency to dehumanize others appears, ironically, to be uniquely human.

Whatever Franklin's beliefs were, he apparently did not offend any of the parties to the Albany Plan. He was respected by the colonists, Iroquois, and the British crown—despite the fact that the parties had competing interests. Franklin was entrusted to draft a plan that balanced these seemingly contradictory interests:

1. the Crown's desire for control
2. the colonies' desire for autonomy, but in a loose confederation
3. the Iroquois wish that the colonies unite in a similar, if not identical manner as they, as that would make negotiations much simpler

To do all this required great diplomatic skill—and Franklin was equal to the task. But before giving Franklin too much credit, it is important to realize that he did not start from scratch. The heart of

Franklin's plan was derived from the already existing governing document of the Iroquois known as *The Great Law of Peace* (at that time, expressed on wampum belts).[63]

In fact, Franklin's plan for the union of the colonies so closely resembled that of the Iroquois that the historian Boyd maintained as recently as 1942 that Franklin "proposed a plan for the union of the colonies, and he found his material in the great Confederacy of the Iroquois." Indeed, Franklin chose the term "Grand Council" for the plan's delegation (the same name the Iroquois gave to their central council); and the number of delegates, forty-eight, was very close to the fifty that comprised the Iroquois Grand Council, amongst other similarities. The greatest difference between the two plans may have been in the selection of delegates. The Iroquois system chose the number of delegates based on tradition, whereas the delegates for the colonies were proportionally allocated based on tax revenues.

The Albany conference did not produce the uniting of the colonies (that did not happen until 1774, thirty years after Canassatego's famous address)—but the conference was still pivotal, as it resulted in the colonies cementing an alliance with the Iroquois.

THE STAMP ACT AND BOSTON TEA PARTY

The Stamp Act of 1765 was the first tax levied directly on the American colonists by the British government, and the vehement protest it provoked succeeded in forcing its repeal the very next year. The colonists were incensed that they were being used as a revenue source without any representation in the government, and this galvanized them to organize into radical opposition groups such as The Sons of Liberty, whose rallying cry was "no taxation without representation." The Sons of Liberty were an underground paramilitary group, and they continued to meet even after they successfully rebuked the Stamp Act. In fact, their opposition to the Crown never ended. It continued to simmer on the back burner of colonial consciousness until it erupted in the Boston Tea Party.

The Boston Tea Party is well known for being a catalyst for the American Revolution, but its origins remain somewhat mysterious even centuries later. When the tea ship Dartmouth arrived in Boston Harbor on November 28th of 1773, a small band of protesting colonists (known as the "patriots") met the ship and demanded it be sent back to sea with its shipment undelivered and duties unpaid. For several weeks, a tense standoff ensued with the patriots refusing to accept the tea and the owner's representative, Francis Rotch, refusing to send the ship back to England. As the crisis grew, Rotch set December 17th as the date for final resolution; if the patriots did not accept the tea by then, Rotch promised to sell the cargo at auction. While the fate of the Dartmouth was being decided, two other tea ships, the Eleanor and the Beaver, arrived in the harbor, bringing the sum total of duited tea to approximately 90,000 pounds. The protest continued to grow, with the Bostonians soon joined by residents from Dorchester, Brookline, Roxbury, and Charlestown and later Newburyport, Worcester, and Plymouth. By December 16th, the day before the deadline, the ranks of the protesters had swelled to an enormous, unruly mob of 5,000.[65]

The group who actually dumped the tea was a much smaller contingent of unknown participants. A half century later, John Adams contended that he did not know the identity of a single participant. Some of the more famous patriots, such as Samuel Adams and John Hancock, were implicated in the planning, but not in the actual deed. Paul Revere was probably the most famous person rumored to have participated, but nobody knows for sure to this day. The most likely culprits were The Sons of Liberty, for their identities were kept secret from the start.[66]

Why Did the Boston Tea Party Participants Dress as Mohawks?

The Patriots who actually dumped the tea were said to be protesting British economic imperialism, but they disguised themselves as Mohawks. I do not find this coincidental. As researchers Stephen Sachs and Bruce Johansen put it, this was not "as if Paul Revere and a gaggle of late eighteen century party animals had stopped by a costume shop on their way to the wharf and found the Mohawk model, the only one available in quantity on short notice."[67] The Mohawks at the time were a ubiquitous symbol for Native Americans, easily recognizable with their unique haircuts and according to Grinde and Johansen, also a symbol of liberty.[68] Clearly, the colonists were not trying to go incognito as much as they were making a statement. The Mohawk and other Native tribes had no kings, no class system, no tariffs, and no courts. They lived in accord with what Paine later called "the natural rights of man." As such, the Mohawks were the perfect symbol to adopt when desiring freedom from imperialists.

The Boston Tea Party, while being the spark that ignited the American Revolution, was also the means through which the radicals finally fulfilled the prophetic words of Canassatego and, at long last, united. It was only one year later that they brought together the Continental Congress of representatives from all the major colonies.

In the summer before the Congress gathered, key leaders of the Iroquois and the colonists gathered to smoke a peace pipe and rekindle the ancient council fire. Again, I do not find this coincidental. It was during this historic gathering in the summer of 1774 that the colonial commissioners repeated nearly verbatim the advice of Chief Canassatego from thirty years ago, and went on to add:

> These were the words of Canassatego. Brothers, our forefathers rejoiced to hear Canassatego speak these words. They sunk deep into our hearts. The advice was good. The advice was kind. We said to one another 'The Six Nations are a wise people. Let us hearken to them, and take their counsel, and teach our children to follow it. . . .' [Today] we thank the great God that we are all united; that we have a strong confederacy, composed of twelve provinces. . . . These provinces have lighted a great council fire at Philadelphia and sent sixty-five counselors to speak and act in the name of the whole and to consult for the common good of the people.[69]

Clearly, the colonists felt a debt of gratitude to Chief Canassatego and the Iroquois for the formation of the Continental Congress (soon to be the United States Congress). Such gratitude was openly acknowledged by the founding fathers for much of the 18th century. However, with the coming of the 19th century, the so-called "Indian Wars" (generally considered to have begun in the 17th century) were greatly intensified—and the US government found it convenient to dehumanize their enemy.[70] Thus the debt to Native America was largely forgotten. Thankfully, within the past quarter century the acknowledgment of the role Native America played in our founding is resurfacing and furthered by the work of modern Native American leaders such as Haudenosaunee elders Oren Lyons, Faithkeeper of the Turtle Clan of the Onondaga Nation, and the social activist and author John Mohawk, who have assisted revisionist researchers Bruce Johansen, Stephen Sachs, Sally Roesch Wagner, Betty Booth Donohue, Donald Grinde, and others, all of whom I owe a debt of gratitude.

DECLARATION OF INDEPENDENCE

People who dismiss the role of Native Americans in the founding of the United States may be surprised to learn that twenty-one Iroquois leaders were invited to witness the month-long debate over potential independence that took place in the hall of the Continental Congress in the late spring and early summer of 1776. And there is evidence their presence was clearly felt, for during the forum John Hancock, the chairman and first signatory to the Declaration of Independence, was moved to address the Iroquois delegation as "Brothers," declaring that the alliance between the two nations shall last "as long as the sun shall shine" and the "waters run."[71]

Hancock's statement was not only hyperbole; it would be proven utterly false within a few, short years. However, it was well-received at the moment—so much so that an Onondaga chief requested permission to give Hancock an Indian name on the spot. Hancock accepted and was given the name *Karanduawn*, or "Great Tree"—which was quite an honor if we can assume this was a reference to the

Iroquois *Tree of Great Peace* (also known as *The Tree of the Great Long Leaves*), whose nature was both peace and strength.[72]

The soaring words of the Declaration of Independence, penned by Jefferson, were deftly edited by Franklin (the primary editor on a committee of five) and later by Congress. The famous phrase "We hold these truths to be self-evident" was originally "We hold these truths to be sacred and undeniable"—a phrase Franklin apparently found too rigid. Most scholars attribute the wording "self-evident" to the influence of Franklin's friend, David Hume, and that may well be.[73]

The phrase "unalienable rights" of "life, liberty, and the pursuit of happiness," assumed to be a derivative of Locke's "life, liberty, and property," may instead have been inspired by the way Native Americans lived—from blessing and wholeness in gratitude for life and liberty (regardless of material possessions). It is known that Locke was greatly interested in Indians, read many reports about them, and spoke with Indians who came to England while developing his views in *The Second Treatise on Government*.[74] The concept of government "deriving their just powers from the consent of the governed" is almost certainly derived from experience with Native American governments—for at that time, no government in Europe would have deigned to give away their power to the people they governed.

The nations of Native America were the salient example of egalitarianism that the colonists drew upon in formulating their own declaration of liberty, even as the Southern states drew upon ancient Greece to some degree (in both government and architecture). It was Native America that primarily inspired the founding fathers, particularly Franklin, Jefferson, and Paine, who sought true liberation from kings and tyrants.

FROM RAUCOUS TO CAUCUS: NATIVE AMERICAN INFLUENCE ON PROCESS

The Native influence on overall philosophy was significant, but the Indians also had a significant effect on decorum and practical rules of order that should not be underestimated in importance. Proper decorum is not merely about rules; it also establishes a process by which respectful relations can be maintained, an important aspect of original politics.

The concept of informally *caucusing*—or listening to each other not to necessarily reach a conclusion but to promote understanding of diverse points of view—is a distinctly Native American ethic that caught on early in American politics and even today remains to some degree. If anyone doubts its origin, consider that the word *caucus* is Algonquin.

The concept of respectful listening for the purpose of understanding rather than to ready a reply—central to fruitful dialogue and consensus decision-making—was also incorporated into early American politics. Some of this influence remains, which is why it is still considered rude to interrupt someone in the American Congress (unlike in the British House of Commons, which is a loud and raucous arena even today). Without the influence of Native America, we would undoubtedly be acting much the same as our mother country continues to act.

The evidence for the Native American effect on process is undeniable. Immediately after the debate and subsequent Declaration of Independence attended by the Iroquois chiefs, two rules changes that were clearly reflective of Native American values were adopted. On July 17, 1776, less than two weeks following the signing of the Declaration of Independence, these formal rules changes were passed:

1. No member shall read any printed paper in the House during the sitting thereof, without the leave of Congress.

2. When the House is sitting, no member shall speak to another, so as to interrupt any member who may be speaking in the debate.[75]

IROQUOIS CIVIL WAR

It is one of the greatest ironies of history that the Iroquois—who did so much to bring the colonies into unity that led to the birth of the United States—did not remain united themselves in the face of the American Revolution.

The reasons for this are complex. For one, the peace that resulted from the end of the French and Indian wars was short-lived. An increasing stream of colonists continued to migrate into Indian lands, even after a treaty was signed at Fort Stanwix that supposedly established firm boundary lines between European and Indian lands. Thus the Great Confederacy was already under duress even before the Revolution.

When the Revolutionary War broke out, the Iroquois Confederacy initially remained neutral, clearly viewing the war as an English civil war that had little to do with them. A long letter was sent from the Oneidas to Governor Trumbull of Connecticut with the request that it be communicated to the four New England colonies. Here is one of the moving passages:

> BROTHERS: We have heard of the unhappy differences and great contention between you and Old England. We wonder greatly, and are troubled in our minds.

> BROTHERS: Possess your minds in peace respecting us Indians. We cannot intermeddle in this dispute between two brothers. You are *two brothers of one blood*. We are unwilling to join either side in such a contest, for we bear an equal affection to both you Old and New England. Should the Great King of England apply us for aid, we shall deny him; if the colonies apply, we shall refuse. The present situation of you two brothers is new and strange to us. We Indians cannot find, nor recollect in the traditions of our ancestors, the like case, or a similar instance.

> BROTHERS: For these reasons possess your minds in peace, and take no umbrage that we Indians refuse joining in the contest. We are for peace.[76]

Unfortunately the Confederacy was unable to maintain neutrality for long because the pressure—from both sides—became too great. The British Crown kept insisting that the Confederacy fulfill its treaty obligations as England's military ally; and while this was true, imagine the confusion it caused since the treaties had been negotiated with colonial mediators such as Franklin. The Confederacy was unable to agree on a unified course of action, and eventually the *Tree of Great Peace* (that united the Confederacy) began to splinter. The Oneida and the Tuscarora were the first to announce their support for the American rebels. The other tribes, perhaps thinking they were choosing the winning side, remained loyal to the British.

The Haudenosaunee effectively collapsed into civil war, and tragically the different nations ended up raiding and destroying each other's villages in the Revolutionary War as they fought under the leadership of either the British or the American rebels. George Washington brutally destroyed forty Iroquois villages with help from the Oneida and Tuscarora, thus truly earning the nickname of "Town Destroyer" originally given to him because of the actions of his great grandfather.

When the war finally ended, a treaty was signed between England and the former colonies. However, it failed to address the fate of the original peoples of this continent. A separate treaty was eventually signed with the Six Nations Confederacy. That treaty, which was deemed to supersede any previous treaties, resulted in the Confederacy giving up significant portions of their lands. A similar fate befell all the other tribes in the area. In this manner, the Revolutionary War ended up weakening all of the nations and tribes of Native America.

ARTICLES OF CONFEDERATION

The Articles of Confederation were the founding document of the United States of America, and yet they are given scant attention. Historians typically gloss over the Articles, characterizing them as a failed experiment that required a do-over, thus implying that the Constitution was the primary founding document of the United States. For our purposes, the Articles are important because of how closely they were based on the Haudenosaunee Confederacy. It is therefore not surprising that the memory of the Articles dimmed as did the vital role Native America played in the founding of the political nation.

The Articles of Confederation were the fruition of the Albany Plan set in motion decades earlier. During the debate called to formulate the Articles, several in the Continental Congress came right out and said that they were proposing a union of the former colonies based on the Iroquois Confederacy.[77]

Of course, the Articles were modeled after the Haudenosaunee way of governing only to the extent that Native ways were understood and considered applicable. Nonetheless, the Articles envisioned a country that was far more of an egalitarian democracy than what was specified by the Constitution that followed, although the Constitution was perhaps the more sophisticated document.

Under the Articles, there was only one governing body: the legislature. The judicial and executive powers were not yet separated into branches of government. The legislature was to operate in a way that was very similar to Indian council circles; all major decisions of the Congress required near unanimous consent (nine of thirteen states). Upon the insistence of Ben Franklin, the Articles also closely followed the Indian concept of public service, limiting the length of time that any person could be a delegate to three years and stating that "no person shall be capable of holding any office under the United States, for which he, or another for his benefit receives any salary, fees, or emolument of any kind."[78] How different that is from today!

Was George Washington Really the First President?

Contrary to common knowledge, there were presidents of the United States before Washington—in fact there were several presidents elected before the Articles of Confederation were even ratified, and eight after they were ratified, John Hanson being the first.[79] Historians typically dismiss these early presidents because they had largely ceremonial powers, presiding over the legislature in a similar manner to how the vice-president presides over the Senate today, and serving no more than a one-year term with the exception of John Hancock, who served twice, once before and once after the Articles of Confederation were ratified.

The presidents before Washington are deservedly thought of in different terms than the presidents from Washington onward, as after the Constitution was drafted the president was given far greater power. Nonetheless, a legitimate argument can be made for John Hanson being considered the first president of the United States. Hanson served from 1781–1782 after The Articles of Confederation was signed and ratified, at a time when other countries (France and Morocco) had already recognized the United States as a sovereign nation, and the United States had already signed a treaty of military alliance with France (negotiated by Ben Franklin). Among other accomplishments, Hanson established the Great Seal of the United States—which all presidents have been required to use on all official documents ever since. In fact, Hanson accomplished quite a bit in his one-year term. Besides designing the Great Seal, he ordered all foreign troops off American soil, removed all foreign flags, established the Treasury Department, and installed the first Secretary of War and the first Foreign Affairs Department. By any standard (weak executive or not), Hanson was productive. So why have historians essentially erased him from the history books?[80]

It could be that any mention of presidents before Washington serves to remind us of how we first modeled the presidential role almost entirely upon Indian ceremonial council government. In council circles, the chief was not considered powerful in and of himself; his power was derived from the consent of the council. This model of power was attractive to the colonists because it could not have been further from the British monarchy. This concern about centralizing power persisted, and even as the Articles of Confederation were superseded by the Constitution, the founding fathers continued to emphasize measures that ensured the president would not rise to the level of tyrant or king. Such measures have been periodically tested over the years, but perhaps never more than today.

THE FEDERALISTS AND ANTI-FEDERALISTS

It cannot be overstated how radical the American experiment was. It was a complete break from any Western government of its day, and while in some respects it hearkened back to ancient Greek democracies, it was uniquely American due to the influence of Native America.

There was no guarantee that the new country would last, however. The years between the signing of the Declaration of Independence in 1776 and the ratification of the Articles of Confederation in 1781, signed two years before the end of the Revolutionary War, were tumultuous, and not just because of the war.

Shortly after the war was over, it became apparent that the Articles were not working—at least not financially. The war had been costly to wage; as a consequence, all the states owed money to the Federal government, but there was no mechanism to compel them to pay. In response, a divide arose between those who wanted to vest the federal level with more power over the states (hence known as the "Federalists"), and those who were opposed (the "Anti-Federalists").

The Federalists, led by James Madison and Alexander Hamilton, did not see the Articles as sufficient for providing a sustainable path forward for the nascent country. Hamilton complained that under the Articles the states were essentially sovereign nations, a situation which left the national government ill-equipped to enforce federal law or to create foreign policy that had teeth. The Anti-Federalists, which included Thomas Jefferson, were wary of ceding too much power to the federal government, fearing a lapse into a monarchy or dictatorship. But even Jefferson realized that there were certain deficiencies in the Articles of Confederation that could prevent the long-term survival of the United States.[81]

The idea began to surface of holding a constitutional convention with the intent of revising the Articles of Confederation. Many assumed that this would only be a slight revision, while Madison and Hamilton had other plans.

In the end, both philosophies—that of the Anti-Federalists who, following the Indians, believed in as little government as possible—

and that of the Federalists who believed in a robust central government being necessary to the survival of the nation—were present at the 1787 Constitutional Convention and its eventual ratification in 1789. Both philosophies of a strong or weak federal government were present during this period (the generally accepted start of the nation)—and both are an inherent part of the American psyche. The two modern political parties have drawn upon this original debate to formulate their political ideologies, but make no mistake about it: The two parties need each other because both aspects of this debate are necessary to constitute the United States as a whole.

CHAPTER FOUR

Preserving the Union for the Long Term: Overcoming Division through Checks and Balances

Alexander Hamilton, like Ben Franklin, was a self-made man, but unlike Franklin he was born outside America and grew up an orphan. Hamilton was blessed with a charisma that earned him many friends and perhaps more than his fair share of enemies—but his greatest gift may have been his vision, and more specifically, his ability to take abstract, lofty ideas and bring them into practical manifestation. Early in life, Hamilton seized upon an opportunity to emigrate from the West Indies to Northeast America. Through a combination of ambition, talent, eloquence, and a knack for showing up at critical moments in the history of the republic, he emerged as one of the driving forces, alongside Madison, that brought the Constitution of the United States into being.

A turning point in the history of the republic was the Annapolis Conference of 1786, convened by Madison for the purpose of addressing interstate disputes. The gathering began inauspiciously, but that quickly changed with the realization that the ostensible purpose to solve tensions among the states could not be accomplished without addressing the flaws in the overall political framework. Thus the idea for a constitutional convention was born.

Hamilton and Madison bonded in Annapolis. They made a good team, even with their opposite temperaments. Madison tended to be a reserved intellectual while Hamilton was more hot-blooded and inspirational—although Hamilton was never accused of lacking intellect. Hamilton began to envision a "finely crafted government of interrelated parts"—something he and Madison were to further develop over time. Their discussions at the Annapolis Conference led to their ongoing collaboration, both during the constitutional convention itself and then on the historic Federalist Papers that were written to make the case for ratification of an American constitution.[82]

Hamilton and Madison pushed for the constitutional convention because they both saw a need to preserve and protect the union for the long term. This required a more foundational structure than the Articles could provide. The key, according to Hamilton, was to establish a strong, central government. He wanted a government that was strong in every way: legally, financially, and militarily—and this, he believed, would provide a pathway to long-term security, prosperity, and peace.

THE AMERICAN CONSTITUTIONAL CONVENTION OF 1787

One of the curious things about the constitutional convention is that the meetings were held in secret. This might seem odd for a convention aiming to design a representational republic, but the founding fathers were aware of the pressure that would have been brought upon them if the meetings were made public, and they studiously wanted to avoid such distractions. They also hoped to facilitate an atmosphere of robust dialogue without being held captive to political factions.

It is important to acknowledge that the founders tried mightily to avoid the development of factions, and to a significant degree, succeeded—and this is one reason I characterize the founding of the nation under the heading of Unitive Consciousness. But unitive does not mean a flat, undifferentiated consciousness. A unitive field can include a wide range of difference and still be unified, provided the integrity of the difference is allowed to coexist.

This is not to imply that the founders were a perfect example of unitive consciousness. Indian councils (both men's, women's, and other tribal councils) were far more unitive, and they were not perfect either. While the founding fathers learned from the Indians and attempted to copy their process, they erred in both their perception and interpretation of what they saw. One obvious blind spot was their failure to include women in any aspect of the political process. Another blind spot was their failure to include people of color or to take a braver stance on slavery, something that has haunted the nation ever since.[83]

Considering the social mores of the time, these were not surprising omissions. Within the constraints of their worldview, the founders set up a container for diverse viewpoints to be heard—at least as diverse as a group of fifty-five all-White male, educated, mostly affluent property owners and lawyers could be.

The reason the founders emerged from the Constitutional Convention with a well-thought out document was that they listened to each other. The process was more dialogic than adversarial, and when two distinct plans emerged (known as the New Jersey and Virginia plans), the impasse was not permanent. This is not to say that the differences were not challenging. In a tense moment, Franklin suggested an opening prayer of intention be said at the beginning of each session—undoubtedly a tribute to how Indian councils operate. Franklin's idea was opposed by Hamilton and not adopted, but I suspect the mere suggestion of invoking a higher power helped break the impasse. In any case, differing views were allowed to breathe together until a solution eventually presented itself. Next I'll examine the details of the two plans.

THE NEW JERSEY AND VIRGINIA PLANS

The New Jersey Plan proposed relatively minor changes to the Articles of Confederation. It had the more modest goal of revising the Articles of Confederation, which after all was the stated objective of the convention. It retained much of the original structure with state sovereignty remaining strong. In lieu of a president, it proposed an executive council—a clause favored by Franklin—with limited powers. (In the worst-case scenario, the council could have been removed by a majority of the state governors.)

The New Jersey Plan continued on the path of incorporating some of the lessons Franklin and other founders had learned from the nations of Native America—in particular, the concept of inclusiveness—that when all voices are heard equally in council, the resulting decisions will be well thought-out and longer lasting. Accordingly, the New Jersey plan proposed a legislature of just one chamber with each state having one vote. It also retained a voluntary system of requisitions rather than giving the power of taxation to the federal government. While this was something that might have worked in Native American councils, it was no longer working in the young country.

The Virginia Plan, proposed by Madison, was much bolder. It was not a revision as much as a new document. Its salient features included a system of checks and balances provided through the articulation of three distinct branches of government: executive, legislative, and judicial; it also proposed a bicameral legislature (the House and Senate). Significantly, the proposal called for a legislature with proportional representation depending upon state population and a much stronger executive—a president with a seven-year term—a huge departure from the one-year presidency defined under the Articles of Confederation. The Virginia Plan also proposed that the Federal government have the power to tax the people in order to build a common defense against foreign enemies. In fact, the Virginia Plan represented a dramatic restart of the republic with a significantly enlarged role for the federal government and a corresponding diminishment of state powers.

As might be expected, smaller states gravitated toward the New Jersey plan—where they would have equal representation—and larger states moved toward the Virginia plan with its proportional representation based on population.

As these two plans were being debated, Hamilton made a passionate and long-winded speech in which he envisioned a hybrid form of government that had the continuity of a monarchy combined with the liberties of a republic with the president continuing to serve an indefinite term provided he embodied "good behavior." Hamilton's intent was to guard against anarchy and tyranny alike, and he distinguished his form of monarchy from its European counterparts by referring to the president as an "elected monarch."[84] William Samuel Johnson quipped that Hamilton's speech was "praised by everybody [and] . . . supported by none," but four states actually voted in favor of Hamilton's proposal of "good behavior," including the delegation from Virginia that included James Madison. Madison even proposed that the federal government be given the power to veto any state laws "as the King of Great Britain heretofore had." Franklin and others strongly opposed a presidential or federal veto, for this smacked of monarchy, and they wanted nothing that too closely resembled that from which they had just broken away. Jefferson, an anti-Federalist, would have certainly opposed such a proposal, but he was not present since he was serving overseas as Minister to France at the time. Hamilton, chastened by those in attendance, never again uttered a kind word about monarchy, "elected" or otherwise.[85]

Nonetheless, the debate of the role of the president aptly illustrates the creative tension between the evolutionary and devolutionary aspects of Unitive Consciousness in our model. The more power vested in the presidency, the closer we flirt with returning to the monarchy we broke away from. To the credit of all those at the Constitutional convention, this did not devolve too far.

Hamilton's radical proposal did serve a purpose, however, in making the Virginia plan seem less extreme. A compromise soon emerged, proposed by Roger Sherman of Connecticut and others (known as the Connecticut Compromise), in which the question of state versus federal power was solved in this way: All states would have equal representation in the Senate while representation in the House would be proportionate to each state's population. And that is the way it remains today.

From Public Service to Professional Politicians

While few would argue that the document produced at the Constitutional Convention is inferior to its predecessor, some of the omissions from the Articles of Confederation are worth noting, as they have proved problematic over time. For instance, under the Articles there was a much clearer call to public service. No person holding office received any salary, fees, or emolument of any kind.

In not permitting salaries or emoluments of any kind for Congressional delegates, and in establishing term limits for delegates, the Articles followed a core ethic of Native American council governments. Franklin was the chief proponent of this radical form of public service, and early in the constitutional convention discussions he made a similar motion, asserting that delegates not receive a salary. Surprisingly, Hamilton seconded the motion, undoubtedly out of respect for the old sage, then eighty-one years old and enfeebled with gout and kidney stones. But the motion was never seriously considered.

If I were to speculate as to why the motion was not seriously considered, I would begin with the differences between Native societies (from which Franklin drew his inspiration) and Western societies. The Western are based on money economies and differences in wealth, whereas Native American societies were based on barter and gift economies. If one were to receive no remuneration in a money economy, only the wealthy would be able to serve. I also suspect that the mostly young delegates—the average age was forty-two—might have envisioned a future career in politics. Many of the delegates were less than half Franklin's age. Hamilton himself was only thirty-two years old; Madison was just thirty-six. Full of ambition to change the world, they probably viewed the notion of term limits and unsalaried delegates as a quaint but obsolete idea; or if given the benefit of the doubt, they could have been concerned that unsalaried delegates would only come from the wealthy class.

This is not to say that the delegates completely ignored Franklin; they retained restraints against the acceptance of emoluments from donors and foreign governments in the final product. But I doubt they foresaw a modern Congress that earns about four times the average person's salary and regularly votes to give themselves raises and other benefits, resulting in an operating budget of approximately $250,000 (paid entirely by taxpayers), the best quality healthcare, a generous pension, and innumerable other perks of the trade, including free airport parking, free health club membership, and weakened insider trading restrictions—while the fate of their constituents is, increasingly, left to the whims of the market.

Clearly, the trade-off in preserving and protecting the union for the long-term was that it created a career path for politicians. While most politicians enter public life with the best of intentions, the virtuous concept of voluntary public service under the Articles was lost. The irony is that with the high cost of running for public office today, it is increasingly only the wealthy—or those who have the backing of wealthy special interests—who can run for office.

THE FEDERALIST PAPERS AND THE PUSH TO RATIFY THE CONSTITUTION

The convention resulted in an initial draft of the Constitution, but that was only the first step toward its adoption. For the next two years, the job of the convention delegates was to persuade the Confederation Congress and the American people of its value. And since the Confederation Congress maintained its legal authority under the Articles, which remained in force unless or until nine states voted for the proposed Constitution, the Federalists had a hard road to victory, and the anti-Federalists were determined to block their path.

Governor Clinton of New York State beat everyone to the punch when he launched a robust publicity campaign opposing the adoption of the Constitution. Hamilton knew he had to respond, so he recruited Madison and John Jay to help him write a series of essays promoting the adoption of the Constitution, known today as the Federalist Papers. Because Hamilton had already earned some enemies in New York State (including Governor Clinton) he kept his identity secret (as well as those of the other contributors, adopting the pen name *Publius* from *Publius Valerius*, one of the founders of the Roman republic).[86]

The original goal of the Federalist papers was modest—to win the vote of the state of New York. But the essays ended up being enormously important. They have been cited in thousands of American legal cases over the years because they are the best existing example of what three of the founding fathers were thinking at the time. Past decisions based on the Federalist Papers have become the legal precedent by which future cases are evaluated, and in this manner, the document lives on almost as if it were part of the Constitution itself.

The plan was for Hamilton, Jay, and Madison to contribute an equal number of essays. After writing five, Jay fell ill, and Hamilton turned out to be far more prolific than Madison. Thus Hamilton wrote the bulk of the essays.

All were in favor of adoption of the Constitution with its built-in checks and balances designed to promote a wiser, more efficient, and stable government prepared to handle the inevitable tensions between federal and state rights, and between minority factions and majority rule, but they emphasized different things. Hamilton was the greatest advocate for strong, central government. Madison's voice was equally powerful, if moderating. He wrote on behalf of decentralization—as an advocate of state's rights and individual freedom. Jay emphasized national security in the few essays he contributed, warning that separate states would be unable to defend themselves against foreign wars.

While the identities of the writers were supposed to remain secret, the differences in style soon led to speculation regarding the probable authors. Madison and Jay were both excellent writers, but Hamilton had an undeniable "skill with the quill," as the modern Broadway musical that bears his name proclaims—and his writing stood out as uniquely persuasive. At times, however, Hamilton overreached, making it seem like the nation would lapse into anarchy at any moment if the Constitution were not adopted. It wasn't only Hamilton who was concerned, as evidenced by Shays' Rebellion of 1786. This armed uprising in Massachusetts—a protest against economic and civil rights injustices that pitted residents against tax collectors—was one of the main drivers for the constitutional convention and its adoption.

DEMOCRACY VERSUS REPUBLIC

It is important to realize that the United States was founded as a republic. It has never been a democracy, although it was arguably more democratic under the Articles of Confederation. Madison succinctly summarized the difference between a republic and a democracy in Essay #14 of the Federalist Papers:

> In a democracy, people meet and exercise the government in person; in a republic, they assemble and administer it by their representatives and agents. A democracy must be confined to a small area. A republic may be extended over a large region.[87]

The founders opted for a republic over a democracy because they felt that only a republic could be sustained over such a broad area as the continental United States—provided there were the requisite checks and balances. Although the United States has never been a democracy, it is understandable that many people assume that it is, considering the opening words of the preamble to the Constitution: "WE the People of the United States . . ."

The truth is that the founders never completely trusted the people—nor did they trust the politicians, and they planned accordingly.

How Could the Founding Fathers Solve the Riddle of Failed Republics?

The founding fathers were determined to solve the riddle of failed republics without resorting to a monarchy that would overly inhibit the freedom of the people. Madison and Hamilton emphasized different aspects of the concern, while also agreeing that the task was to design an efficient government that would stand the test of time. In pursuing this goal, Hamilton became known as a master innovator of governmental procedures. He was not content to sanction the federal government's assumption of the debt incurred by the Revolutionary war. He also designed an efficient, legal process for the government to tax the public and thereby offset the federal obligation. He was convinced that the nation was at risk as long as the states only paid these debts on a voluntary basis. As the first Treasury Secretary in the modern era of four-year-term presidents, Hamilton not only designed an efficient tax system; he also founded key institutions, such as a central bank, the stock exchange, the customs service, and the Coast Guard, among other innovations. His uncanny ability to create structures and regulations to manage money and resources earned him the moniker of "evil genius" from Noah Webster.[88]

In the Federalist Papers, Madison played the role of counterpoint to Hamilton, calmly assuaging any fears about federal overreach. In Essay #45, he claimed, "The powers delegated by the proposed Constitution to the federal government are few and defined. Those which are to remain in the State governments are numerous and indefinite."[89] He also stated that "the operations of the federal government role will be most extensive and important in times of war and danger; those of the State governments in times of peace and security."[90] He asserted that the new Constitution does not so much consist of "the addition of *new powers* to the Union than in the invigoration of its *original powers*."[91] He concluded that, rather than enlarging the powers of the Union, the Constitution merely substitutes "a more effectual mode of administering them."[92]

On the whole, the Federalist Papers provided a cogent rationale for adopting the Constitution, and Hamilton, Madison, and Jay deserve credit for articulating that argument. Oddly, the Federalist Papers did not accomplish its original, limited purpose since New York State was not easily persuaded. (New York only voted in favor after nine other states had done so and its fate was sealed.) But that is an aside. In the end, the Federalist Papers ended up accomplishing far more than the authors ever set out to do, becoming an integral part of American history.

THE BILL OF RIGHTS

During the final days of the constitutional convention, George Mason, the delegate from Virginia, made a proposal to include a bill of rights in the body of the document to explicitly protect the rights of individual citizens throughout the union. The proposal, which proved controversial, was dismissed rather perfunctorily, probably because taking up the subject would have required considerable dialogue, and the convention was winding down by then; delegates were tired and wanting to go home. Mason, who had already written and adopted a Bill of Rights in his home state, felt so strongly about his proposal that he did not sign the Constitution when the closing ceremony was held in Independence Hall.

Oddly, the authors of the Federalist Papers almost ignored the question of whether the Constitution should include a bill of rights. Neither Jay nor Madison took a position on it, even as Madison explored the overarching issue of majority rule versus minority rights in Essay #10. Hamilton was the only one to address it, and he took a defiant stance against a Bill of Rights in Essay #84, claiming, "the Constitution is itself, in every rational sense, and to every useful purpose, A BILL OF RIGHTS." Hamilton considered bills of rights a thing of the past—something that in their origins served as stipulations between kings and their subjects. He saw the United States Constitution as heralding a new era, and pointed to the opening sentence of the Preamble as evidence that the document was written for the people, in the people's voice (when it was, of course, written by a few men).

Despite Hamilton's rebuke and the lack of support from Madison or Jay, a clamoring arose for the inclusion of a bill of rights in the Constitution almost as soon as the campaign for ratification began. Thomas Jefferson was one of the lead proponents, even as he was still in France. Writing to Madison from Paris, he expressed his dismay that the Bill of Rights was not included, adding, "a bill of rights is what the people are entitled to against every government on earth, general or particular, and what no just government should refuse, or rest on inference."[93]

Madison would soon sit down and craft what is now known as the Bill of Rights for inclusion in the Constitution, but make no mistake about it: His main motivation was to appease the Anti-Federalists so that the Constitution as a whole would pass into law. He first tried to insert the bill of rights within the body of the document but then proposed they be included as a series of amendments.

THE AMAZING STORY OF THE 27TH AMENDMENT

When Madison first submitted a bill of rights to Congress, it included seventeen proposed amendments. Of the seventeen, only twelve were passed (which required a ⅔ approval vote in both the House and Senate), and of those twelve, two were not ratified by enough states (¾ of the states must ratify an amendment before it becomes affixed as an addition to the Constitution). Thus, only the first ten amendments became adopted, and these became known as The Bill of Rights.

Of the two amendments not ratified at the time, one was intended to be the Second Amendment, an indication of how important Madison considered it to be. Once the amendment failed, however, it was forgotten—only to be resurrected from the trash bin of history in an unlikely and somewhat miraculous manner. A University of Texas student, Gregory Watson, was assigned to write a paper on governmental process in 1982. Mr. Watson was studying books on the US Constitution when, in his own words, this happened:

> "I'll never forget this as long as I live," Watson begins. "I pull out a book that has within it a chapter of amendments that Congress has sent to the state legislatures, but which not enough state legislatures approved in order to become part of the Constitution. And this one just jumped right out at me."[94]

The unratified amendment read as follows:

> No law varying the compensation for the services of the Senators and Representatives shall take effect until an election of representatives shall have intervened.

In other words, if Congress were to vote to give itself a raise, it would not take effect until after the next election, thus giving constituents the opportunity to decide if they deserved it.

Watson was amazed by both the content of the memo and the fact that it had not been ratified into law. In proposing the amendment, Madison said at the time, "There is a seeming impropriety in leaving any set of men without control to put their hand into the public coffers, to take out money to put in their pockets."[95] To which someone employing modern slang might respond, "Ya think?"

Watson submitted his paper and got a C grade. He was none too pleased about that and thought to himself, "*I'm going to get that thing ratified.*"[96] To make a long story short, Watson spent the next ten years doing exactly that, and the 27th amendment was ratified. And when his old professor, Sharon Waite heard about it, she changed his grade from a C to an A.[97]

THE ENDURING INFLUENCE OF NATIVE AMERICA ON CURRENT US POLITICS

Had the 27th Amendment passed and become the Second Amendment, as Madison originally intended, congressional delegates might not be as handsomely compensated as they are today. They would also be closer to the spirit of our original politics, a spirit found in the Articles of Confederation. Yet, while the discarding of some of the more noble intentions of the Articles of Confederation might cause the reader to surmise that the Constitution represented a complete parting with Native American ways, that would be a false conclusion. For despite the fact that Hamilton and Madison considered the checks and balances of the United States Constitution to be on the cutting edge of political science—equivalent to other advances in sciences of their time—the ancient Iroquois Great Law of Peace contained many similar checks and balances. Again, I do not find this coincidental.

Many point to the Great Law as the reason the Iroquois Confederacy endured for so long; and indeed, the Great Law outlined a wise and balanced approach. Each of the nations had an assigned role. The Onondaga were acknowledged as the firekeepers, which can be interpreted as a form of executive branch that oversees the entire process. In terms of decision-making, the Mohawk and Seneca were considered the "Older Brothers," and the Oneida and the Cayuga were the "Younger Brothers," acting in a manner that foreshadowed the House of Representatives and the Senate. The Mohawk and Seneca, when they reached consensus on a question, would report to the Cayuga and the Oneida. The Mohawk would then present the consensus to the Onondaga, who would render a decision. However, if the Onondaga decision did not resonate with the Younger and Older Brothers, they could reconsider the question. If they remained united in opposition to the decision of the firekeepers, the Onondaga would be compelled to accept this outcome.

Thus the modern Congress of the United States in many ways mimics the Great Law. The House of Representatives is akin to the Younger Brothers (Cayuga and Oneida) since they serve a shorter term in office (two years). The delegates of the Senate, who serve a six-year term, are akin to the Older Brothers (Mohawk and Seneca). The Executive Branch of the United States (comprised of the judiciary and the president) is akin to the Onondaga Council. The judiciary has the right to overturn a law on the grounds that it is unconstitutional; likewise the president has the right to veto a law. But just as in the Great Law, that veto can be overridden if Congress is united against the decision of the Executive branch. The threat of a veto can also be nipped in the bud if the passage of a bill occurs with a veto-proof majority, something that happened as recently as when Congress overwhelmingly voted in 2018 to not allow President Trump to overturn sanctions against Russia.

Missing Pieces of the Great Law

While there are striking parallels in the governmental structures of both the Haudenosaunee and that of the United States, particularly in terms of checks and balances, certain aspects of Native American governance were completely ignored or rejected by our founding fathers. While there was initially no role at all for women in United States politics, women in Haudenosaunee politics held an integral role—and in certain instances, *were the oversight body that controlled the actions of the men.*

It was the role of the women's council to nominate the chief (or sachem). The chief was always male, and his nomination was in part based on his being a good family man who respected and took good care of women and children. It was also the role of women to remove any sachem that did not properly fulfill his responsibilities or brought dishonor to the community by his actions.

The right to remove an elected official in the United States, including the right of the House of Representatives to initiate Articles of Impeachment against an American sitting president, was likely derived, at least in part, from the right entrusted to Haudenosaunee women.[98] While Hamilton and other founders attributed the concept of impeachment to English parliamentary law, there was, significantly, no precedent in Europe for the impeachment and removal of a King. The King was above the law. In America, however, the Haudenosaunee women were empowered to remove the chief. Many of the framers, including Franklin, Washington, and Jefferson, were well aware of this practice. The ability of Iroquois women to remove the men from power was not a fact the Iroquois men kept from the founders, nor was it a source of any sort of shame. They highly valued the women and recognized their important role in maintaining the continuity of the tribe, not just through childbearing, but through their ability to consider what was best for the longevity of their children.

In fact, the entire Iroquois society was matrilineal, and this is still the case in many Native societies today. I discuss this—and other aspects of the balance of power between women and men among Haudenosaunee society—in more detail in chapter seven.

FEDERALISM AND THE PROPER ROLE OF GOVERNMENT

Today, with increasing partisan tension over the concept of federalism—or the balance of power between states and the federal government—the origin of this concept has been lost. It, too, can be traced to the Iroquois. The Onondaga Nation had a form of federal (or central) government that acted in concert with the other Indian Nations (or states), each of which had sovereignty over their territories. Only the central government could determine certain things—such as the decision to go to war—but the individual nations were responsible for many of the decisions that applied to their particular territories without interference from the central government.

During the Constitutional Convention, the founding fathers felt it important to strengthen the role of the president with regard to war-making powers, making the president the Commander-in Chief of the Armed Forces. However, the Constitution continued to give only to the Congress the right to declare war (Article 1, Section 8, Clause 11). Congress has not used its power to declare war since 1942. It has instead abdicated much of its control over war-making powers to the president. The intent of the founders, however, was to have a balance between the power to declare war and the power to prosecute war. Both the Articles of Confederation and the Constitution were closely aligned with the Iroquois Confederacy on this point. A balance of power between the central government and the states is the core intent of federalism.

THE 1988 UNITED STATES CONGRESSIONAL RESOLUTION HONORING INDIAN NATIONS

In the aftermath of an academic conference held at Cornell University in 1987—during which a considerable amount of research was presented that demonstrated the influence of Native American nations on the formation of the United States government—Congress made a startling resolution, in which the debt to Native American nations, and particularly the Iroquois, was explicitly acknowledged. Moreover, they chose to make this Congressional Resolution the very next year at an occasion marking the 200th anniversary of the signing of the US Constitution. I quote a salient passage of the resolution below:

> Whereas the original founders of the Constitution, including most notably, George Washington and Benjamin Franklin, are known to have greatly admired the concepts, principles, and governmental practices of the Six Nations of the Iroquois Confederacy; and whereas the Confederation of the original thirteen colonies into one Republic was explicitly

modeled upon the Iroquois Confederacy, as were many of the democratic principles which are incorporated into the Constitution . . . Be it resolved by the Senate (The House of Representatives concurring) that the Congress on the occasion of the 200th anniversary of the signing of the US Constitution, acknowledges the historical debt which the Republic of the USA owes to the Iroquois Confederacy and other Indian Nations for their demonstrations of enlightened, democratic principles of government and their example of a free association of Independent Indian Nations.[99]

CHECKS AND BALANCES TODAY

The intent of the founding fathers was to maintain stability over the long term, and so far the checks and balances built into the Constitution have mostly held together over the almost two-and-a-half centuries since they were implemented. Certainly there have been tensions between the various branches of government, each being accused on occasion of overreach. But that was to be expected.

The dynamic tension of checks and balances has been tested from the beginning, as soon as the Adams administration passed the Alien Sedition Act and began to crack down on free speech in potential violation of the First Amendment. Andrew Jackson was the first president to seriously challenge the limits of the presidency, and was censured by the Senate in 1833 for doing so (although the censure was rescinded in 1837).[100] Andrew Johnson was impeached in part because of his contempt for Congressional authority. Modern presidents, beginning with Woodrow Wilson and Franklin Delano Roosevelt, have continued to expand and test the limits of the executive branch, increasingly relying upon executive orders to carry out their respective agendas when faced with a recalcitrant Congress.

Perhaps no administration to date has provided a greater test of the checks and balances of the US government than the Trump administration. It is almost as if the founders anticipated a person

like Trump, someone who might be tempted to take advantage of the
position to enrich himself. They designed the Emoluments Clause,
prohibiting presidents and congressmen from profiting from gifts
and other contributions from foreign governments, but that check
has never been legally tested with a president until now. I delve more
deeply into the Trump administration and the stresses it has placed
on the integrity of the country in part III.

RESPECTING THE LIVING ROOTS OF OUR NATION'S FOUNDING

Native American influence on the founding of our nation is not just
an historic fact. It is ongoing. To put our country back together in
full integrity requires us to remember and respect the living roots of
our nation's founding.

It is not enough, however, to simply remember our Native American roots. Native Americans became who they were by establishing an intimate relationship with the land and then by continuing to
engage in ceremonies of renewal with all that is sacred—the light,
the air, the water, and the moist, fertile soil—that they and the sacred
plants, minerals, and animals living with them on Earth all depend
on. That connection was immediate, visceral, and real. It spoke to
them, called to them, and nourished not only their bodies, but also
their hearts and souls.

It was the call of wild rivers, lush forests, and wide open vistas—
an intimate connection from the human heartbeat to the heartland
initially transmitted through Native Americans to open-minded individuals such as Williams and Franklin—that also infected Jefferson,
Paine, Madison, Washington, Jay, and many of the other founders. It
may have even affected the ambitious Hamilton, for it impacted all to
varying degree. The spirit of the land was in our blood from the beginning: in the Declaration of Independence, the Articles of Confederation, and the Constitution; and it remains in our blood today, even if
somewhat dormant, like the once wild rivers.

The spirit of the land never goes away. It is not a cultural relic; it is still relevant, still guiding us in unseen ways—especially during the times that "try men's souls," which seemingly describes today as much as when Thomas Paine penned those words. It is therefore not only Native America that we must learn to respect. It is what underlies Native American nations. It is the spirit of the land that we must turn to; it is the spirit of the land we must feel again in our breast. We must remember that we are the land. We are the light, air, water, and earth—and every time we breathe, drink, or wake up and see the light, we are renewing our relationship with all there is. It is this that has the potential to heal us—for it is this that we share with all people and all living beings on this planet.

PART TWO

DANCE OF THE OPPOSITES

"Having and not having arise together.
Difficult and easy complement each other.
Long and short contrast each other;
High and Low rest upon each other."[101]
—LAO TZU

"The path is the goal and the goal
is the path."[102]
—CHÖGYAM TRUNGPA

"We must all obey the great law of change.
It is the most powerful law of nature, and
the means perhaps of its conservation."[103]
—EDMUND BURKE

CHAPTER FIVE

Dual Aspects of Wholeness

art I focused on Unitive Consciousness because the desire to unite was the driving force behind the creation of the United States, as it was for the Iroquois Confederacy before. The colonists had to unite before they could conceive of breaking away from their mother country. Once separated, the Dance of the Opposites could begin.

In uniting, the colonists were following the advice of Onondaga Chief Canassatego who urged them to do as the Iroquois had done in forming their confederacy. It took nearly thirty years before they followed Canassatego's advice, but the colonists eventually modeled their own confederacy after the Iroquois both in terms of structure and in the primacy given to the values of liberty and equality. Of course, the colonists adopted Iroquois values only to the extent that they understood them or felt them appropriate—and their perception of Native beliefs was always colored by their own.

At the time of contact, the Iroquois already had a long-standing worldview that was one of interrelated wholeness. The colonial American worldview, on the other hand, was still developing. Thus when European Enlightenment science met Native American egalitarianism, it gave rise to a hybrid form of science that attempted to reconcile these dual strands: a new science of egalitarian politics—the colonist's version of unitive consciousness. This experiment was a radical departure from European politics, but not nearly as inclusive as the Native American origins from which it was derived.

EVOLVED AND DEVOLVED MODES OF
UNITIVE CONSCIOUSNESS

As already pointed out, Unitive Consciousness has both evolved and devolved modes of expression. The evolved mode celebrates *unity in diversity*, which I have come to see as the *sacred purpose of America*, destined to unfold. The devolved mode seeks unity as a reaction to what is perceived as too much diversity. The devolved mode heads in the direction of totalitarianism or monarchy. It strives to create a society based on homogeneity of race or religion, or both.

During the founding of the United States, both the tradition of monarchy and the new idea of a diverse, representational republic were present and in conflict with one another—even as the diversity of the young republic didn't go nearly as far as it does today. Only White, male property owners were fully empowered members of the society. Even this was a departure from the prevailing monarchies of Europe (where social class made life much more restrictive for many); but it wouldn't have amounted to much if the seed idea of equality had not grown and blossomed over time.

There is every reason to believe that the founding fathers foresaw the need to build a system that would be flexible enough to change over time. They knew the nation must evolve. The famous phrase from the preamble to the Constitution, "to form a more perfect union," implies both an improvement from the Articles of Confederation and a task left to their descendants. The founders may have been courageous in forming a representational republic, but there were limits to their bravery. None had the audacity to suggest freeing the slaves, even when some were abolitionists. None suggested the inclusion of women in any part of the political process, even though John Adams' wife Abigail clamored for it, beseeching her husband in a written letter, saying "Remember the Ladies, and be more generous and favorable to them than your ancestors."[104] The omission of women was a carryover from British common law in which women were subordinate to their husband. This was *not* something they learned from Native America, as we have discussed. There, women held an integral role in political decision making.

"The arc of the moral universe is long, but it bends toward justice," said nineteenth-century abolitionist Theodore Parker, words later made famous by Dr. Martin Luther King Jr. and President Obama. Indeed, the overall arc of American history has been in the direction of our sacred purpose of unity in diversity (as evidenced by increasing inclusivity of women and people of color)—but there also have been periodic calls to return to a simpler era when the United States was less diverse—and this is happening again today.

HAMILTON AND JEFFERSON: TWO PATRIOTS WITH OPPOSING VIEWS OF THE COUNTRY

The birth of this nation, like real birth, was a bloody affair. We were born out of the Revolutionary war, and immediately after, experienced a degree of separation anxiety in leaving our mother country. This is one explanation as to why many of the founders advocated maintaining strong relations with Britain.

The legacy from the mother country of Britain was the third element of early American politics in addition to Enlightenment science and Native American egalitarianism. Some founders, like Hamilton, admired certain aspects of British government and wanted to establish a similarly stable, if different, government for the United States.

Hamilton's desire to maintain continuity with the country we had just declared independence from was controversial. Jefferson accused Hamilton of being a monarchist at heart, while Hamilton accused Jefferson of holding not just malice toward him but toward all of government. In both cases, the accusations were misguided. The quarrel was not really with each other as much as it was over what identity the newborn nation should take. Neither was seeking to abort the experiment.

Hamilton and Jefferson were locked in a struggle between evolved and devolved forms of unitive consciousness. They both wanted to form a singular republic of diverse viewpoints as expressed in the motto *e pluribus unum* (out of many, one). But they argued over what the foundational principles were for such a government. They each wanted their version to prevail. This form of unitive consciousness was devolved because it amounted to self-aggrandizement—an attempt to achieve unity through enlarging one's own view to engulf all others.

Then at the most critical times in our nation's early history, Hamilton and Jefferson rose above their disputes to compromise. They did so because they both loved their country and recognized that love in the other. Hamilton and Jefferson were the leaders of the Federalists and Anti-Federalists, respectively, but the founders were determined to avoid political parties, and so that division never hardened. In fact, Jefferson once said, "If I could not go to heaven but with a party, I would not go there at all."[105]That's how determined he was to avoid being pigeon-holed as an anti-Federalist. Neither one were true party leaders; but they were the harbingers of modern political parties in certain respects. Their disagreement over the size of government, for instance, has continued to this day.

While Jefferson was purported to say that "the best government governs least," there is no evidence that he ever said those exact words. The source of his desire to minimize the role of government was clearly influenced by Native America, for he did say:

> In so much that it were made a question, whether no law, as among the savage Americans, or too much law, as among the civilized Europeans, submits man to the greater evil, one who has seen both conditions of existence would pronounce it to be the last."[106]

In his appreciation for the minimalist quality of Native American government, Jefferson was aligned with Franklin, who was similarly impressed. Franklin noted that Native societies had "no prisons, no officers to compel obedience, or inflict punishment." He attributed this to the Indians living in a "natural state," a theme taken up by Paine, who I discuss shortly. Franklin elaborated on the concept of a natural state:

> [T]he Indians were constrained by no laws, having no Courts, or Ministers of Justice, no Suits . . . The Persuasion of Men distinguished by Reputation of Wisdom is the only means

by which others are governed or rather led . . . and the State
of the Indians was probably the first State of All Nations.[107]

The idea that Native Americans were representative of the first,
or natural, state of humanity was widespread among the founders.
Franklin, Jefferson, Paine, Washington, and others believed this.
These founders were partly in error because Native American societies
had changed and matured over time, but they were also partly correct
in their perception, for while Native cultures were never static, they
continued to emphasize living in accordance with perennial wisdom
passed down by oral tradition. Comparable perennial wisdom in
Europe had been forced into retreat by the advent of science, and
pre-Christian spiritual wisdom was relegated to secret societies. The
founding fathers were attracted to one secret society in particular:
the Freemasons (who became a prominent society during the heyday
of medieval church construction, although the sacred geometry they
employ dates back to Pythagorean times). The Freemasons still exist
today. Gerald Ford was the last US president to have been a member
(although Reagan was made an honorary member). Among the founding fathers, Washington, Franklin, Hamilton, Hancock, and many
others were all reputed to be Freemasons. Some say Jefferson was a
Freemason, but that has never been well established.[108]

Hamilton, intent on promulgating a new science of egalitarian
politics, did not give credit to either Freemasonry or Native America
for his inspiration. As I have already demonstrated, Hamilton's new
science was likely influenced by long-standing Iroquois practices of
checks and balances. At the very least, there were uncanny parallels.
And Hamilton must have had some contact with Native Americans
since Natives and non-Natives lived in close proximity in those days,
and everyone interacted to some degree.

At the same time, Hamilton's penchant for designing complicated structures of governmental bureaucracy was divergent from
both Native and European politics. An immigrant who thrived in
his adopted city of New York, Hamilton was more aligned with
urban intelligentsia than either rural or Native America. He believed

government could be efficient, even elegant, and did not feel any compunction about limiting its size.

Hamilton, the urban self-made man, became the counterpoint to Jefferson, the Southern aristocrat. Their personal differences played out in the growing divides between North and South, urban and agrarian, Black and White, big and small government—and all of these themes are still present in modern day politics.

It is misleading, however, to say that Jefferson was a prototype of modern conservatives and Hamilton the prototype of modern liberals. While Jefferson was for small government and gradual social change when it came to issues like slavery, he also supported radical political reform on many fronts, and was open even to revolution if necessary. Moreover, Jefferson fervently opposed Hamilton's plans for modern banking and capitalism, something conservatives today wouldn't think of opposing. Hamilton, for his part, may have been for larger government and capitalism, but this was not because he was a big government ideologue. Hamilton was a pragmatist who delighted in designing systems to get things done. While Jefferson held different views from Hamilton on many points, he was also a pragmatist. This is undoubtedly the common ground that enabled them to compromise so successfully.

In a famous compromise between them that took place over dinner, Hamilton agreed to move the nation's capital to Virginia in exchange for Jefferson's support of his plans for a central United States bank. Later when Jefferson ran for president against Burr, Hamilton supported Jefferson over Burr, who was Hamilton's nemesis and ended up mortally wounding Hamilton in a dual a few years later.[109]

Thomas Paine and Edmund Burke and the War of the Pamphlets

Perhaps nothing demonstrates the principle of the *dance of the opposites* more aptly than the famous "war of pamphlets" that took place between Thomas Paine and Edmund Burke. Their pivotal interaction—which began in 1775 and lasted more than two decades—

riveted public attention at the time, and proved to be of lasting importance.

In many respects, Paine was a prototype for modern liberals and Burke for modern conservatives, and their arguments in the pamphlets often seem to reflect those positions. But rather than dwell on whether Paine or Burke as individuals were right or wrong, I choose to consider them together—as two sides of the same coin—because much of their work, particularly in the latter decade, was done in reaction to the other. Considering them together, as two aspects of one whole, enriches our understanding.

Ironically, Paine would disagree with my approach, for he believed in absolute right and wrong. I am not attempting to dismiss their dispute, for clearly, the two men passionately disagreed with each other. But there was something about the way they worked in tandem, each triggering a response in the other, that brought out the best in both of their perspectives; and the fact that Paine and Burke looked at the same situation and came up with vastly different interpretations and prescriptions of action does not diminish either approach. Each philosophy had its own integrity. Both were necessary, at different times, depending on circumstance. They still are. A liberal response begets a conservative answer, and a conservative response begets a liberal one. They are two aspects of one pendulum that need each other to stay in balance. It has always been this way, and continues so today.

The Arrival of Thomas Paine in America

One of the curious things about Paine and Burke is that they were both immigrants who became famous in their adopted countries, just like Hamilton. Burke came from Ireland to settle in England; Paine was born in England, and after an undistinguished career as a tax collector, emigrated to America in 1774.

How Paine arrived in America was a bit of a miracle because he was penniless at the time. But as fate would have it, a chance meeting in London with none other than Benjamin Franklin resulted in

Franklin sponsoring Paine to come to America. Franklin obviously saw something in the young Pain (who added the "e" to his surname later), and sent him off on a boat to America armed with a note that read: "The bearer Mr. Thomas Pain is very well recommended to me as an ingenious, worthy young man."[110] Paine arrived in America sick and penniless, but with Franklin's recommendation in hand, not surprisingly, he became a near immediate success as an editor and then an author.[111]

The timing of Paine's arrival in America was near-miraculous. He came less than two years before the Revolutionary war began—a war that would have happened without him, of course—but arguably would not have been successful for the colonies. John Adams certainly thought so, anyway. Adams claimed, "Without the pen of the author of *Common Sense*, the sword of Washington would have been raised in vain."[112] And John Adams was a rival, not a friend of Paine's.

Common Sense was Paine's first book, and it immediately became a best seller. On the very first page, he passionately endorsed the revolution, proclaiming that "The cause of America is in a great measure the cause of all mankind." But what is perhaps his most famous passage came from an essay called "The American Crisis," composed while traveling with the army in New Jersey. To lift the troop's morale, he wrote:

> These are the times that try men's souls. The summer soldier
> and the sunshine patriot will, in this crisis, shrink from the
> service of their country; but he that stands by it now, deserves
> the love and thanks of man and woman. Tyranny, like hell,
> is not easily conquered; yet we have this consolation with us,
> that the harder the conflict, the more glorious the triumph.
> What we obtain too cheap, we esteem too lightly: it is dear-
> ness only that gives every thing its value.[113]

Paine went on to write several more very influential works, including *The Rights of Man* and *The Age of Reason* as well as many pamphlets, articles, and letters that have become part of the historical lexicon of the times. He had a talent for putting complex ideas in simple, accessible language, and everything he produced sold well. This included his final and most controversial book, *The Age of Reason*, in which he so thoroughly denounced religion that nearly all of Paine's associates ended up denouncing him and destroying his reputation. It is a tragic fact of history that Paine died in much the same state as he was in when he first came to America, alone and destitute. Legend has it that only six people attended his funeral.

The Influence of Edmund Burke

Edmund Burke was born in Dublin, Ireland, and educated there, first at a Quaker boarding school and then at the renowned Trinity College. Afterward he went to England to study law but soon became involved in the literary circuit of philosophical and political debates, which led to his first published work, *A Vindication of Natural Society*. It was a satire of Lord Bolingbroke and the well-known deist's final work, *Letters on the Study and Use of History*, which criticized all organized religions as artificial. In his satire, Burke mirrored Bolingbroke's style while adopting a completely different position, writing in support of religion and other social institutions. Burke then went on to write another book, *A Philosophical Enquiry into the Origins of Our Ideas of the Sublime and the Beautiful*, in which he argues that human nature depends not only upon rational thought, but also upon emotions and aesthetic appreciation of beauty. He later applied this insight to political discourse, arguing that politics must be governed less by the abstract and more by the real. Burke was irritated by what he felt were the more abstract arguments of Paine, who argued for the sanctity of the individual and the existence of unalienable human rights. Burke saw things differently, contending that rights evolved with the growth of society and could not be disconnected from societal obligations.[114]

Burkes' most famous work was his argument against the French Revolution called *Reflections on the Revolution in France*. It was very well received, selling over 7,000 copies in its first week in publication.

Paine and Burke and The French Revolution:
The Birth of the Modern Right and Left

The way the two men met was actually quite ironic. Paine reached out to Burke to seek his assistance in support of the French Revolution, expecting to find an ally in Burke, who had supported the American Revolution. Jefferson, too, expected that Burke would support the French Revolution; and upon learning otherwise, quipped, "The revolution in France does not astonish me so much as the revolution in Burke."[115]

Paine and Jefferson were both taken aback by Burke's refusal to support the French Revolution, but only because they never understood why Burke supported the American Revolution in the first place. Burke supported the American cause not because he found it so noble, but because he was disturbed by Britain's inept failure to govern the American continent.

Burke was a pragmatist who advocated for change when appropriate, but especially as he grew older, he valued stability—or rather, he valued a balance between stability and change. Paine, on the other hand, came from a completely different perspective. He fervently believed that the American experience was only the beginning of a worldwide revolution—a transformation from illegitimate government to government of the people—and such reforms should be made in as rapid a fashion as possible. His goal was clear: "to rescue man from tyranny and false systems and false principles of government, and enable him to be free and establish government for himself."[116]

It was during the period of the French Revolution when the battle of the pamphlets between Paine and Burke caught fire. Burke kicked off the debate with his famous missive *Reflections on the Revolution in France*, published in 1790. *Reflections* had begun as a letter in response to Richard Price, a Unitarian, but ended up as a long dissent against the revolution. In *Reflections*, Burke not only defended the monarchy; he defended the traditions of civilized society. He lamented the loss of civility in this famous passage:

The age of chivalry is gone. That of sophisters, oeconomists, and calculators, has succeeded; and the glory of Europe is extinguished forever. Never, never more, shall we behold that generous loyalty to rank and sex, that proud submission, that dignified obedience, that subordination of the heart, which kept alive, even in servitude itself, the spirit of an exalted freedom. The unbought grace of life, the cheap defence of nations, the nurse of manly sentiment and heroic enterprise, is gone! It is gone, that sensibility of principle, the chastity of honour, which felt a stain like a wound, which inspired courage whilst it mitigated ferocity, which ennobles whatever it touched, and under which vice itself lost hale its evil, by losing all its grossness.[117]

Reflections on the Revolution in France provoked many responses, but none more famous than Paine's *Rights of Man,* the book he published in 1791 that sold tens of thousands of copies. In Paine's reply to Burke, he forecasts the ending of hereditary government, writing:

It is not difficult to perceive, from the enlightened state of mankind, that hereditary governments are verging on the decline, and that Revolutions on the broad basis of national sovereignty and Government by representation, are making their way in Europe.[118]

One of the many reasons Burke and Paine are so strongly associated with modern conservatism and liberalism, respectively, is that the terms "right" and "left" have their origin from this time in history. During the French Revolution this referred to seating arrangements in the French parliament where those who supported the monarchy sat to the right of the chairman and the dissenters to the left. Burke can be considered the first prominent philosopher of the conservative right, and Paine of the liberal left.

In *Reflections on the Revolution in France*, Burke formulated the central metaphor of his political thought: the concept of *equipoise*, or the balance between stability and change. He also came out against radical individualism, arbitrary usurpation of power, degradation of social institutions, and abstract, metaphysical politics. Paine, in his response, defended the revolution, not on moral grounds but as part of a well-developed philosophical treatise, expounding upon the necessity of returning to the origins to learn the true nature of man, pre-government. Paine advocated rebuilding government from the ground up to reflect the natural state of man, asserting that man was an individual first, and a social creature second. [119] If governments became corrupted and did not represent the people, it was necessary to overthrow the government and begin anew.

Burke also based his philosophy on nature, but he had a markedly different take on nature's attributes, choosing to see nature as primarily based in heredity, or the handing down of genes and traits. To his mind, this was a justification for family traditions of leadership, if not monarchs. Burke was open to the possibility of a hybrid of monarchy and democracy, as was Hamilton (at least at the constitutional convention), and both realized that the idea went back at least as far as Cicero. To Burke, a pure democracy posed as much danger as a pure monarchy because in his view a democracy could devolve into a different form of tyranny—that of the majority over the minority—a point which Madison argued in Federalist #10.

Paine wasn't having any of Burke's arguments, however. He believed that any accommodation for royalty was merely a corrupt way of justifying the status quo—and it is hard to argue that this was not a possibility.

The Major Differences Between Paine and Burke

Paine and Burke differed in their views on time and history, the pace of change, the importance of the individual in society, the principles of nature and human rights, the origin and purpose of society and government, and the philosophical underpinnings of justice and order—among other things. The difference over justice was crucial. For Paine, justice was an abstract, unchangeable principle. For Burke, justice was a relative concept that evolved along with the nature and history of a particular nation.

The differences in viewpoints regarding time, history, and nature are predictive of the other differences between the two men. Paine looked to the past only from a philosophical point of view to establish his argument about the abstract (timeless) principles of natural or unalienable rights that have been with us since the origins of humanity. According to his theory, the individual existed prior to the forming of society, and the earliest societies were a collection of individuals joined together to meet individual needs—something Paine felt was only natural. Paine likened society to a function of nature; government, on the other hand, was a product of art or science.[120] He considered a government legitimate only if it began from a knowledge of nature that was acquired through reason and then consciously constructed through laws and practices that respected individual liberty and equality. Any government that did not live up to this standard should be replaced by any means necessary, including revolution. Every generation must be free to begin anew with a just form of government designed by and for the people.

Burke began from a different premise, believing that human, society, nature, history, and government were all inextricably connected. He could not conceive of a pre-social individual. People are born into a society, and any rights they may have cannot be divorced from the societal obligations they inherited at birth. He found Paine's concept of individuals being endowed with abstract, unalienable rights to be naïve and illusory. Burke's objection might be difficult for modern Americans to understand because Paine's idea of unalienable rights, undoubtedly inspired by Native American beliefs, was taken up by Jefferson in the Declaration of Independence and became a foundational aspect of the American psyche. But Burke believed otherwise. He considered rights not as endowed but granted by societies in the course of their natural evolution —and therefore governments should not be installed, but built on past traditions. The fact that governments have a leadership class was only natural to Burke, mimicking the way nature passes down genes and traits from one generation to another.

In sum, Burke believed that government should function in accordance with the forms and traditions of society. While Burke distrusted abstract principles of justice, the practice of justice was important to him. And he was not against reform or challenging the monarchy when he deemed it appropriate. Burke was, after all, a member of the Whig party, which aligned itself with Britain's revolution of 1688 when parliament overthrew James II, a Catholic king, and replaced him with William and Mary as joint monarchs. But Burke interpreted the 1688 revolution as a means of maintaining continuity, not upsetting it. He was steadfast in believing that reforms should, whenever possible, be implemented gradually so as not to uproot the social order.

Why Paine and Burke Are Both Right

In my view, Paine and Burke were both right, although individually they each had a piece of the puzzle that the other helped to complete. They were like dance partners moving in response to each other, covering up for the other's missteps when necessary. Paine inspired the masses to imagine a better future; Burke reminded us of the value of past traditions. Paine heralded a new age of reason and ethical government, justifying the overthrow of corrupt governments; Burke reminds us of the potential hypocrisy in the usurpation of power in the name of light and reason. Paine upholds the sanctity of individual, natural rights; Burke counters by cautioning that rights cannot be removed from societal obligations. Paine points to justice as an abstract, unchangeable principle; Burke distrusted man-made concepts of abstract justice used as justification for overthrowing governments and was more of a natural law philosopher who derived his moral code from what was evident in nature. Burke favored gentle, gradual change in accordance with nature.[121]

In these and many other ways, Paine and Burke tempered each other's passions. They noticed what was being neglected in each other's arguments and called each other out—and they were right to do so because without both of their contributions, American politics, and American society in general, would have been less balanced and whole.

The Root of the Philosophies of Thomas Paine and Edmund Burke

To better understand Paine and Burke, it is helpful to consider the origin of their worldviews. Thomas Paine's philosophy was rooted in the ethos of the European Enlightenment: an optimistic view of humankind's capacity to resolve the conundrums of the time through the application of rational thought. The scientific advances of his era were enormously exciting to Paine and many of the founding fathers. It was an era when people began to imagine all things were possible, for the advances of science revolutionized the way humanity conceived of reality and our place in the world. A rush of creativity and innovation was unleashed that could, seemingly, only benefit humanity.

Edmund Burke, on the other hand, was more aligned with those known as the "Romantics"—who rebelled against the European Enlightenment, bemoaning the end of an era of passion. The Romantics were pained by the growing trend of favoring scientific reason over emotion—and they forged a counter-cultural identity. Wordsworth, Shelley, Coleridge, and other romantics sought to counterbalance the modern fixation on linear, scientific progress; instead, they praised imagination over reason, emotions over logic, and intuition over scientific rigor.

This is not to take anything away from Thomas Paine's vision, for in many ways, Paine was prescient about the future. The founding of the United States was unquestionably important; it heralded a new era of greater democracy and the advancement of modern science that quickly spread around the world. Not only did America become a successful and powerful country; it came to wield enormous influence on the world stage—and continues to do so.

In other ways, however, Burke was the prescient one, and not just because the quintessentially British form of government, a hybrid between monarchy and republic, persists nearly two-and-a-half centuries later. In my view, Burke's more important contribution was his clarity about the shadow side of Enlightenment values, even as these had already radically remade society. The Industrial Revolution, with its concomitant emphasis on economic growth, has led to great progress. Yet it has also had devastating consequences, particularly with regard to the environment. We are currently experiencing mass species extinction amid the unprecedented degradation of our oceans and waterways; soil, and air. The root cause of all of this environmental destruction is arguably found in the Enlightenment ethos (now called "neoliberal") that results in the economic engine being pushed forward at the expense of everything else. True conservatism, dating back to Burke, would be against this (too rapid) development. In chapter thirteen, I discuss how environmental (green) conservatism is still alive and well in contemporary Europe, but has become forgotten or overrun by corporate interests in the United States.

The Native American Influence on Paine

Burke accused Paine of relying too much upon the abstract, and this is a noteworthy objection, since it is certainly possible to become enamored with theory at the expense of practical implementation. But there is one thing Burke may not have realized—and that is how much Paine was influenced by living examples of Native American governments while developing his theory. This could be in part because Paine was famously reticent in revealing his sources, claiming he rarely read the work of others and did his thinking for himself. Paine was undoubtedly influenced by Locke and Rousseau, but he was also clearly influenced by his mentor, Franklin, and by the Native Americans Franklin introduced him to. Therefore, Paine's vision for egalitarian government was less abstract than Burke imagined.

It is probable that Paine came to his assumption regarding the natural state of man by observing Native American societies. Moreover, Paine's emphasis on individual autonomy also was likely influenced by Native culture. Paine was influenced by Native American communities in other ways—in particular, by the strength of their democracies. Paine had ample opportunity to observe Native democracies that empowered the people and valued liberty and justice for all. He observed and/or participated in council talking circles, and he was introduced to the concept of informal caucusing. Perhaps most significantly, Paine was able to witness a functioning society in which equal distribution of wealth was not theory, but practice—and he took note of this.

Why the Differences Between Paine and Burke Matter Today

In their day, Paine and Burke were widely influential authors who carried on a spirited debate. But why do they matter today? They matter because they were foundational thinkers. Their differing perspectives provide a basis for understanding the root of today's liberal and conservative political positions, a basis that is often lost or ignored in a climate of reactive opposition.

Paine and Burke were so popular that they were followed by many—supporters and dissenters alike. In the political arena, there is nothing comparable today—for instance, there's no war of pamphlets between the conservative George Will and liberal Chris Matthews. Both conservatives and liberals write best-selling books, but for audiences who already agree with them. The media has obviously exacerbated (if not created) this situation; networks such as Fox or MSNBC market to one side or the other in virtual isolation. Audiences on each side of the political divide hear only one side of the story. It is rare to have intelligent discourse between the parties. It is no wonder that people have begun to imagine they have a corner on the truth.

While Burke and Paine have influenced modern politics, it is not because their ideas have become fixed in stone. Ideas are living things that grow and change from generation to generation. Thus, Burke and Paine have been reinterpreted over time, and our understanding of their central ideas evolved and repositioned.

The 20th century transdisciplinary thinker, Gregory Bateson, exemplified how ideas can be repurposed when he wrote *Steps to an Ecology of Mind*. He transplanted principles of ecology into epistemology and justified his method by saying he was loosening up the soil of the mind, bringing it to compost so that it can give birth to new, organic reformulations.[122] His youngest daughter, the author and filmmaker Nora Bateson, understood the efficacy of repurposing ideas when she wrote "The idea that ideas are fixed or permanent is just an idea."[123]

ENANTIODROMIA

Fundamental to my way of thinking is that all ideas are related, even ideas that seem antithetical to each other, because in time everything turns into its opposite—a principle that Heraclitus first called "enantiodromia." A generation after Heraclitus, Plato added: "Everything arises in this way, opposites from their opposites."[124]

To see how ideas are related, one must dig deep into the soil of the mind to uncover the connecting roots. It is worthwhile revisiting Paine and Burke for this reason. In truth, so much has changed since their day that it is barely possible to recognize the original roots of what is now the so-called right and left of the political spectrum. Contrary to the visions of Burke and Paine, the right is now the champion of the individual; the left is the champion of environmentalism. Most recently, it has been the right that has been more aggressive in seeking changes in society, even if it is only of the kind that rolls back changes made by the left. When Donald Trump said "Make America Great Again," he was repeating Ronald Reagan's words. But when Reagan accepted the Republican nomination for president in 1980, he invoked Paine in calling for a transformation of failed government. Barack Obama, on the other hand, was known to describe himself as a Burkean because he was comfortable with incremental change (to the chagrin of the hard left).[125]

The dance of the opposites is never as simple as it seems, or as opposite, because political parties are not static; they are ever-changing in relation to each other. Political parties are like dance partners, because their actions are dictated by what their partner does. In time, the parties will unconsciously assume the position of their counterparts, just like dance partners end up on different sides of the dance floor. This happens not through lack of attention but from fixation upon the other. Political actions are not based in principle as much as they are a reaction to what the other side does. They may begin by hating what the other side does, but in time might adopt it, which is why William Irwin Thompson wisely said, "We become what we hate" (a subject I will return to).

The following chapter introduces the birth of the modern Democratic and Republican Parties, and shows how much they have changed, however unwittingly, while dancing together. Because political parties are dynamic, ever-changing entities, it behooves us to carefully observe this dynamic. Even in times that seem mired in polarization, such as today, there is growth, change, and transformation. This is the way things have always been. As the Buddha understood, the only constant is change.

CHAPTER SIX

The Birth of the Modern Democratic and Republican Parties

When the United States was first formed, the founding fathers discouraged factions and political parties because they wanted to present a unified front to the world. I therefore characterize the birth of the nation as a form of *Unitive Consciousness*, even if it was not the most evolved nor long lasting. Although divisions quickly arose, such as the Federalists and Anti-Federalists, it would be a mistake to consider these the equivalent of modern political parties. The modern Democratic and Republican two-party system took nearly a century to evolve.

Today's parties are organized in a manner that inspires loyalty to their brand, something that was done intentionally, if somewhat disingenuously. In truth, neither party has a fixed ideology and both parties have changed enormously over time. The result, one hundred and fifty years later, is that both parties now occupy nearly opposite positions from where they started. The Republicans of today are remarkably like the Democrats of Lincoln's time, and the Democrats are considerably closer to the original Republicans than to their own origins. It is therefore not surprising that our political system is nearly as polarized now as it was during the Civil War or that similar issues, such as race relations, are cropping up again.

The founding fathers tried mightily to protect us against this kind of situation. They knew that the development of hardened political factions would paralyze the nation; and they were successful for quite some time in preventing this from happening. When Thomas

Jefferson, prominent leader of the Anti-Federalists (also known as the Jeffersonian Republicans or Democratic-Republicans), ascended to the presidency in the early nineteenth century after a notorious, mud-slinging campaign, he immediately reached out to the Federalists, attempting to soothe divisions and unify the country. This kind of gracious post-election overture has remained a constant in American presidential politics ever since. The most ruthless of campaigners, such as Andrew Jackson, John Quincy Adams, Lyndon Johnson, and even Donald Trump, were magnanimous to their opponents upon victory (although Trump went on to govern almost exclusively to his base).[126]

THE BIRTH OF THE MODERN DEMOCRATIC PARTY

Andrew Jackson is considered to be the first president representing the Democratic Party. This is a half-truth, as the Jackson presidency led to the official birth of the Democratic Party, but only after he left office. Moreover, many complicated factors led to both the Jackson presidency and the birth of his party. First, it was necessary for the Federalists—who had produced our first two presidents after the Constitution was ratified—to tumble into disarray, which they did, after opposing the war of 1812. When the Federalists declined, the Jeffersonian Republicans (i.e., the Anti-Federalists) rose in stature; and for a time, everyone who ran for president claimed a link to Jefferson's heritage. But for the modern Democratic Party—*the party of the people*—to form, it was necessary for Jackson to *lose* his initial bid for the presidency in 1824 *while also receiving the most popular votes*. Because Jackson did not receive enough electoral votes to be elected, Congress installed John Quincy Adams as president. The loss then propelled Jackson to run again in 1828 as the populist candidate. But that wasn't all. Behind the scenes, then-Senator Martin Van Buren (who later succeeded Jackson to the presidency) and John C. Calhoun (then Vice-President to John Quincy Adams) put their heads together to forge what would become a lasting coalition between the "planters of the South and the plain Republicans of the North."[127] The intent was to reform the old Democratic-Republican Party (originally started by Jefferson and Madison) into a new vision of "the people's party" by bringing Jeffersonian ideas of liberty and equality together with support for the common man. The plan was to promote Jackson to the presidency, but this was initially kept secret until the central idea took root. Finally—and only after Jackson left office—the party dropped "Republican" from its name, and the Democratic Party was born.

It was in this way that Jackson became thought of as the first Democratic president, in part because he was a champion of the common man, and in part because the "party of the people" came into prominence after he left office. Jackson had little political experience (serving two short terms as Senator) and no defined political ideology; but what he did have was a force of personality. Calhoun and Van Buren capitalized upon his celebrity to create a populist campaign that would outlast the moxie of Jackson's personality.

Because political parties are ever-evolving entities with shifting ideologies, there comes a time during their evolution when the center cannot hold, creating growing dissent behind the scenes (if not out in the open). It is during such a time that something new—a new party or new version of the party—is potentially gestating. Such a gestation is typically gradual and surreptitious, making it nearly impossible to see it as it is unfolding.

Few imagined that the 1828 campaign between Jackson and Adams would foster the beginning of a new, two-party system. At the time, both Jackson and Adams laid claim to the principles of Jeffersonian Republicanism that had reduced the Federalist Party to impotency.[128]

The Jackson camp prevailed by successfully tagging the once-Federalist, wealthier Adams with the label of "monarchist," effectively recasting the campaign as a battle between democracy (Jackson) and aristocracy (Adams). Because Jackson was the first president not to come from the aristocracy, there was some credence to his claim. Moreover, the Jackson camp successfully labeled Adams as a corrupt Washington insider, turning Adams' political and diplomatic experience into a disadvantage (in somewhat similar fashion to what Trump did to Clinton in 2016).[129]

THE JACKSONIAN BANK WARS

Jacksonian democracy transformed itself into the Democratic Party of the people through the strength of Jackson's personality and also his support of the common man versus wealthy special interests (as long as the "common man" was white). Jackson divided the country by pitting Whites against Blacks and Indians and poor (White men) against rich (White men). In pitting the poor against the rich, he was reminiscent of how Jefferson rallied farmers against the Federalist aristocracy. But, unlike Jefferson, who was a complex thinker, Jackson tended to see things in simplistic and extreme terms. This was evident in his attitude toward the banks, which he saw as evil because they were beholden not to the common man, but to their largest donors.

Jackson had a particular beef with the Second National Bank, questioning its constitutionality from the very beginning and believing the bank was out to get him. "The bank," Jackson told Martin Van Buren," is trying to kill me, but I will kill it"—and then proceeded to do just that through the following actions: he immediately moved to veto legislation intended to re-charter the Second National Bank; he stopped using the bank to make federal deposits (paying government bills out of deposits already made); and finally, he shifted the funds to state banks he favored. These actions not only killed the bank; they effectively declared war on the business community, which struck back by organizing a new political party—the Whigs—in opposition to Jackson.[130]

The Whigs took their name from the party of Burke that opposed the British King in the 18th century, and they dubbed Jackson "King Andrew I." The Whigs were an important political development. Not only did they put multiple presidents in the White House; they were Lincoln's first party. But they made little impact during Jackson's presidency, as Jackson remained popular due to the force of his personality.[131]

Jacksonian-style democracy produced a long-lived Democratic Party that has intermittently emphasized the common man while being a mostly socially conservative, pro-business party until the mid-twentieth century. Today's socially-liberal Democratic Party could not be more opposite from its beginnings. The only link across time is the claim to being the party of the people. This catchphrase denotes unity-in-diversity, although at its inception, the Democratic Party was a far cry from that. This is because the party began under the shadow of its founder, Andrew Jackson. While touted as the champion of the common man, Jackson was also the greatest force in the 19th century for white supremacy through ethnic cleansing.

THE MERGING OF NATIONAL SECURITY WITH WHITE SUPREMACY

Andrew Jackson viewed the suppression of the nonwhite population as an inviolable aspect of national security. This was not the first time—nor would it be the last—that white supremacy has emerged as a response to perceived national security concerns in America. It has reoccurred many times in our history, resulting in the Chinese Exclusion Act of 1882 under President Arthur; the Japanese internment camps in WWII under Roosevelt; the Nixon administration's "law and order" that targeted minority populations and, most recently, the Trump administration's select targeting of Muslim and other nonwhite immigrants. In every case, the nation was seeking unity through exclusion, or what I am calling the *devolved mode* of unitive consciousness.

Jackson formed his beliefs about national security and white supremacy long before he became president. His primary fear was that a foreign army, such as the British or Spanish, might marshal the forces of nonwhites against the United States. Jackson explicitly stated that a foreign power could "excite the Indians to War, the Negroes to insurrection, and then proceed to the Mississippi." [132] Thus, he contended, it was necessary to "pacify" the Mississippi Valley by leading a campaign that targeted Native Americans, Africans, African-Americans, and any so-called disloyal Whites who might sympathize with a potential foreign invader.

Specifically, Jackson saw the destruction of the Muscogee (a member of the Creek Confederacy)—whose territory stretched from northern Florida to all of Alabama and western Georgia—as essential to US security. Thus when the Muscogee broke out into civil war, Jackson seized upon the opportunity to declare war on the entire Creek nation. In the 1813–1814 Creek War, Jackson's legend grew, for it was during this war that he endured both a gunshot wound and a near-mutiny from his starving and exhausted troops—and still, he prevailed militarily.

It was then, over a fifteen-year period from 1817–1832, that Jackson, first as general and then as president, directed the ethnic cleansing and racial subjugation of the entire Southeastern United States. He began with Florida, at the time a Spanish territory. As a general, his official charge was to move the Seminole away from the Gulf coast (since this is where it was assumed an invading army would likely establish a beachhead). When he quickly exceeded his mandate, he hired a private army of soldiers to wage an illegal war against the Spanish. In so doing, he was violating both federal and international law, but he was never prosecuted for this—and all was forgiven when the Spanish ceded Florida to the United States in the Adams-Onis Treaty of 1819. Jackson did not stop there, as his goal was to make Florida a safe haven for White settlers and, by extension, the expansion of slavery. Such a mission compelled him to not only vanquish the Spanish, but to subdue the Seminole Indians and the escaping slaves who took up with the Seminole. [133]

After he was done with the Seminole, Jackson turned his attention to relocating the Chickasaw who were then based in present-day Alabama and Tennessee. To entice them to leave their ancestral home, Jackson promised them comparable land west of the Mississippi, but the Chickasaw were not amused. They pledged "to lose every drop of blood in their veins before they would yield to the United States another acre of land."[134]

It was then that Jackson employed a three-pronged strategy that he would use again and again to achieve his desired results. Harvard professor Walter Johnson described this ploy succinctly:

> First, he threatened that the Chickasaw would simply be deprived of their land by force and offered nothing in return;

then, he bribed a portion of the tribal leadership with secret payments and land grants; finally, having bought off a portion of the Chickasaw, he signed a treaty that he claimed represented the wishes of the people as a whole.[135]

Jackson's subsequent removal of the Cherokee was perhaps the most complicated and bitter of all Indian removals. The Cherokee, originally located in a widespread area that included the Cumberland Basin of Tennessee and Kentucky and the Southern Appalachian Mountains in parts of present-day North and South Carolina, Georgia, Alabama, and Virginia were not willing to relocate west of the Mississippi without a fight. And the way the Cherokee fought back was unusual. They did so through legal means, despite the fact that the Supreme Court had previously issued an 1823 ruling that Indians could occupy lands but could not hold title to their lands within the United States. The rationale for the 1823 ruling was controversial, to say the least. It was deemed that while Native Americans had the "right of occupancy," that right was subordinate to the United States' "right of discovery." The so-called right of discovery dates back to a mid-15th century Papal Bull, called the *Doctrine of Discovery*, which justified the seizure of non-Christian lands by European colonial powers (a doctrine still in effect and cited by the US Supreme Court as recently as 2005, although Pope Francis is reportedly considering rescinding it).

In their Supreme Court case, the Cherokee contended that they were a sovereign nation, and thus should not be subject to Georgia state law. Initially, they lost that fight, but the Cherokee did not give up and ultimately prevailed because of a loophole they found in an 1830 Georgia state law which prohibited Whites from living on Indian territory after March 31, 1831 without a license from the state. The law had been put in place with a completely different intent—to dissuade missionaries from building alliances with Indian tribes and helping them resist removal. But the highest court in the land sided with the Cherokee anyway, stating that they had the right to self-government and declaring Georgia state law (over them) to be unconstitutional.

What happened next was extraordinary. While it is often said that the United States is a country governed by the rule of law, *this was not the case when the Cherokee won in court*. Instead, Georgia refused to honor the law and the Jackson-led federal government did nothing to enforce it. And that was only the beginning of the woes for the Cherokee.

THE INDIAN REMOVAL ACT

President Jackson then signed the Indian Removal Act of 1830. The Act required the various Indian tribes in today's Southeastern United States to give up their ancestral lands and relocate to federal territory west of the Mississippi River. When the Cherokee refused to leave, Jackson employed his often-used strategy. He persuaded a small faction of the Cherokee to sign the 1833 Treaty of New Echota. This treaty was illegitimate, as signees were not the recognized leaders of the Cherokee nation, and over 15,000 Cherokees—led by Chief John Ross—signed a petition in protest. But this time, the Supreme Court ignored the tribe's demands, and the treaty was ratified in 1836.

The Cherokee nation was then given two years to voluntarily migrate from their lands east of the Mississippi River, after which time any remaining Cherokees would be forcibly removed. Nonetheless, only 2,000 had migrated by 1838, and at least seven times that number remained on their traditional homelands. The US government then took the extraordinary step of employing 7,000 troops to force the Cherokees into submission at bayonet point, ordering them to leave their homeland without being allowed time to gather their belongings. The Cherokee were then forced to march over 1200 miles on foot to reservations in present-day Oklahoma. The forced relocation is known as the *Trail of Tears* because along the way approximately 4,000 Cherokee people died of cold, hunger, disease, and exhaustion. For these actions, the Cherokee dubbed Jackson "Sharp Knife."

Many historians consider the Trail of Tears to be a culmination of the Jacksonian era. In reality, it was just the beginning of a century-long effort to uproot Native American civilizations from their homelands.

The Indian Wars

The Indian Removal Act ignited the so-called Indian Wars of the 19th century—which were really *wars on Indians*. While wars with Indians began centuries earlier, it was not until the 19th century that they became a coordinated mass-extermination campaign. This produced another effect that, for our purposes, is highly significant. They changed the way the nation looked at American Indians. The founding fathers, while not devoid of racism, had given proper credit to the influence of Native America on the nation's founding principles. In the first fifty years of the United States, the entire world understood that what made America unique was its hybrid character: half-Native, half-European. In fact, while the founding fathers used the word "American" to describe themselves as being born in America, the word "American" was originally synonymous with the word "Indian."[136]

Before Andrew Jackson, the federal government's relationship with the tribes was mostly one of equals: nation to nation. In fact, the newly established American government frequently relied upon Indian tribes as partners in military and other alliances.

But when Jackson's Indian Removal Act undertook ethnic cleansing on a massive scale (killing or relocating the Creek, Choctaw, Chickasaw, Cherokee, and Seminole nations), the national attitude toward Native America shifted. It is a common occurrence in times of war: the enemy must be dehumanized if soldiers are to kill without remorse. The dehumanization of the American Indian, however, was deeply counter to the original spirit of America, because that spirit had been significantly shaped by contact with Native American traditions and values. Over the long century of Indian Wars, when the Indian Removal Act remained in effect, recognition of the Native American influence on our European ancestors was suppressed, along with acknowledging the genocide that followed. These inconvenient truths were buried deep in the American psyche.

In short, we retained the high-minded ideals of liberty and equality but forgot their source. Instead, we gave all credit to the founding fathers, elevating them as moral leaders, which is a dubious claim at best. None of this erases the truth of Native American influence; it only explains why it is a larger task to reacquaint the public with the facts.

WHAT IS JEFFERSONIAN EQUALITY?

It should now be apparent that the Democratic Party was founded on a paradox. Inspired by the immortal words of Jefferson that "all men are created equal," the party saw itself as a voice for the common man in a manner that hearkened back to principles of equality passed down from Native America—but that equality was initially only applicable to a select few: White, male property owners. At the founding of the party, the full flowering of Jefferson's words had yet to occur, and still have not.

The Jackson presidency was the precursor to the Democratic Party, but Jackson himself was a dubious beneficiary of Jefferson's legacy. On the one hand, Jackson furthered the goal of equality by extending suffrage to all White males (not just property owners); and for this reason, Jackson was considered progressive for his day. But Jackson's populism, like much of what passes for populism today, had an undeniable association with white nationalism. In Jackson's time, the support of the common man was synonymous with the expansion of Whites into new territory at the expense of both Native Americans who were removed and Black slaves who were forcibly removed along with them.

One of the great ironies in American history is that the modern Democratic Party and the modern Republican Party, founded less than twenty years later, were both formed for the same reason: to fight aristocracy, something they claimed existed only in the other party. Democrats and Republicans alike said they represented the common man, and they both traced their roots to Jeffersonian equality. There was one issue in which they made no pretense of agreement, however, and that was slavery.

THE BIRTH OF THE REPUBLICAN PARTY

The Republican Party emerged out of the collapse of the Whig Party, which splintered into pro-slavery and antislavery factions after the passage of the Kansas-Nebraska Act in 1854. The bill threatened to overturn the Missouri Compromise of 1820 and open new American territories to slavery. Convinced that wealthy, slave-owning Southerners were trying to take over the country, a group of 30 Northern Whigs, including Abraham Lincoln, gathered the morning after its passage. Lincoln later recalled that "We were thunderstruck and stunned; and we reeled and fell into utter confusion." Nonetheless, the group acted decisively, and determined to found a new political party. As it turned out, that party was destined to become the Republican Party of Lincoln.

The demise of the Whig party was also hastened by the rise of the American Party in the 1850s, better known by their more colorful name, "The Know-Nothing Party." The Know-Nothings were a Protestant-based, nativist, anti-Catholic, anti-immigration party that originally began as a secret society. (They were called "Know-Nothings" because members of the society would reportedly say "I know nothing" when asked about their membership). Because the Know-Nothings were organized before the Whigs disbanded, they were America's first major third party, and they had an impact. Pushing a radical xenophobic agenda, they successfully placed over one hundred congressmen and eight governors during the 1850s. While the Know-Nothing Party lasted only a few years, an element of xenophobia continued to exist in the shadows of the American psyche.

Make no mistake about it. The overall arc of American history has been in the direction of increasing unity in diversity. Our sacred purpose will be eventually fulfilled. The Know-Nothing Party may have been one of the more successful attempts at a devolved mode of unity consciousness—attempting to achieve unity through exclusion—but it only inspired an even stronger movement back in the direction of increasing diversity. The Know-Nothings folded, and the Republican Party of Lincoln was born. Lincoln was the first Republican presidential candidate in 1860.

Like the Democratic Party before them, the Republican Party began by pledging to be the party of the common people. The Democratic

Party had already become the party of the wealthy, at least according to the Republicans. This was partly true because the slave-owning population was rapidly becoming an aristocracy. It is also true, that, no matter who is in power, the wealthy try to exert their influence. And they often succeed. Again and again, this occurs, affecting both parties. Neither political party has clean hands.

The stands taken by the early Republican Party were mostly opposite those of today's Republican Party. The party held more socially liberal attitudes regarding government spending on infrastructure, and progressive taxation. The original Republicans were the party of social change.

The contemporary Democratic Party is nearly as far from its origins as the Republicans are from theirs. The Democrats may be the more socially liberal party today, but they began as the socially conservative party. They initially opposed federal spending on infrastructure and were for the expansion of slavery, citing state's rights. Ironically, today's Democratic Party is again moving back to embrace state's rights—something they see as a last resort (with many states, and especially California, suing the federal government a record number of times).[138] The modern Democratic Party move to embrace state's rights is likely temporary, or it could potentially split the country apart as it did during the Civil War era.

LINCOLN'S ACTIVIST POLICIES

In announcing his candidacy, Lincoln made it clear that he believed the Declaration of Independence—not the Constitution—was the document that best expressed America's fundamental principles. The Declaration of Independence had proclaimed that "All men are created equal," but then, thirteen years later, the Constitution codified slavery into law. Lincoln would eventually free the slaves, but he did not start out being an abolitionist. Lincoln's political position on slavery was similar to Jefferson's. He was morally opposed to slavery and made that clear in public and private; but his official political position was that he was merely against expansion of slavery to the new territories.

Even still, the candidacy of Lincoln alarmed the South. They saw Lincoln as an existential threat to their way of life, and upon his election quickly seceded from the union, thus setting the stage for the bloodiest war—by far—in American history.

One of the ironies of the Civil War is that the Republicans dominated Congress because the Southern Democrats had been expelled. Such scant resistance was fortuitous because it enabled Lincoln to implement sweeping changes during times that demanded decisive action.

To begin with, the war could not be fought without adequate funding—and the nation was deeply in debt. Lincoln moved quickly to shore up the financial health of the union by aggressively shifting revenue collection away from the states and into the coffers of the federal government. It was under Lincoln that the Internal Revenue Service was created, a fact most modern-day Republicans would be horrified to acknowledge (which only goes to show how the origins of the Republican Party could not be further than its current beliefs). [139] In the 1860s, it was the remaining Northern Democrats (those not expelled from Congress) who most vehemently protested the idea of a stronger federal government. They resisted, but their numbers were too weak to prevent the tax reform legislation from sailing through. As it turned out, this was only the beginning of radical social change. Everything about the federal government would change under Lincoln.

Before the Civil War era, the federal government did little other than to conduct foreign affairs, collect customs duties, and deliver the mail. Within two short years, the Lincoln administration had completely transformed the entire system of finance and revenue, transforming the federal government in the process.

Lincoln began by freely imposing high tariffs, averaging 37 percent. Tariffs were not a radical notion, having been employed ever since Hamilton. But tariffs had become a contentious issue between the North and South. This was because the North was the country's manufacturing base, while the South was dependent upon trade with Britain. The Southern secession removed the resistance to tariffs. Lincoln soon found out, however, that revenues from tariffs are notoriously unpredictable (which is one of the reasons tariffs fell out of favor in the 20th century, only to be revived by the Trump administration). The revenue from tariffs is unpredictable because of the ripple effects they cause—something that was true in Lincoln's day, but even more so in today's interconnected world. In fact, the Lincoln tariffs did not produce the revenue needed to offset the war funding, and so Lincoln had to devise other measures.

Needing still more revenue, the government took the extraordinary step of mass marketing—for the first time ever—US bonds directly to individuals. Those that could afford it jumped at the opportunity.

Thus, the finance system was reformed by shifting the levers of finance away from wealthy bankers and into the hands of the people themselves. Of course, the people had to pay for this privilege. Suddenly, every American who purchased anything had to pay national taxes; and every American who could afford it, purchased US bonds. One important benefit was that every American who did so now had a vested interest in the success of the Union war effort.

But that wasn't by any means the entirety of Lincoln's vision. He next implemented the Homestead Act of 1862, which granted to all citizens—and even to immigrants who merely announced their intention to become citizens—160 acres of Western land. All that was required was to live on the land for five years. The intent was to give hard-working farmers an incentive to own their own land, providing a means for individuals to rise, just as Lincoln's own family had done when they moved west to Illinois. The Homestead Act took the expansion of the West away from land speculators and put it into the hands of the average person. To help these novice farmers, the federal government provided education; and to do that, the Lincoln Congress created the Department of Agriculture.

But none of this would have worked without an easier way to travel to the West than on wagon trains. So the Lincoln administration took the exceptional step of committing to construct over one-thousand miles of transcontinental railroad track all the way to the Pacific Ocean (a project that was, considering the era, about as equally audacious as Eisenhower's national interstate highway project undertaken nearly a century later). To make the rapid expansion of railroad tracks financially feasible, the government took the radical step of chartering a national railroad, called appropriately enough, the Union Pacific Railroad. They then allowed the newly chartered railroad to sell US bonds to fund its construction; and finally, they granted right of way to the newly chartered railroad. These actions combined to enable railroad tracks to be built prior to the economic development of towns. This had never happened before.

But that wasn't all. Lincoln then ensured that the new territories would have economic hubs by funding public colleges through land grants—one for every state, which is why every state has a university today. Thus, not only did the Homestead Act provide citizens a way to settle open land; it also ensured that there would be an intellectual (and economic) hub in each state.

Of course, there were at least two parties the Homestead Act did not benefit: Native American Plains Indians and the bison they depended upon. In combination, the Homestead Act and the railroad brought enormous numbers of White settlers to the West. These settlers eventually clashed with and then overwhelmed Native populations with the help of the US military, under the continuing policy of mass extermination. From 1860 to 1890, the American non-Indian population doubled, going from 31 million to 62 million, while the Indian population was decimated. The buffalo suffered a similar fate. Seeking clear passage for new railroad, the US military killed thousands upon thousands of bison on sight, not even bothering to pick up, let alone eat, the carcasses.

Lincoln's Policy Toward Native America

Lincoln's policies resulted in the upward mobility of all peoples, with the notable exception of America's First Peoples. While the Civil War (through the absence of congressional resistance in the southern states) allowed Lincoln to implement a radically revised role for the federal government and to eventually free the slaves, the Civil War did not change American policy toward Native America.

A forgotten element of the Civil War occurred in the Western territories. To properly understand these events, we must remember the context. The Civil War was initially fought, not over the morality of slavery per se, but over whether the practice of slavery should be condoned in the new territories. In this matter, Lincoln's policies were not so different from those of Jackson and other 19th century presidents. *The Indian Wars were fought so that the White population could expand into new territories*, and this was justified by the idea of Manifest Destiny (the idea that the country, and specifically, the White population, was destined to expand across the entire continent). Any opposition to slavery in the new territories was rarely based on moral grounds. Instead, slavery was opposed by Whites that felt they would prosper more if slave-owners did not corral the bulk of the land into large plantations. Whether one was for or against slavery in the new territories, both sides were united on the need to remove the Indian populations. That is the reason the genocide continued throughout the 19th century.

While Lincoln was more moderate on this issue than Jackson before him, the US policy of removal of Native peoples from their traditional homelands continued during his tenure. The Navajo were relocated in a particularly brutal, 300-mile trek known as The Long Walk, with eerie similarities to the Cherokee Trail of Tears. After surrendering to Kit Carson and the US Army in Canyon de Chelley, the Navajo were marched from that area of modern-day eastern Arizona to Fort Sumner, NM (also known as Bosque Redondo or Hwèeldi to the Navajo). Hundreds of Navajo died along that walk because much like the Cherokee before them, they were removed without adequate time to prepare and were nearly starved before surrendering.

The ill-conceived plan was to turn the Navajo into farmers, alongside their traditional enemies, the Mescalero Apaches, who also were relocated to Fort Sumner. But the soil and water there were both inadequate, and the experiment failed in every way. In a rare reversal for the US government, the Navajo were allowed to return to their traditional homelands about three years later, and the Mescalero Apaches also managed to escape and return.[140]

Many other Indian massacres occurred while Lincoln was in office, including the devastating Sand Creek Massacre in Southern Colorado, which resulted in approximately 250–500 deaths and the subsequent relocation of the Arapahoe and Cheyenne. Clearly, Lincoln did not extend the same view of equality toward Native populations as he did to all other peoples. While Lincoln occasionally moderated the violence perpetrated upon Native Americans—including a noteworthy intervention that saved all but 39 of 300 scheduled to be executed for war crimes—the moral failing of the era of the Indian Wars continued. Because Lincoln was assassinated, it is impossible to know what might have happened if he had completed a second term in office. But there is no indication that he would have made a dramatic reversal in his policies toward Native Americans comparable to what he did for African Americans.

COMING FULL CIRCLE

Lincoln was an incredibly activist president, something not seen before in America, which is why the initial years of the Republican Party would come to be denounced by today's Republican Party as government overreach. The Democratic Party of Lincoln's day claimed exactly that, and also complained that Republican policies were lifting African Americans at the expense of White America. The Democratic Party of today likes to think of itself as always having been the inclusive party of the people, but for much of its history it was overtly racist.

It was the Democratic Party that supported the expansion of slavery to the new territories; and it was the Democrats who had the strongest association with the Ku Klux Klan. The Klan was first formed after the Civil War. It fell out of favor around the turn of the 20th century but was revived in the 1920s after the film *The Birth of a Nation* celebrated the Klan as heroic. It was at the brokered and chaotic 1924 Democratic convention that the KKK openly marched in the streets.

The Democratic Party remained the party of the South right up until President Lyndon Johnson, a Democrat, succeeded in passing landmark civil rights legislation (begun by President Kennedy) with more Republican votes than Democratic votes. It was only then that the Southern Democrats began to flee the party and eventually became the base of the Republican Party. At that point, we had come full circle and the parties were now at completely opposite positions from where they began.

THE PROCESS OF BECOMING WHAT WE HATE

It should now be apparent that, beyond the publicly stated positions of the political parties, there is a larger dynamic at work. In broad terms, that dynamic moves in the following way: Each party establishes its identity in contradistinction to the other. The fixation on the *other* precipitates reactive behavior that eventually compromises one's own principles, and this creates an inauthenticity within one's own party, known as a psychological shadow (or unseen awareness of self). Eventually, the political parties diverge so much from their center that resistance develops from within. When that happens, an entirely new party—or a greatly revised version of the same party— may be on the verge of forming.

When a new party is born, it appears suddenly, like a chick breaking out of an egg or an amoeba dividing. From a single unitive consciousness, two distinct entities are formed. They typically present themselves as opposite philosophies, but the energy from the original union continues to drive their subsequent evolution.

The new party still derives its identity through its opposition to the old party. Eventually, however, the new party often ends up becoming what they originally rebelled against. William Irwin Thompson understood this dynamic when he said, "We become what we hate," a powerful statement that bears repeating. Heraclitus also understood this when he formed the concept of *enantiodromia*: opposites turning into the other over time. And Navajo elder Grandfather Leon Secatero understood this too when he said, "In time, a negative becomes a positive and a positive becomes a negative."[141] And of course, a rebellious teenager often discovers this dynamic later in life, when he/she wakes up and realizes they have become like their parents.

In a two-party political system, this dynamic is destined to occur; in fact, it has repeatedly occurred throughout American history, and it was there at the very start when we rebelled against our mother country of Great Britain. The colonists ostensibly rebelled to become a country of greater equality, but glaring inequalities remained—between men and women, between Whites and Native Americans, Whites and African Americans, and also between classes (to a lesser extent than in Great Britain but to a greater extent than the founding fathers admitted). All these inequities persisted, either unseen or unacknowledged, for quite some time—until they eventually began to be addressed.

The most important unseen variable was the profound influence Native America had on our founding principles. The Native influence on the 19th century abolitionist and women's movements also remained unacknowledged. In truth, the women's movement and the antislavery movement owe an enormous debt of gratitude to Native America, and I dedicate the next chapter to exploring this contribution.

Not only did nineteenth century America not acknowledge the influence of Native Americans; it sought to expunge Native America from our cultural memory altogether. Our effort to destroy Native American history is tantamount to what Mao Tse Tung did in China, seeking to erase centuries of his own country's history. But stories are held in the land. And while they can be suppressed and forgotten, they can never be destroyed. The original wisdom of this land—a wisdom that spoke to and through our Native American brethren—is still present today. The concept of Manifest Destiny did not, and could not, expunge a greater idea—the concept of the radical interrelatedness of all peoples, of all beings, and of all with the soil, air, and waters of this fruited plain. It is this underlying value of unity in diversity that is America's sacred purpose. It may lie dormant today, but it still exists, and eventually will be manifest. I do not know how long it will take for America to reach this higher vision. It could be millennia. But it will eventually be revealed, since a future society based in unity in diversity is our true destiny.

CHAPTER SEVEN

Historical Influences on the Politics of Gender and Race Relations

Any contemplation of a *dance of opposites* would be incomplete without consideration of gender and race, as the dynamic between the sexes and races fleshes out the various expressions of what it is to be human. The mating dance between women and men is most basic, serving to perpetuate the species and underlying much of human creativity. The interplay between different colors of humanity—once separated by different traditions born of different continents—is also important as we increasingly interact together in a globally connected world.

The United States has become a place of maximum diversity where all the world's peoples meet on one soil. But our nation was originally founded through the mix of two primary (although aggregate) cultures: European Enlightenment science meeting Native American place-based wisdom. The politics of gender and race in America are still affected by this initial encounter between Native American and European peoples.

There is a carryover from colonization that, even today, pits some White, Euro-Americans against people of color. While this is often characterized in simple terms of racism, what underlies this is a continuing dispute between worldviews—between different ways of seeing and relating to time, space, and place.

Racism emerges out of a fear of difference. In extreme form, this fear manifests as hate or a desire to annihilate the other; but more commonly, people harbor prejudice against an unfamiliar group or individual, causing them to avoid contact in some cases or to attempt to convert the other to their (presumed correct) point of view. Of course, many open-minded people thrive when encountering different cultures, recognizing an opportunity to learn. Roger Williams and Ben Franklin were two such people, as were many of the Native people they encountered, such as Miantonomi, Canonicus, Massasoit, and Canassatego. Later, in the 19th century, Emerson and Thoreau continued this important dialogue with William Apess (Pequot), Joseph Polis (Penobscot), and other Native Americans to help to create a new American philosophy that emphasized the importance of place and the valuing of diversity.

America will always be a hybrid of Native American and European values, even if this is rarely identified, acknowledged, and understood. It is important to realize that there were colonial roots of white supremacy *and* positive intercultural interaction between European settlers and Native Americans. It was not one or the other, but both. To see these two realities together is not only possible; it is helpful to do so—for it affords us an opportunity to see through misunderstandings, recognize gifts from other cultures, and begin to heal.

THE ROOTS OF COLONIZATION AND WHITE SUPREMACY

Most of modern world colonization has been done by White, male Europeans. Why is that? What is the root cause of colonization? And what, other than greed, was their motivation and rationale?

The roots of colonization go back to antiquity and are difficult to trace; but there is a particular thread that emerged in the European Renaissance with the advent of linear perspective in art that I chose to emphasize in my earlier chapters for an important reason. Linear perspective—and its concomitant view of linear time—produced such a radical change to the Western worldview that the map became confused with the territory. In other words, the resulting abstraction of reality was taken to be reality itself—what Whitehead called "the fallacy of misplaced concreteness."[142] This is why we call the kind of art that employs linear perspective *realism*, even though humans are not *really* apart from the world.

As I pointed out earlier, one of the consequences of linear perspective was that it yielded a new view of time. Time, once universally understood to be cyclical, became reimagined as a line stretching outward away from the viewer and into the future. In effect, *time replaced place*, because *origin* once referred to *where* you came from and only later became associated with the *beginning of time*. What was once distance from the origin was renamed *progress*.[143]

It was in this way that the European view of time and nature became the seed of colonization—for without the notion that knowledge could be removed (abstracted) from one place and transported (progress) to another, modern colonization might never have occurred. The notion of colonization required both the concept of human linear progress and the belief of the colonizer that they were at the head of the parade. The colonizer believed their own imported knowledge was more advanced than local, place-based knowledge.

Colonization is the attempt by one culture to create unity by subsuming another; it is therefore an expression of a *devolved form of unitive consciousness*. This is not to say that colonization has resulted in only a one-way transmission of knowledge—for, whenever cultures meet, there is always some form of knowledge exchange. In fact, even if the colonizers of America felt superior, they soon realized their survival depended upon learning from the native inhabitants of their new continent.

THE INCOMPLETE VISION OF AMERICA'S FOUNDERS

The European settlers needed considerable inspiration, encouragement, and practical knowledge from Native America before eventually determining to break away from their mother country. The specific example of a participatory democracy set by the Haudenosaunee (Iroquois) Confederacy and other Native American tribes was a key ingredient. But this would not have mattered if the founding fathers did not have the requisite intelligence, imagination, and resourcefulness to envisage and implement their vision of a representational republic.

Of course, the founders selectively adapted any input they received from Native America, and in doing this made broad, sweeping generalizations about both human nature and the nature of Western society. They established a republic that was based on diverse colonies uniting; yet this did not represent the highest form of unity in diversity, which would have guaranteed liberty and equality for all its citizens. Instead, they limited equality and reserved the highest liberty—the right to vote and run for office—for those like themselves who were White, male property owners. And contrary to common belief, women who owned property had the right to vote in many colonies prior to the formation of the United States. Thus the founding fathers did not just deny women the right to vote; *they took it away from them*, only to be regained in 1920.[144]

It can be seen that the founding fathers, while brilliant, were at times also arrogant. Hamilton and Madison believed that they had invented a new science of politics akin to other sciences like physics or biology. Their arrogance stemmed partly from intellect and partly from privilege. Not only were all the founders White, male property owners; they were almost all born into the aristocracy, with the notable exceptions of Franklin and Hamilton. The first six presidents (after the Constitution was ratified) were of the aristocracy, with only Jackson breaking the mold. While the founders may have created a daring experiment that benefited the common man far more than any European monarchies had, they did not give up their privileged position to do so, holding onto a sense of entitlement and superiority.

This was particularly true when it came to relationships with Native Americans, African American slaves, and women. The founders were indebted to Native America for much of their inspiration but were somewhat reluctant to acknowledge it. Nor did they include Native Americans in positions of power. The founders were similarly conflicted over the issue of slavery. But they made little attempt to end it in the early years of the republic, setting a lasting precedent. Thus even after Europe ended slavery early in the 19th century, the United States did not follow suit. The founding fathers also made no effort to include women in the political process; and there is little evidence to suggest that they were morally conflicted over this. Our founding fathers were apparently comfortable with proclaiming lofty ideals of equality while ignoring the fact that certain elements of society enjoyed nothing of the sort.

This view of white male supremacy remained relatively unchallenged in the United States for many years due to an elaborate system of repression that included both external coercion and the projection of inferiority, which then became internalized in varying degrees by nonwhites and women. Then came the rise of both the antislavery movement and the women's movement of the mid-1800s.

THE INFLUENCE OF NATIVE AMERICA ON THE 19TH CENTURY WOMEN'S MOVEMENT

How did the first radical suffragists of the United States—Elizabeth Cady Stanton, Lucretia Mott, and Matilda Gage—come to a vision of equality for women? All these women were living in 19th century America, a time when a woman fleeing a violent husband would be routinely returned to him by police, just as runaway slaves were returned to their masters. How did these women—who lived in a society where they were required to pay taxes but had no voice in the direction of government; could not vote; could not run for office; lost all property rights once they married; had no right of divorce, and if they separated from their husbands, lost all custody rights to their children; whose oppression was sanctioned by the Bible, with their husbands having the legal right and religious responsibility to physically discipline them;—HOW in the world did these women, who were not even permitted to speak aloud in church, have the courage to ask for equal rights?[145]

They did so because they were living nearby Native women who befriended them and showed them another way. These Native women were fully equal in their society—their responsibilities were in balance with men; their children were members of the mother's clan, and they controlled their own use of property. The Native women's work was satisfying and done alongside other women (as opposed to the mostly isolated drudgery of the colonial household), and they were responsible for agriculture in addition to the home life. Moreover, the women were understood to be spiritually related to Mother Earth herself, a relationship that ensured respect. In fact, they lived in a society where rape and violence toward women was almost unheard of and severely punished if it were to occur. These Native women happened to be Haudenosaunee (Iroquois)—the same group that strongly influenced the founding fathers of the United States—but, in truth, they could have been from any number of other tribes with similar traditions of equality for women.

Through association with their Native sisters, the early suffragists learned that the Haudenosaunee women were responsible for caring for nourishment from everything *in* the earth (such as planting, cultivating, and harvesting), while the men had responsibility for everything *on* the earth (hunting, fishing, and so forth). They learned that the Clan Mother nominated the male chief that represented their clan in the Grand Council—and that she had the right to remove him (by taking off his deer antlers, the symbol of authority) if he committed acts of malfeasance, or acted inappropriately in any way, especially toward the women. Their nomination was based on certain criteria. Specifically, the nominee had the following restrictions:

- He could not have committed a theft.
- He could not have committed a murder.
- He could not have abused a woman.
- He must be a responsible family man.[146]

Haudenosaunee women were arguably in the highest position of governmental authority, as the Clan Mothers were the overseeing body. For any declaration of war or treaty to be signed, two thirds of the clan mothers needed to approve it. If, at any time, the mothers were dissatisfied with the subjects considered by the male council, a Grand Council would be called during which time the women joined in and asserted their voices in the affairs of the nation. The women did not seek to usurp the men's authority, only to redirect it. The men respected the women as carriers of the "Dream of the Earth" (what the sentient, living Earth wants to happen) and listened to their guidance.[147] The women were the wisdom council that set the tone, determined the agenda, and oversaw the men who then enacted that agenda on behalf of the women and the whole tribe. If all were running smoothly, it might appear to an outsider that the men were in charge, but the women were always empowered to intervene as necessary. Imagine how things would change if similar traditions were in place in America today.

Stanton, Mott, and Gage wrote extensively about the influence of the Haudenosaunee on the incipient women's movement, as did many of their women colleagues, such as Frances Wright, Harriet Maxwell Converse, Harriette Phillips Eaton, Helen Troy, and Erminnie A. Smith, and their accounts were published in magazines, newspapers, and books.[148] In response, these brave women were mocked, cast out of social circles, and often labeled as heretics; but they were undaunted, because their experience with Native American women taught them a better existence was possible.

It is hard to overstate the impression the Native women made upon the early suffragists. European-American women had been led to believe that their lower status in society was normal, sanctioned by the Bible, and that conditions were the same for women everywhere. But Native women opened their eyes to a whole new world of possibility. In fact, it is a bit of a misnomer to call these feminists "suffragists," since Stanton, Mott, and Gage were not content to seek only suffrage; they wanted equal rights in every way. It was only years later, after Susan B. Anthony became a nationally known figure for being arrested trying to vote, that the women's movement strategically limited their goal to suffrage alone. They did so for practical reasons—mainly because it was considered more achievable.

THE SENECA FALLS CONVENTION OF 1848

Stanton and Mott teamed up to organize the first ever women's rights convention in the United States, the groundbreaking Seneca Falls Convention of 1848. Stanton was the principal author of the treatise produced at the conference—The Declaration of Sentiments—which Stanton later referred to as "The Woman's Declaration of Independence"—for, in effect, their audacious declaration served to launch a second American Revolution, only this time it was for women. And its first two paragraphs were clearly influenced by the US Declaration of Independence:

> When in the course of human events, it becomes necessary for one portion of the family of man to assume among the people of the earth a position different from that which they have hitherto occupied, but one to which the laws of nature and of nature's God entitle them, a decent respect to the opinions of mankind requires that they should declare the causes that impel them to such a course.
>
> We hold these truths to be self-evident; that all men and women are created equal; that they are endowed by their Creator with certain inalienable rights; that among these are life, liberty, and the pursuit of happiness; that to secure these rights governments are instituted, deriving their just powers from the consent of the governed. Whenever any form of government becomes destructive of these ends, it is the right of those who suffer from it to refuse allegiance to it, and insist upon the institution of a new government, laying its foundation on such principles, and organizing its powers in such form as to them shall seem most likely to affect their safety and happiness. Prudence, indeed, will dictate that governments long established should not be changed for light and transient causes; and accordingly, all experience hath shown that mankind is more disposed to suffer, while evils are sufferable, than to right themselves, by abolishing the forms to which they are accustomed. But when a long train of

abuses and usurpations, pursuing invariably the same object, evinces a design to reduce them under absolute despotism, it is their duty to throw off such government, and to provide new guards for their future security. Such has been the patient sufferance of the women under this government, and such is now the necessity which constrains them to demand the equal station to which they are entitled.[149]

Important Writings of the Women's Suffrage Movement

Three years after the Seneca Falls convention, Elizabeth Cady Stanton met Susan B. Anthony, and they went on to collaborate on women's rights for the rest of their lives. Stanton and Anthony enjoyed an extraordinary partnership even though they had very different strengths. A mutual friend described them as follows:

> Mrs. Stanton is a fine writer, but a poor executant; Miss Anthony is a thorough manager, but a poor writer. Both have large brains and great hearts; neither has any selfish ambition for celebrity; but each vies with the other in a noble enthusiasm for the cause to which they are devoting their lives.[150]

Stanton and Anthony, together with Matilda Gage and Ida Husted Harper, wrote a comprehensive, six-volume history of the women's rights movement. *The History of Women's Suffrage*, which chronicled the movement from 1881 to 1922, was one of the best-known pieces of literature to emerge from this era.

Gage went on to author her own magnum opus, *Woman, Church, and State*, published in 1893. In her comprehensive book, Gage, who was adopted into the Wolf clan of the Mohawk nation and given the name Ka-ron-ien-ha-wi or "She who Holds the Sky," explores many of the ancient civilizations in which women had equal rights. She also had the courage to confront Christianity for its part in promoting the inequality for women and for misrepresenting history. She opens *Woman, Church, and State* by asserting:

Woman is told that her present position in society is entirely due to Christianity; that it is superior to that of her sex at any prior age of the world. Church and State both maintain that she has ever been inferior and dependent, man superior and ruler . . . *Such assertions are due to non-acquaintance with the existing phase of historical knowledge*, whose records the majority of mankind have neither time nor opportunity of investigating.

Christianity tended somewhat from its foundation to restrict the liberty woman enjoyed under the old civilizations. Knowing that . . . *in many ancient nations woman possessed a much greater degree of respect and power than she has at the present age,* this subject will be presented from a historical standpoint. . . . [This] . . . will prove that the most grievous wrong ever inflicted upon woman has been in the Christian teaching that she was not created equal with man, and the consequent denial of her rightful place in Church and State (italics mine).[151]

In a later chapter, on the subject of witchcraft, Gage goes on to make an important clarification regarding its history:

Before the introduction of Christianity, no capital punishment existed, in the modern acceptation of the term, except for witchcraft. But pagans, unlike Christians, did not look upon women as more given to this practice than men; witches and wizards were alike stoned to death. But as soon as a system of religion was adopted which taught the greater sinfulness of women, over whom authority had been given to man by God himself, the saying arose "one wizard to 10,000 witches" and the persecution for witchcraft became chiefly directed against women. The church degraded woman by destroying her self-respect, and teaching her to feel consciousness of guilt in the very fact of her existence.[152]

Other writers from the 19th century women's rights movement included Lydia Maria Child, author of the novel of *Hobomok: A Tale of Early Times*, who grew up among the Abenaki people of Maine and was a strong supporter of Indian rights and women's rights, and favored the abolition of slavery; and Catherine Maria Sedgwick, who was adopted into the Oneida nation and authored *Hope Leslie: Or, Early Times in the Massachusetts*, an important novel that followed Child's *Hobomok*. Both Child and Sedgwick stressed the importance of place, valued diversity of thought, and painted a much more positive picture of Native Americans and women than was customary at the time. Child included numerous Indian stories in *Hobomok* as she sought to overturn mainstream moral principles and transform European thinking to accept cultural differences. Sedgwick was a scholar who read Roger Williams's *A Key into the Language of America* and quoted him in *Hope Leslie*, knowing that Williams was the forerunner for co-existence between peoples. *Hope Leslie* also included a strong Native woman character, Magawisca, who provided a bridge between European and Indian worldviews.[153]

An important cross-fertilization occurred between women writers, Native American civil rights leaders such as William Apess, and the American philosophers Emerson and Thoreau. The influential Margaret Fuller, the first woman writer at the *New York Tribune* and the first woman foreign correspondent to serve under combat conditions, was both a friend to Emerson and to the woman suffragists. Emerson was a close friend of Thoreau, who had more direct contact with Apess and other Native Americans than Emerson had.

MARGARET FULLER'S VISION OF DIVINE LOVE

Margaret Fuller wrote an important book: *Woman in the Nineteenth Century*, in which she re-envisions the relationship between women and men as an awakening to divine love. Unlike Gage, she utilized Christianity to support her case for the equal divinity of men and women, citing as evidence the existence of both male and female saints.

Fuller articulated ideas that were both ahead of her time and a revival of ancient wisdom. She asserted that equality between men and women would fulfill the lives of both, and also bring divinity itself to new heights.

Fuller's father raised her to be a precocious intellectual, and she went on to support intellectual and religious freedom for women equal to that of men. She foresaw the transition of marriages of convenience into marriages that expressed a union of souls. She outlined four types of marriage, with each progressive higher stage including the lower stages as displayed in the following pyramid.[154]

Fuller specifically did not exclude unmarried women from the possibility of divine union, saying they have opportunities for communion with the divine that married people often do not have. In this and other matters, Fuller always asserted the importance of women developing themselves as individuals. Women could not simply demand that men remove their dominating influence; women must also proclaim themselves as equal to, and independent from, men.

The
Religious
Union

Intellectual
Companionship
(Friends and Confidants)

Mutual Idolatry
(Infatuation of the other as perfection to the
exclusion of the rest of the world)

Household Partnership
(Man as provider, Woman as housekeeper)

Fuller's Four Levels of Marriage

The challenge for 19th-century women, however, was that Euro-American men and women did not simply represent polar opposites because the male occupied both the positive *and* the neutral pole (representing humanity in general), as Simone de Beauvoir pointed out a century later in her groundbreaking opus *The Second Sex*.[155] This idea has been remarkably resistant to change, for, until recently, the word "humankind" had not yet come into common use and "mankind" was understood to represent all of humanity. For true equality to occur, any vestige of male as neutral pole must be erased.

RELATIONSHIP BETWEEN NATIVE AMERICA, ABOLITION, AND WOMEN'S MOVEMENTS

I have made the case that Native America planted the original seed of unity in diversity in America and that the Iroquois (Haudenosaunee) Confederacy, in particular, were the primary inspiration for this unfolding. The Haudenosaunee were an important inspiration for both the founding fathers and what we might call the "founding mothers" who were the founders of the women's movement—and they and other Native Americans were important inspirations for both the women's movement and the abolitionist movement.

Ironically, at the very same time that they were serving to empower women and the freed slaves, Native Americans were themselves under siege from the Jackson administration. The intent of the Indian Removal Act was to divide in order to conquer—a philosophy that goes back to Phillip of Macedonia, whose *divide et impera* (divide and conquer) became the blueprint for controlling the masses. Jackson tried to divide the country in every conceivable way: East versus West, North versus South, Black versus White, and White versus Red—but in some respects his strategy backfired and brought people together in ways he did not anticipate. In herding "undesirable" people away, The Indian Removal Act created opportunities for Native Americans, runaway slaves, and women (both Black and White) to mix in ways that otherwise would not have occurred. They mixed in every way, which is to say that there were interracial sexual relations and occasionally intermarriage, particularly within Native communities. Thus an impetus of hatred that attempted to cast away an entire group of people ended up generating love, respect, and the formation of new families and communities. This literally changed the complexion of the modern era to come.

Everything I am speaking of here is a common effect of what I call a *devolved form of unitive consciousness*. Jackson was trying to achieve *unity through exclusion*, and succeeded to some extent; but he also was a catalyst for accelerating a higher-level reunification at a later time. This underscores another important aspect of the model: Devolution is sometimes a necessary prelude to higher integration.

An even more direct effect of the Indian Removal Act was that it changed the philosophy of the abolitionist movement. Before the Indian Removal Act, most antislavery proponents favored relocating free Black Americans back to Africa. (Even Abraham Lincoln was a proponent of this "solution" for a time.) But as a consequence of witnessing the effects of the Indian Removal Act, many of the same abolitionists recognized the cruelty of relocation and changed their thinking. By 1831 the leading abolitionists including, most famously, William Lloyd Garrison, shifted away from advocating the repatriation of free slaves to Africa in favor of immediate emancipation. Garrison, not coincidentally, was also an important voice for women's suffrage. In fact, Garrison promoted women's rights within his organization (The Massachusetts Anti-Slavery Society) to such an extent that some members left to form another abolitionist society, one that excluded women. This forced the hand of women who supported abolition, prompting them to stand up for themselves as well. Thus, the two issues of Black suffrage and women's suffrage were conjoined into one nascent civil rights movement promoting the greater inclusion of voices.

ALLIANCE BETWEEN SUFFRAGISTS AND ABOLITIONISTS

The alliance between the abolitionist and women's movements was there at the start. In asserting this, I am not simply referring to prominent Black women who were abolitionists and later became women's rights activists, such as Harriet Tubman and Sojourner Truth. Mott and Stanton first realized the need for the women's movement through working together on the abolitionist movement. In fact, Mott and Stanton were two of only six women delegates at the groundbreaking World Anti-Slavery Convention held in London in 1840. It was there where Mott and Stanton first kindled their friendship—and also where they experienced hurtful segregation. The women attendees were confined to a separate area of the meeting hall, but several of the men in attendance, including William Lloyd Garrison and Wendell Phillips, protested the women's exclusion. Three men (William Adam, Nathaniel Peabody Rogers, and Charles Lenox Remond) broke ranks and caucused with the women.[156]

Then during the Seneca Falls Convention, the great social reformer Frederick Douglass ended up having a pivotal role. Douglass, who was the only African American to attend, made a passionate speech in favor of a suffrage statement being included within the Declaration of Sentiments, which was then signed. In his speech, Douglass referred to men ruling over women as a fallacy, with those backward-thinking people who believed in it equal to those who believed the sun revolved around the earth. He proclaimed that "right is of no sex, truth is of no color."[157]

Douglass first became involved in the women's rights movement in 1847 upon moving to Rochester, New York (which became a hotbed for both the women's and abolitionist movements). It was in Rochester that he published *The North Star*, a weekly abolitionist newspaper. At that time, he was active in the Western New York Anti-Slavery Society; and it was there that he first met Elizabeth M'Clintock, who was the person that invited him to the Women's Rights Convention.

In 1866, Elizabeth Cady Stanton, Susan B. Anthony, Lucy Stone, and other women suffragists who also supported abolition, partnered with Frederick Douglass and Henry Blackwell (husband of Lucy Stone) to found the American Equal Rights Association, an organization that demanded not just universal suffrage, but full equality for women and people of color. [158]

THE BREAK BETWEEN ABOLITIONIST AND WOMEN'S MOVEMENTS

The strong partnership between the abolitionist and women's movements came to an impasse after the Civil War when Stanton and Douglass could not agree on a future strategy. Stanton wanted the two movements to remain in lockstep so that they might simultaneously achieve suffrage; but because Black suffrage seemed imminent at the time and there was no such assurance for women's suffrage, Douglass resisted. Stanton feared that Black suffrage coming first would set the women's movement back decades. And she was right. But Douglass feared that insisting on simultaneous suffrage for Blacks and women would set *both* back for decades—and he may have also been right. We will never know. In any case, Douglass continued to work on behalf of women's rights, including suffrage, years after Black suffrage was achieved. But women's suffrage was not achieved on a national level until one hundred years ago, in 1920, nearly 150 years after the founding of the nation.[159] In the meantime, the divides in our country remain, as the next chapter makes clear.

CHAPTER EIGHT

A Country in Conflict:
The Civil War Era Comes Full Circle

While we tend to think of the Civil War as ancient history, in some ways we never left the era because our national divide over race has never left us. Nor has our divide over gender. When Blacks won suffrage, women's suffrage and women's rights were delayed. Even after the passage of Black suffrage, there was a 100-year period of Jim Crow segregation before the enactment of Civil rights legislation, and that did not end our racial divide. It just pushed it into the shadows. And now it is reemerging, as history seems to be repeating itself. The country is arguably as divided today as then; even if we never devolve into outright civil war, we have come to a similar crossroads. "A house divided against itself cannot stand," cautioned Lincoln, and clearly we cannot remain this divided much longer. We are essentially reliving the Civil War—at least verbally—only it is anything but civil.

POLARIZATION IN THE MEDIA

Perhaps the most striking similarity between today and the Civil War era lies in the polarity of media coverage. In the 1850s, newspapers were sponsored by one political party or the other. In New York, there was the Democratic-controlled *New York Herald*, first established in 1835 and the Republican-controlled *New-York Tribune*, founded in 1841, long before the two merged in 1924. If you read about the Lincoln-Douglas debates in the *Tribune* or other Republican papers, you learned that Lincoln was brilliant and triumphant; but if you read the Democratic papers, you were told that "Lincoln was so terrible he fell on the floor in humiliation and they had to carry him out," according to historian Doris Kearns Goodwin. The closest equivalent today is cable television. Flipping the channel from MSNBC to Fox News, particularly in the evening hours, might seem like peeking into alternate universes.

THE FAIRNESS DOCTRINE

How did the media become so polarized? A particularly profound event occurred during the Reagan administration, and I am not referring to the collapse of the Berlin wall but to a different kind of wall that came down around the same time: the Fairness Doctrine of the FCC. Originally established in 1949—and in place until 1989—the Fairness Doctrine ensured that broadcast networks presented controversial issues of public importance in an honest, equitable, and balanced manner. If one point of view was presented on a controversial issue, broadcast networks were required to present a contrasting view. The networks were given wide latitude as to how they presented the opposing view. They could do so through editorials, news segments, or other programming. Before the demise of the Fairness Doctrine, it was not uncommon for the same network to broadcast a conservative talk show followed by a liberal talk show.

Reagan tore down the "fairness wall" because he saw it as a restriction on the freedom of the press. Reagan's stated intention was for the press to compete, as every other business did for public attention. This sounds reasonable, but without the stabilizing force of the Fairness Doctrine, we became subject to a marked increase in segmented programming that accented extreme views on both the right and left, and particularly on the right. Prior to the end of the Fairness Doctrine, there was some validity to the conservative claim that the media had a liberal slant; however, the media also used to have a mandate to adhere much more closely to truth than today. Although the demise of the Fairness Doctrine lowered the intelligence of the public discourse, it was celebrated by some conservatives who believed they had been "liberated from the East Germany of liberal media domination," as talk radio host Rush Limbaugh proclaimed in the inaugural year of his show.[161]

The Fairness Doctrine only applied to broadcast networks, not to cable networks, but its demise ended up not only creating polarization among broadcast networks because the emergent polarization was then exploited by cable networks (such as FOX News and MSNBC) that exclusively catered to one side of the political aisle. Thus, the tearing down of the fairness wall initiated a slide away from reality—and, potentially, into oblivion. We entered into an era of "alternative facts," as White House strategist Kellyanne Conway proclaimed in the early days of the Trump presidency.

CITIZENS UNITED SUPREME COURT DECISION

Besides the polarization of modern media, another important factor contributing to the decline of truth was the 2010 Supreme Court landmark case resulting in what is referred to as the Citizens United decision, whereby corporations were equated with individuals in terms of the free speech clause in the First Amendment. When pertaining to campaign finance, this freedom prohibits the government from restricting independent expenditures for political campaign communications. In 2010 the court extended this to include corporations, labor unions, and other associations. This decision led to the creation of "Super Pacs," political action committees that are permitted to receive unlimited corporate contributions, which they then funnel to specific political campaigns. The net result was that media became increasingly controlled by wealthy magnates such as conservative icons Rupert Murdoch, Shelden Adelson, and Roger Ailes as well as liberal icons like Michael Bloomberg, George Soros, and Jeff Bezos. The lion's share of today's news media is owned by just 15 billionaires.[162]

The consolidation of media has had a chilling effect on creativity. At the end of 2018 *The Weekly Standard*, a critically acclaimed conservative magazine, announced its closing, mainly because its new parent company, the *Washington Examiner*, wanted to cannibalize the parts to help the *Examiner* expand its market. *New York Times* columnist David Brooks lamented that "this is what happens" when

> corporate drones take over an opinion magazine, try to drag it down to their level and then grow angry and resentful when the people at the magazine try to maintain some sense of intellectual standards. This is what happens when people with a populist mind-set decide that an uneducated opinion is of the same value as an educated opinion, that ignorance sells better than learning.[163]

Social Media

The consolidation of media outlets by the wealthy also happened in Lincoln's day. But one important difference between today and the 1850s is degree of complexity. During the 19th century, newspapers, pamphlets, and letters were the only sources of topical information available to the public. By the mid-twentieth century, radio and television had emerged, vastly increasing the speed and power of mass communication. With the advent of the internet at the end of the century, email largely replaced postal communication. This further hastened speed, if not intimacy. Speed increased even more with the popularity of text messages and smart phones during the early 21st century. All of this was a prelude to social media, which dramatically changed the landscape of modern life.

The arrival of social media such as Facebook, Twitter, and Instagram was, like smart phones, touted as a means of connecting people together. When Arab nations began a series of pro-democracy uprisings (known as the Arab spring of 2011), Facebook and Twitter postings of tweets were credited with empowering the people to organize and overthrow totalitarian regimes—and, at that time, it unquestionably helped people circumvent state-controlled media. But the promise of social media and smart phones never fully materialized.

Authoritarian regimes have found ways to limit access to social media and, more recently, to exploit its use *against* their people and against democratic societies in general. The latter was inevitable because the major purveyors of social media have a financial incentive to collect data on individuals for marketing purposes—data that can be readily exploited by totalitarian regimes seeking to sow discord among democratic societies.

Thus the net effect of social media so far has not been to increase media literacy, critical thinking, and social cohesion (as once hoped) but to increase fragmentation, division, misinformation, and general social incoherence. While social media giants can mitigate the damage, and are attempting to do so (if for no other reason than to protect their product and profitability), it remains to be seen whether social media will make civil unrest more likely, or less likely, in the future.

How Close Are We to an Actual Civil War?

In 2017 Keith Mines, a national security expert, estimated the likelihood of the United States breaking into civil war (or at least some form of violent political conflict) within the next ten to fifteen years at 60 percent. [164] The makings of a civil war may have already begun in 2017. The FBI reported more than a 15 percent increase in hate crimes for 2017 and 2018 over 2016. In 2019, mass shootings occurred at a rate exceeding more than one per day for the first time.[165]

Two events from 2017 stand out. In June, at a charity congressional baseball game, Republican Congressman Steve Scalise was shot and wounded, but thankfully survived. Then, in August of 2017, neo-Nazis marched in Charlottesville to protest the decision to take down the statue of Confederate General Robert E. Lee. Nineteen people were injured, and a counter-protester was killed when a man drove his car through the crowd.

One might wonder why the Charlottesville marchers chose to chant the anti-Jewish Nazi slogans "Blood and Soil" (translation of the German *Blut und Boden*) and "Jews will not replace us" in a rally that was ostensibly protesting the removal of a Confederate General. But anti-Semitic and anti-Black rhetoric have long been merged together in American history. The Ku Klux Klan was created by ex-Confederate veterans and other Southerners opposed to Recon-struction in the aftermath of the Civil War. But it was the second wave of the KKK in the 1920s that specifically merged anti-Black and anti-Jewish sentiment.

The Trump administration gave cover for white supremacist orga-nizations to mobilize because Trump consistently failed to condemn their actions, not only at Charlottesville, but ever since the launch of his campaign. This has inspired a near record number of protesters against him and his administration, beginning with the Women's March on day one. Millions have been involved in nearly daily protests, much of it because of objections to Trump's anti-immigrant, anti-Latino, and anti-Muslim rhetoric. Five-hundred people were arrested at a June 2018 rally protesting the administration's family separation policy at our southern border.[166]

The uptick in right-wing extremism has also inspired the mobi-lization of Antifa (short for Anti-Fascist) counter-protesters. Antifa dates back to anti-fascist citizen protests of the 1920s and 1930s. Its members believe a show of force is necessary to combat the rise of fascism. The tactics of Antifa have been frowned upon by mainstream and conservative commentators alike, but some, including President Trump, have sought to draw a false equivalency between Antifa and white supremacist groups. (No known murders have been attributed to Antifa activities in the United States, while thousands have been killed by white supremacists). Nonetheless, there is still cause for concern regarding the increase in Antifa activity. Violence against violence tends to only produce more violence, bringing us closer to a civil war.

THE SEEDS OF PRESENT-DAY CONFLICT

As I have been asserting all along, the seeds of our present-day conflict date back not only to the Civil War. They go back to the original founding of our government. If the founders had incorporated the full range of Native American egalitarianism, they would have given people of color and women equal participation in the political process.

Instead, they spoke in high-minded terms about liberty and equality while cherry picking who would benefit: only White, male property owners. Women, people of color, and non-property owners were omitted from what otherwise would have been an exemplary vision of equality. The unwillingness of the founders to address the rights of women and people of color pushed those issues into the national shadow, making them harder than ever to fully resolve, but certain to reemerge later. The current tensions between race and gender are a direct result of unaddressed shadow issues coming to the surface.

All of this became plain with the election of an African American president, Barack Obama. Yet the Republican backlash to Obama's election never would have occurred if the Republican party had not already moved sharply to the right in the past half-century.

The seeds of the modern Republican era began with President Johnson's passage of the Civil Rights Act in the mid-1960s. Johnson, like Kennedy, was a Democrat, but Johnson knew he needed Republican votes to pass the civil rights legislation that Kennedy had initiated, and in the end, he succeeded in securing more Republican votes than Democratic. As tragic as Kennedy's assassination was, it may have required Johnson, a skilled politician known for horse trading, to pass that particular legislation. Johnson knew he could count on the party of Lincoln to care more about civil rights (at that time) than Democrats. But Johnson also knew that the passage of civil rights legislation would hand the South to the Republicans for generations. And that was exactly what happened.

Because a Democratic president passed civil rights legislation, Southern Democrats fled the party and became the base of today's Republican Party. It didn't happen overnight. First, Barry Goldwater and then Richard Nixon capitalized on this shift. Nixon devised his infamous "Southern strategy" to recapture the White House for the Republican Party, running a campaign that emphasized "law and order." Such a campaign enabled him to employ the strategic use of "dog whistles," statements that did not seem overtly racist, but could be heard as such by those who opposed equal rights for Black people and other minorities. In turn, Nixon's Justice Department prosecuted far more Black than White persons for certain offenses, such as drug-related crimes. Such actions appealed to many White Southerners. This also moved the Republican Party to the right, cementing its shift from the progressive party of Lincoln to the party of conservative traditions (marketed as family values). It was left to the Democrats to fill the vacuum and become the socially progressive party.

This was all part of the natural dance of opposites between the parties. One party always needs to be the party of fiscal restraint and gradual, incremental change; and the other party needs to be the party of progressive forward movement. An important result of this do-si-do on the political dance floor was that the Democratic Party became the party of diversity, and the Republican Party became increasingly whiter—and increasingly male.

The Republican Party is now appealing to the same base that supported the likes of Governor George Wallace, the Democrat who fiercely opposed desegregation, proclaiming "Segregation now, segregation tomorrow, segregation forever" in his 1963 inaugural address.[167]

Because the country itself has continued to become increasingly diverse, many thought the Republican Party would have to expand their tent or become extinct. Then, along came Donald Trump.

Trump ignored the advice of the Republican Party elites and won the 2016 election by getting out the White male vote at levels not seen since Andrew Jackson. He eked out an electoral college victory by capitalizing upon the backlash against Barack Obama and Hillary Clinton (and with significant help from Russia, as we came to more fully understand). While only a certain percentage of Trump's base may be overtly racist, Trump employed the tactic of dog whistles to reach racist and sexist voters without offending others in his base. He never would have won the election if Obama had not won two terms before him; it was Obama's success that generated a backlash within certain sectors of the White working class that are against Black upward social mobility.

The Election of Barack Obama

The election of Barack Hussein Obama was the perfect recipe for bringing the collective shadow of America to the surface. Why? Let's face it. There are a lot of people in the United States who harbor racist inclinations, even if they ordinarily remain hidden or unknown to themselves. When a Black man with a Muslim-sounding middle name was elected president 150 years after the slaves were freed (15–20 percent of whom were Muslims), the shadow was awakened. It was as if these racist tendencies were stored in the attic like old firecrackers and someone took a torch to them. They exploded.

The Tea Party movement was the vehicle. While the movement was ostensibly about fiscal responsibility, it created a platform for raging against the president. And because our president was Black, the inevitable happened, and much of the expression became overtly racist. It was the election of President Obama, not President Trump, that ushered in the what we can call the modern civil war era. But that is not where the similarity ends between Lincoln and Obama.

The Character of Lincoln and Obama

The mid-19th century and the turn of the 21st century saw the rise of two historic, if unlikely, figures of American history: Abraham Lincoln and Barack Obama. Whether or not Obama appears to be the reincarnation of Lincoln, he might as well be since so much about Obama's story completes the story of Lincoln. Lincoln was the president who freed the slaves; Obama was the first African-American president. And Obama in many ways emulated Abraham Lincoln. He arrived in Washington by traveling along the same route as Lincoln and used Lincoln's Bible to take the oath of office.[168] But the similarities do not end there.

They both came from humble origins. Neither was born in Illinois, yet they both moved a relatively long distance to make a life there—Lincoln went from Kentucky via Indiana, and Obama went from Hawaii to New York and Massachusetts and then to Chicago. Both became attorneys, served a short time in the Congress, and then won the presidency as distinct underdogs.

Lincoln and Obama shared many character traits. They were renowned public speakers, achieving some fame through their oratory skills before running for the presidency. They were both known for honesty and integrity. While Lincoln was a voracious reader and fiercely ambitious from a young age, Obama started more slowly. But by the time he went to college he had become a stellar student and was the first African American to head the *Harvard Law Review*. Lincoln was mostly introverted and sometimes melancholic but was a renowned storyteller who often illustrated his points through parables with a keen sense of humor. Obama is also a gifted storyteller with impeccable comedic timing.

Perhaps most significantly, Lincoln and Obama both maintained a dignified presence while in office. They were models of poise under pressure. Lincoln presided over the bloodiest war in American history and showed steadfast leadership. Not only did Lincoln weather the war; he did so while accomplishing an ambitious agenda of legislative accomplishments and suffering great personal tragedy, including the death of his third son while in office (and during his lifetime suffered the loss of two of his four sons). Lincoln was the first president to visit troops in battle, something future presidents have emulated. He boosted morale while demonstrating courage, arriving at the Richmond, Virginia, battlefield in April of 1865 only hours after Jefferson Davis had retreated, with the city still on fire.[169] He wrote and made his own speeches. Many speeches, including the Gettysburg Address and Second Inaugural, continue to inspire us to this day.

No president other than Lincoln has had to endure a civil war, but Obama took office with two wars raging while also inheriting a financial meltdown (with the economy bleeding 800,000 jobs a month). Obama and his hand-picked staff (including Treasury Secretary Timothy Geithner) avoided what could have been a second Great Depression by turning around the economy and presiding over the longest period of sustained growth in American history. Perhaps the most dramatic moment of Obama's presidency came as he was overseeing the special forces operation that captured and killed Osama

Bin Laden. As the operation unfolded, Obama was making jokes at the 2011 Annual White House Correspondents Dinner. The next day, we learned of the successful operation.

Both Lincoln and Obama governed during the most divisive times in the history of our nation. The Civil War represented the epitome of division; but Obama also governed in a time of great division, what can only be characterized as the *uncivil war*. Obama has the dubious honor of being the only president heckled at a State of the Union address by a sitting congressman; but Obama remained unflappable.

Lincoln had an easier time legislating than Obama did, and his list of accomplishments is long in part because the Republican Party controlled Congress the entire time he was in office (the Southern Democrats having been expelled for the duration of the war). Obama governed for a full two terms. But it was only in the first two years that his party controlled Congress—and it was during that time that he passed historic healthcare reform with significant help from Speaker Pelosi. For the remaining six years Obama had to compromise or horse-trade to enact his agenda, which he did skillfully, if differently, from previous presidents such as Clinton who faced a similar outcome in the first mid-term election of his tenure.

Obama accomplished certain things that Lincoln could not—or did not want to do—such as improving relations with Native America. Lincoln may be beloved by African Americans for freeing the slaves, but he was not beloved in Native America because he did little or nothing to slow the momentum of the 19th century Indian Wars. Obama, almost as if he were Lincoln's reincarnation returning to complete unfinished business, pledged to rectify the neglect and dishonor of the federal government regarding treaty obligations—and he kept his promise. Obama settled more than 100 tribal claims to the tune of more than 3.3 billion dollars and gave another 3.4 billion dollars in compensations. Additionally, he settled 492 million dollars in lawsuits with 17 different Native American tribes for mismanagement of their lands. Russell Begaye, president of the Navajo nation at the time Obama left office, said "Reaching out to Indian nations has been one of the hallmarks of his administration."[170] Then Trump became president and, as with many other of Obama's initiatives, did the opposite.

SIMILARITIES BETWEEN TRUMP AND ANDREW JOHNSON

Former White House strategist Steve Bannon envisioned President Trump as a modern-day Andrew Jackson and went so far as to bring a portrait of Jackson into the Oval Office. There are some similarities between Jackson and Trump; both of them shook the establishment to its core, and both primarily advocated for a White male population. But the Trump presidency is closer to the administration of President Andrew Johnson in many respects.[171] For one, Johnson and Trump both succeeded historic presidents. And Johnson, like Trump, did his best to reverse or mitigate the accomplishments of his predecessor. Both were highly unpopular presidents who came to office through unusual means, and the similarities only begin there.

It was a quirk of fate that Johnson inherited the presidency after Lincoln was assassinated. Johnson was a Democrat, the opposite party of Lincoln, but he was specifically chosen for that reason in an attempt to unite the country. Unlike his namesake Lyndon Johnson, who succeeded Kennedy from the same party after assassination, Andrew Johnson did not take risks to achieve his predecessor's agenda because his main concern was getting re-elected. During the Reconstruction, Johnson sought to soften the impact on the South, hoping to win Southern support. He contemplated forming a new party of Southern Democrats and Republican moderates to support his re-election. For a time, Johnson successfully masked his strategy until eventually his own racism gave him away.

Johnson was not only known for his racism; he also demonstrated a combination of self-aggrandizement and self-pity. He repeatedly invoked his own name in speeches and gave the same stump speeches over and over. He demanded loyalty and verbally attacked those who opposed him. He was accused of surrendering the dignity of the office and sparring with hecklers. Supreme Court Justice David Davis described Johnson as "obstinate, self-willed, combative, and totally unfit for office,"[172] traits that may sound familiar to those who disapprove of the 45th president's demeanor.

Early in his presidency, Johnson was able to win over Republican moderates who were hesitant to grant suffrage for Black people but favored civil equality for them. This was the 1860s equivalent of modern moderates who favored civil unions for gay couples but not gay marriage. Two closely related bills came up in 1866 addressing civil rights: the second Freedman's Bill that was a follow-up to the bill of the same name from 1865 and the Civil Rights Bill that specifically defined all persons born in the United States (with the notable exception of American Indians) as citizens without regard to race, enjoying "full and equal benefit of all laws and proceedings for the security of person and property."[173]

To the surprise of many, Johnson vetoed the Freedmen's bill, saying Congress had never been previously called upon to provide economic relief, establish schools, or purchase land for "our own people" and claimed that providing Black people any such aid would strip away their desire to work for a living. In vetoing the Freedman's bill in this manner, Johnson anticipated some modern conservative arguments, but to do so at a time immediately after slaves had been liberated was heartless. Johnson then vetoed the Civil Rights Bill in its entirety, again employing a dog whistle to signal to those who wanted to keep Black persons under the thumb of White persons, saying it violated "all our experience as a people." In a speech given immediately after the veto, he rhetorically asked, "What does the veto mean?"—and the audience cried out, "It is keeping the nigger down," to which Johnson offered no rebuttal.[174]

It turned out, however, that the veto of the Civil Rights bill was Johnson's greatest political miscalculation. He managed to annoy not only radicals, but many moderates. In response, a movement began with the goal of fixing the problem through veto-proof means: a constitutional amendment. The 14th amendment ended up giving citizenship to all persons born in the United States, including former slaves.

With support rapidly waning, Johnson became increasingly desperate. He sought to overturn his Cabinet, throwing out dissenters and replacing them with loyalists, something President Trump also did after his support began to wane. For both Johnson and Trump, these initiatives failed and led to their inevitable impeachments. The reason cited for Johnson's impeachment was his attempt to remove Edwin Stanton, the Secretary of War, from his Cabinet, in violation of the Tenure of Office Act; but Congress also objected to his "loud voice . . . and intemperate, inflammatory, and scandalous harangues." Trump's impeachment was similarly precipitated in part by his suspicious removals of FBI Director James Comey and Ambassador to Ukraine Marie Yovanovitch. Trump was eventually impeached for Abuse of Power and Obstruction of Congress, but he, like Johnson, was also partly impeached due to his temperament. I discuss the Trump impeachment further in part III.[175]

The Unveiling of the Shadow Side of America

It is hard to say exactly what would have happened to the Reconstruction of the South if Lincoln had not been assassinated. At the time, the Republican Party was itself divided into radical and moderate factions. The radical reconstructionists favored suffrage for the Black population and government support that would assist in upward social mobility for Black people, while the moderates favored increased civil rights, but not suffrage or any other governmental support for Black people. There was no consensus at the time of Lincoln's death about suffrage for non-White people or any other so-called radical reforms.

It is safe to assume, however, that if Lincoln had lived, the path forward would have been more dignified, if no less difficult. It is at least possible that some of the shadow elements of the American psyche would have been addressed. Instead, they were suppressed. While the legal right of citizenship was extended to Black men and women, the Reconstruction changed little, particularly in the South. Black people were citizens, but were considered second-class citizens. Although they were no longer slaves, their avenues for success were limited. The Ku Klux Klan, founded in Tennessee in 1866, soon spread into nearly every Southern state, launching a "reign of terror" upon Republican leaders, both Black and White.

Although the Reconstruction enabled the South to reenter the union, the distrust between North and South continued. Many in the South did not look upon secession with shame. In the late 19th century, Jim Crow laws were enacted to segregate Blacks from Whites, and around the same time, statues were commissioned to commemorate Confederate heroes such as Jefferson Davis and Robert E. Lee. Legal challenges to segregation were rebuffed in the 19th century. The Supreme Court upheld the right of segregation in the Plessy versus Ferguson decision of 1896, claiming that separate could still be equal.

Over time, Black people left the rural South in droves. During the Great Migration of 1916 through 1970, six million African Americans moved to urban cities in the North, Midwest, and Western US where opportunities were better, but racism persisted throughout the country. As a whole, America lost an opportunity to face our collective shadow. While overt racism gradually became publicly unacceptable, it went underground in covert form. A century after slaves were freed, Lyndon Johnson initiated civil rights reforms aimed at ending segregation. Still, racism persisted, often going even further underground.

Then the election of Barack Obama brought it all back to the surface. The fact that Obama was the first African American president produced a backlash, or what political commentator Van Jones called a "blacklash;" this indirectly led to the creation of the "birther movement" and the candidacy of Donald Trump. In a sense, Trump began running for office a full five years before the 2016 election by becoming a leading proponent of the movement that claimed Obama was not born in America. Trump did not invent the birther theory. This was the brainchild of conspiracy theorist Jerome Corsi. But Trump was its most famous and unabashed advocate. The claim that Obama's birth certificate was a fraud was a very thinly disguised dog whistle to racists who could not cope with the election of a Black president. As a presidential candidate, Trump continued in the same vein. Whether or not Trump is a racist, he clearly understood that he could win by cultivating support among Whites who felt hopeless and dispossessed and projected their fear and resentment onto others, particularly minorities. In so doing, Trump skillfully played upon another shadow element: an attitude of entitlement among Whites because of their race.

As president, Trump has continued to serve as a vessel for the expression of our collective shadow. At no time was that more evident than after the events in Charlottesville. To the astonishment of much of our nation, Trump hesitated to condemn the actions of neo-Nazis during his August 15, 2017 official press conference from Trump Tower, 48 hours after the violence. Here is some of the dialogue:

> REPORTER: You said there was hatred, there was violence on both sides. Are you—
>
> TRUMP: I do think there's blame—Yes. I do think there's blame on both sides. You look at both sides. I think there's blame on both sides and I have no doubt about it, and you don't have any doubt about it either and–and–and–if you reported it accurately you would see that.
>
> REPORTER: Neo-Nazis started this in Charlottesville. They showed up at Charlottesville, they—
>
> TRUMP: Excuse me.
>
> REPORTER: To protest the removal of that— (statue of Robert E. Lee)
>
> TRUMP: [inaudible] You had some very bad people in that group, but you also had people that were very fine people on both sides. . . .[176]

And following this Trump said something of note, something that was true, but ordinarily never voiced by other presidents.

REPORTER: Do you support white nationalists, then?

[Cross talk] Reporters shout questions

TRUMP: Well, George Washington was a slave owner. Was George Washington a slave owner? So, will George Washington lose his status? Are we going to take down—excuse me. Are we going to take down, are we going to take down statues to George Washington? How about Thomas Jefferson, what do you think of Thomas Jefferson? You like him? . . . OK good. Are we going to take down the statues, because he was a major slave owner. Now, are we going to take down his statue? So you know what? It's fine . . .

And then he later added: "You know, you really do have to ask yourself, where does it stop?"[177]

In those words, Trump made us question the foundations of our nation—and he also demonstrated why he is the perfect catalyst for revealing the shadow of the United States. Unlike his predecessors, who studiously avoid the inconvenient truth of slave-owning past presidents, President Trump bluntly addressed the situation. His lack of filter presents an opportunity for America to see who we have been and who we are, and in the process, make corrective changes. By ripping apart conventions and challenging all of our existing institutions, Trump is forcing an identity crisis, just as one occurred during the Civil War.

And every crisis has both danger and opportunity.

The only certainty in this crisis is that the old order is dying. We may be in a relatively peaceful hospice period, during which time the old order dies due to the introduction of a foreign element or disruptive cancer such as the Trump administration; but once that factor is removed or concludes, a higher-level order can be born. However, we could also be entering an actual interregnum—an ugly period when normal government is suspended and the United States is no longer viable or recognizable—before a new government is installed that is not necessarily a higher order, and could be lower. As the Italian Marxist philosopher, Antonio Gramsci put it: "The crisis consists precisely in the fact that the old is dying and the new cannot be born; in this interregnum a great variety of morbid symptoms appear."[178]

PART THREE

MAXIMUM DIVERSITY

"Love serves the whole."[179]

—JAMES O'DEA

"Peace is not unity in similarity but unity in diversity, in the comparison and conciliation of differences."[180]

—MIKHAIL GORBACHEV
June 5, 1991 Address accepting Nobel Peace Prize

"In our dreams, we struggle against fragmentation and move toward wholeness."[181]

—MONTAGUE ULLMAN

The Apocalypse: The Ending of the Neoliberal World Order?

The Black Dog

An old woman has been long at work weaving a beautiful rug. As she nears its completion, she pauses to stir a soup. When she stirs the soup, however, her black dog, asleep in the corner, awakens, pulls on a loose thread, and causes the rug to unravel. Where there was beauty and harmony, there is now confusion and chaos. But the old woman, returning from stirring the soup, is unfazed. She stares into the disorder, picks up a loose thread, and reimagines a new way to restore beauty and harmony.[182]

A White Mountain Apache Story

Politicians often claim the next election will be the most consequential of our lifetime—a refrain so often repeated that we tend to tune it out. The 2016 US presidential election, however, was a genuine inflection point. The election of Trump set in motion forces that will forever change the United States and the world. Like the black dog in the story, Trump is a trickster figure that has begun to unravel the world order. The country and world have been altered, perhaps irreparably. Things may never return to normal, whatever that is, but they can be transformed—into something far worse, or perhaps into something much better.

Trump is not, of course, the cause of all that ails America in our time; nor has he necessarily changed the country and world as much as it might appear. His election was arguably as much a symptom as a cause of how far liberal democracies have fallen.

In any case, the 2016 election presented a stark choice for our national future. That campaign is now over, but the choice remains.

The race was fought over two themes: Are we *"stronger together?"* (Clinton's slogan that implied unity in diversity) or Should we *make America great again*? (Trump's slogan implying a return to the way we were, a simpler time when America was less diverse). The campaign was never about two individuals as much as it symbolized which direction the nation should take.

The election was also a referendum on masculine and feminine leadership. If Clinton had prevailed, she would have been the first female American president, and the end of her first term in office would have coincided with the 100-year anniversary of American women getting the right to vote. Clinton's election would have represented a continuation of a trend toward unity in diversity and more diverse leadership in politics. But Hillary Clinton was also a unique figure. It was Clinton, not Trump, who represented a continuation of the status quo, even though she would have been the first female president—a major departure—and he was a White male. Clinton represented the status quo because she had been an integral part of the political mainstream for the past quarter-century, whereas Trump came from completely outside the system. Before Trump, there had never been a president without political or military experience. The election of a political novice (and trickster) shook the system to its core.

THE ORIGINAL MEANING OF APOCALYPSE

The 2016 US presidential election was like none other in American history, in part because Clinton and Trump held the highest unfavorable ratings of any two presidential candidates ever. Many voted for Clinton out of fear of Trump becoming president; and many Trump voters, rightly or wrongly, were similarly frightened at the prospect of Clinton being elected. I therefore call this the election "apocalyptic" because both sides felt that their world would collapse if the other were to win.

It is worth reiterating, however, that the original meaning of *apocalypse* was not disaster, but an "unveiling" or a "revelation." The

2016 election was unique in that it helped reveal what ordinarily lies beneath the surface of the American psyche, including our sexist and racist roots. It presented us with an opportunity to see the truth of America—with one eye toward the unhealed wounds of our past—and another toward the open field of potential that is our future.

It is not only the past that makes us who we are. In some ways, the future creates the present by pulling us in the direction of our destiny. I have contended that our nation's destiny is to bring all the world's peoples together on one soil—to be a model of unity in diversity. And despite periodic resistance (if not regression), the country has moved over time toward greater inclusivity, albeit unevenly and incompletely—first with African Americans, then women, then much of the world through immigration. As America has become increasingly diverse, cultural mores have shifted. The shift in mores has been followed by the passage of laws protecting individuals from discrimination based on race, gender, ethnicity, and, most recently, sexual orientation and sexual identity.

Native Americans, ironically, may be the last to be fully included and appreciated for their seminal role in creating this country—and for making an enduring connection to this sacred land. Nonetheless, it was Native Americans who originally planted the seed of inclusivity. It is that seed idea to which we are returning, effectively completing a circle back to our origins, *going back to the future*. This might sound confusing if you view time as a line, but nature always unfolds in a circle: from seed, root, bud, fruit, and back to seed again in preparation for the next cycle. Our country has unfolded in this same way. Now that we have arrived in the time of Maximum Diversity, it is appropriate to revisit how we got here. Therefore, I reintroduce the diagram of this circular process originally presented in the introduction to this book.

In the diagram, Unitive Consciousness represents both the original impetus to establish a singular national identity and the direction to which we are now returning. Note the positions of Unitive Consciousness and Maximum Diversity. They are at opposite ends of the spectrum. In a time of Maximum Diversity, the devolved mode is anarchy, which is the opposite of monarchy, the devolved mode of Unitive Consciousness. It is not a coincidence that the founding fathers were as concerned about anarchy as they were about monarchy. In breaking away from a monarchy in favor of a republic, they understood they were giving up stability in exchange for freedom. They knew the republic could degenerate into anarchy—or revert to monarchy—if not properly maintained. They further understood that a republic was a dynamic entity that must grow and change of necessity. Yet, even as we learn and grow, the original tension between Unitive Consciousness and Maximum Diversity—or monarchy and anarchy—has never left us.

We are now at Maximum Diversity, the turning point of the diagram. We appear to have reached the maximum diversity the system

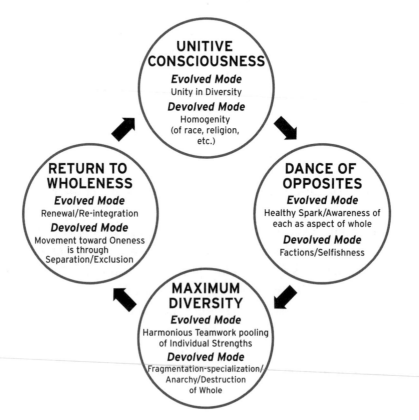

can bear. Amid the stress and chaos of our current situation, we have come to a choice point: between unity in diversity or unity through sameness. The direction we choose as a nation will determine our future identity. The America we knew is already gone. We are in a chaotic, undefined period of identity crisis. In the midst of this chaos, it is hard to see clearly. The first thing we ought to do, then, is to step back and view today's events and the way we view chaos in a larger context.

CHAOS AND ORDER

In seeking a larger context to view our identity crises, it is helpful to consider how the Western world has traditionally approached chaos. Western origin stories speak of a world created from primeval chaos; but ever since Western civilization began, it has been seeking its opposite: order. Our politics establish communities based on law and order; our science attempts to harness laws of nature to predict and control the environment; our arts and religions strive to build museums, cathedrals, libraries, concert halls, gravestones, mausoleums, and other monuments that preserve and protect our place in posterity. Everything about Western science and culture is predicated upon establishing and maintaining order. We cling to the status quo and want things to remain as they are—but that is an exercise in futility. Disorder, decay, and death cannot be avoided. Order unravels. Chaos returns. It is only in the past century that Western science has begun to appreciate the role chaos plays in evolution.

Other cultures are less frightened by chaos. Many, including probably all Asian and Native American cultures, recognize chaos and order as two aspects of one whole. In the Apache story that opens part III, the black dog (a trickster figure) periodically intervenes, whenever necessary, to recreate the world. Author Michael Meade, in speaking of this story, says, "Be thankful for the trouble you find in the world":

> Be thankful for the black dog that unravels the whole thing.
> For the black dog acts out the role of chaos, which eventually

undoes and dismantles everything made manifest in this world. They [the Native American people who told the story] knew that the dog is black in order to remind people that this world must be repeatedly rewoven from darkness as well as light, that those are the enduring threads of existence that were separated at the beginning of creation and that must be handled again each time re-creation is required.[183]

It takes wisdom to recognize and accept the periodic disruptions that cause temporary chaos and disorder but ultimately end up revitalizing the order. Many of us resist change, especially those who benefit most from the status quo. Many of our most powerful political leaders fight tooth and nail to avert changes to the status quo. Those leaders have a vested interest in preserving the existing state of affairs because they are the ones who created it. Let's not fool ourselves. Even if the world order were to benefit all citizens, it would benefit those who designed it most of all. Normally speaking, our leaders resist change. They are doing so now even as Trump is in power. Trump, ever the paradox, acts in unprecedented ways that disrupt the world order. At other times, he himself resists change or doubles down on protecting aspects of the world order that benefit him personally.

In any case, the world order requires periodic review and revitalization. And because Trump is a different kind of leader who rebels against many aspects of the world order, it gives us a unique opportunity. The disruption of norms allows us to see more clearly how things used to operate. This can enable us to make the necessary substantive changes to our government to meet the challenges of the coming era. This is the role of the black dog.

DIVERSITY: THE DEFINING CHARACTERISTIC OF THE UNITED STATES

It is significant that Maximum Diversity is the turning point on the wheel of our diagram.

A strong argument can be made for diversity as the defining characteristic of the United States. I believe it is our diversity that has enabled us to be a uniquely creative and resourceful country. There are advantages and disadvantages to our multicultural composition. We excel at innovation far more than countries that are mostly mono-cultural, such as Japan; but this also helps explain why Japan has a much more orderly, coherent society.

Too much change—too rapidly—can make anyone feel unsettled. Nearly all of us are struggling to grasp, and keep pace with, our rapidly evolving, complex culture. We are tired of being divided. We yearn for unity in our solar plexus. But just as Hamilton and Jefferson could not agree on what country to create, we cannot agree on what form of unity we want to manifest.

Significantly, this choice point is not only happening in America. A similar choice between unity in diversity—or unity through same-ness—has cropped up in liberal democracies around the world. That is because the American crisis was originally spawned out of a world-wide crisis. Democracies were faltering in many places, particularly in Europe, as we headed into the 2016 US presidential election. To understand America, we must understand the world context and the role America has occupied in the world order. We must understand how the current world order came to be before considering its flaws, vulnerabilities, and how it might be improved. I turn to this next.

THE WORLD AT THE TIME OF THE 2016 US PRESIDENTIAL ELECTION

In the 20th century, liberal democracies (or representational republics) around the world achieved many milestones. Some of these achievements we have already chronicled: universal suffrage for people of color, women, and other civil rights gains. There were additional benefits, including establishing a modest safety net for all citizens through government programs such as Social Security, Medicare, and unemployment insurance. These kind of programs became popular over much of the world, not just in the United States. Citizens became accustomed to the right to vote, an increasing standard of living, and some assurance of financial and retirement security. In the United States, a strong middle class emerged and continued to prosper from the mid-1940s through the mid-1960s. The citizenry was relatively content during this period; there was greater trust in the government and in our economic system compared to now.

The socioeconomic system currently underlying liberal democracies has been labeled *neoliberalism*, a confusing term because it includes both liberals and conservatives.[184] So let us examine this more closely. Who are neoliberals? They are politicians who favor a globally integrated, capitalist economy of free trade that combines market deregulation with socially liberal economic policies—or, in other words, every US political leader from the past three-quarters of a century up to, but not including, President Trump. He is the lone exception. (I will later address the ramifications and consequences of this departure from the norm).

The overall intent of neoliberal economics was adeptly captured by President Kennedy when he said, "A rising tide lifts all boats." Neoliberal economic policies are a rough hybrid of supply-and-demand brand of classical capitalism of Adam Smith and the economic policies of John Maynard Keynes (and variant theories descending from Keynes).[185] Keynes was the father of macroeconomics (the science of large-scale national or international economics). He rose to prominence in the 1930s, spearheading a big picture economic policy that was adopted by President Roosevelt and helped lift the US and world out of the Great Depression. Keynes is sometimes only associated with his advocacy for government intervention, via stimulus, in times of recession or depression. However, that is only a partial picture. During times of full employment, he advocated reliance on the private sector to rebalance market forces. Keynes was not a socialist, although he did push for international organizations that could regulate world markets. Keynes died in 1946, one year after the United Nations was formed. The following year, GATT (General Agreement on Tariffs and Trade) was established, and GATT helped regulate and liberalize world trade for five decades until it gave birth to its successor, the World Trade Organization (WTO). The World Trade Organization and other international organizations, such as the International

Monetary Fund (IMF), help maintain multilateral trade and balanced economic growth or, in other words, they help maintain the global status quo integral to neoliberal economics.

After WWII ended, the United States became the undisputed leader among neoliberal democracies, working closely with our NATO allies to provide mutual military and economic support. The idea of American exceptionalism was strong during this period, and America's influence was felt all over the world, both economically and culturally. As a result, liberal democracies were on the rise for more than forty years after the conclusion of WWII. Even the Soviet Union made a short-lived move in the direction of liberal democracy in the 1980s. Mikhail Gorbachev, the last leader of the Soviet Union, began ambitious social reforms, both economic and cultural. (Economic reform was known as *perestroika* and increased freedom of expression and information was known as *glasnost*). With the fall of the Berlin Wall in 1989, it seemed that capitalism had triumphed over communism. But this conclusion was premature. It was premature in part because it did not account for the rise of China and state-sponsored capitalist societies; but also, because liberal democracies were not as healthy as they appeared.

With the benefit of hindsight, we can see that stress fractures had been developing in the United States since the late 1960s—first with the anti-war movement, race riots, White flight to the suburbs, and the degradation of public education (especially in the inner cities)—and then with the 1973 oil shock that led to double-digit inflation. Then, from the late 1970s to the present, a disturbing trend emerged: growing income inequality and wage stagnation in America at levels not seen since the 1920s. For the first time, younger generations could not look forward to a higher standard of living than their parents. The similarities to the 1920s were foreboding. It should therefore not have been that shocking when the Great Recession of 2008 hit at the close of the George W. Bush administration.

The Obama administration deserves credit for pulling the economy out of a possible depression; for rescuing the US auto industry;

presiding over the longest period of sustained growth in our nation's history; and for passing the Affordable Care Act, which like Social Security and Medicare, has proven popular, if flawed. But the economy never recovered to its mid-twentieth century heyday. Economic growth remained relatively low; wage stagnation persisted; real estate did not rebound as much as after previous downturns; and most significantly, the US manufacturing base appeared hopelessly irretrievable. Factory workers (who once enjoyed a middle-class income) were left in the lurch. This was particularly true in fossil fuel industries such as coal, oil, and gas that the Obama administration was seeking to transition away from (even as natural gas fracking was ramped up to record levels). All this affected the 2016 election.

Perhaps the two most important factors that impacted the 2016 US presidential election were the reemergence of totalitarian rule in Russia under Putin in the late 1990s and the destruction of the World Trade Center Towers on September 11, 2001. It is important to realize that Russia was not only undergoing a reemergence of authoritarianism; it was also experiencing a resurgence of the intelligence state, headed by Putin, a former KGB operative. Putin was ensconced in power well before the World Trade Center attack occurred. The attack on the World Trade Centers—the first attack on US soil since Pearl Harbor—inflicted a wound upon the American psyche from which we have yet to recover.

Donald Trump eventually took advantage of the 9/11 wound in the 2016 presidential election, using Islamic terrorism as a foil. But Putin did so immediately. While Europe was busy rallying to the defense of the United States in the aftermath of 9/11, Putin went to work undermining democracies. His efforts bore fruit in Europe and beyond, and over the following two decades the liberal democratic world order started to fracture. Leaders with authoritarian and xenophobic tendencies emerged in several Eastern European countries: in the Czech Republic (Milos Zeman), in Hungary (Viktor Orban), and in Poland (Beata Szydło), among other places. These new authoritarian leaders were elected in liberal democracies and then began imposing autocratic rule from within. Authoritarian leaders also cropped up in Turkey (Tayyip Erdogan) and in the Philippines (Rodrigo Duterte) at the same time as leaders in already repressive regimes, such as Syria (Bashar Al-Assad) consolidated their power. To consolidate power, autocratic leaders require an enemy to rally against. Immigrants and refugees make convenient targets.

Xenophobia, in a nutshell, is fear of diversity. With the outbreak of the Syrian Civil War and continuing war in Afghanistan, a European migrant crisis began that precipitated a marked increase in xenophobia and a rise in support for right-wing parties who opposed immigration. With German Chancellor Angela Merkel continuing to permit asylum seekers, hordes of refugees poured into Europe. Border fencing was erected in many places, including a fence on Hungary's border with Serbia and Croatia. To Putin's delight, the European Union began to fracture over the immigration issue. Then, just before the 2016 US presidential election, Britain shocked the world by voting to exit the European Union (known as Brexit). Russia was suspected of meddling with the British referendum, but the extent to which that might have affected the outcome has never been determined.

In sum, the 2016 US presidential race took its place alongside a worldwide unfolding of events that challenged the post-WWII world order of liberal democracies based in global capitalism and free trade. Trump was not so much the cause of rising xenophobia and racism as a symptom of an already changing (or reverting) world order. Dissatisfaction with international trade deals was at an all-time high coming into the 2016 election, and both Donald Trump and Bernie Sanders capitalized on this, if we can use such a term in this case. Trump broke with over seventy years of free trade policies among Republicans, but Sanders was also breaking with long-standing Democratic acceptance of free trade—something all modern presidents had previously favored. Sanders and Trump both recognized frustrations in the working class; but of the two, Trump was more successful in exploiting that resentment.

It is during times like these—when the rate of change seems to have exceeded the country's capacity and feelings of disconnection abound—that a nation becomes most vulnerable to a strong personality, particularly one who promises a return to a simpler era. Such a leader offers him or herself as the solution. Thus, in a manner strikingly similar to that of past authoritarian leaders, candidate Trump boasted, "I alone can fix it" and found a receptive audience among the people who were most vulnerable: members of the working class who had previously held high-paying manufacturing jobs that did not require advanced education. These people—mostly White males—who hailed from a once powerful manufacturing base had become jobless or underemployed. The loss in manufacturing jobs was due mainly to advancing automation, but these workers were persuaded that they were unfairly displaced by immigrants or because of bad trade deals—deals that failed to put "America first."

The preponderance of the manufacturing base was in the Midwest of the United States, a previous Democratic stronghold. Trump, with a highly unorthodox approach, penetrated that Democratic (blue) wall, aided by Russian intelligence to a significant, if unknown, degree.

PROBLEMS WITH THE NEOLIBERAL WORLD ORDER

Trump's election and presidency, disruptive as it may be, affords us an opportunity to see how the neoliberal world order has been working until now and to also see another side of neoliberalism—its shadow side. There were, and continue to be, many problems with that world order. Yet these problems often escape proper scrutiny. Why? Because the American worldview and the neoliberal world order are so tightly interwoven. Like a fish in water, America is immersed in the neoliberal world environment, and what we are immersed in goes unseen. Since it is important that we both see and question the world order, I turn next to the questioning.

I begin with economics because the spine of the neoliberal world order rests upon modern economic theory and because politicians depend upon economists to guide many of their most important decisions. There is a hidden fallacy in economics, however, that propels economists to unwarranted conclusions.

Economics is a deductive, abstract discipline, modeled after another deductive discipline: physics. The advantage of a deductive discipline is that it is capable of producing results suitable for statistical analysis, prediction, and control; the disadvantage is that it draws deductive conclusions about the real world from a set of abstractions (with little awareness of the inherent danger in doing so). The practice of mistaking the real from the abstract is why Whitehead labeled this the fallacy of misplaced concreteness.

Whitehead said this of modern economics:

> It is arguable that the science of political economy . . . after the death of Adam Smith . . . did more harm than good. It riveted on men a certain set of abstractions which were disastrous in their effect on modern mentality. It dehumanized industry. . . . It fixed attention on a definite group of abstractions, neglected everything else, and elicited every scrap of information and theory which was relevant to what it had retained. The method is triumphant provided the abstractions are judicious. But, however triumphant, the triumph is within limits. The neglect of these limits leads to disastrous oversights.[186]

The most common abstractions used in modern economic theory are well-known: They are the market, the Gross National Product (GNP) and the Gross Domestic Product (GDP). GNP and GDP are useful measures of the state of the nation, but only in purely economic terms. They are deeply inadequate for measuring the health and well-being of a people or the natural environment upon which we all depend. For instance, in the aftermath of hurricanes, tornadoes, and floods, GNP and GDP go up because the economy is stimulated to make repairs and rebuild homes. Something similar occurs after oil spills, chemical spills, or other human-caused ecological disasters, including indirect consequences of human induced climate change. Economic growth may be considered good in strictly economic terms, but clearly economic growth of any type is not good in overall human terms. Lives can be ruined while the economy supposedly improves.

The most significant abstraction economists make is, not coincidentally, about human nature. Economists reduce human beings to economic machines of insatiable desire. The blanket assumption is that humans seek to obtain the greatest amount of necessities, conveniences, and luxuries while expending the least amount of labor and self-denial. Critics of this view, including the economist Herman Daly, have denounced the field for creating an artificial human being: *homo economicus*.[187] "Homo economicus (*economic man*), which Gregory Bateson once described as the "dullest of all imaginary organisms,"[188] is a large and misleading abstraction. It focuses all its attention on one single aspect of human behavior, leaving out the best of human behavior—including altruistic acts of caring, cooperative, and loving behavior. These behaviors are an integral part of being human. They are important for our joy and well-being.

Today many of the important political decisions are made for one reason alone: economic growth. How did we get so fixated upon growth and profit above all? How did the ideals of democracy become merged with capitalism?

RAMPANT CONSUMERISM: THE MERGING OF DEMOCRACY WITH CAPITALISM

Remember what President Bush told the nation after the 9/11 attack? "Go about your lives, fly on airplanes, go shopping. . . . go on with your normal life." Our fixation upon consumerism as a healing salve was (and is) so strong that Bush's statement, absurd as it was, sounded compassionate, almost wise at the time. But rampant consumerism has not always been the American way. It had to be cynically and systematically inculcated into our consciousness and then skillfully interwoven into our national identity and exported around the world as the American lifestyle, thereby increasing profit by opening foreign markets for American goods. Today, the merging of capitalism with democracy—and nearly every other aspect of our lives—is taken for granted. We may be mildly annoyed by the ubiquitous nature of advertising, publicity, and promotion, but most of us accept it as normal.

Much of what we take for granted today as the American way of thinking about commercial brands and products is largely traceable to one man—Edward Bernays, the nephew of the famed Austrian psychoanalyst Sigmund Freud. In the 1920s, Bernays adapted Freud's theories of the unconscious mind and mixed these together with existing principles of war propaganda to create the fields of modern advertising and public relations. Before the influence of Bernays, products were advertised in utilitarian ways. After Bernays, they were sold through emotional triggers, as they are today. Bernays understood that the faceless masses could be manipulated to buy products. He devised strategies to sell goods and services in a way that (temporarily) alleviated the alienation and suffering of the masses.[189]

Bernays was enormously influential in changing both the landscape of modern advertising and modern life in general. Bernays not only founded a new form of advertising; he invented the field of *public relations*, known before simply as "propaganda." Bernays was also the first to merge celebrity identification with politics, thereby rehabilitating President Calvin Coolidge's reputation by associating him with a parade of celebrities, mainly film stars.[190] He then invented the art of product placement in films in a subliminal form of advertising to complete the circle.

Bernays understood how alienated the average citizen felt in a highly atomized and competitive society. He took advantage of this deep-rooted loneliness to sell people a sense of belonging. Consumers were not purchasing goods so much as membership in a class based on what products people bought.

If people did not actually need the product, Bernays knew how to create a perceived need. For instance, Bernays famously sold cigarettes to women during an era when women's smoking was frowned upon. He did so brilliantly, if cynically, by rebranding cigarettes as "Torches of Freedom" that associated women with independent thinking at the same time he was manipulating them into smoking. Once again, he reinforced his advertising through product placement in films. Once women saw other women smoking, particularly women movie stars, his success was all but assured.

It is not an overstatement to say that Bernays became one of the driving forces merging democracy with capitalism. Advertising bonanzas like the Torches of Freedom campaign endeared Bernays to businessmen and politicians alike. Politicians saw how marketing and public relations could make a happier society, with employed people making for docile, content consumers. Bernays did not create the need for perpetual economic growth in the United States, but he made it *seem* possible. He was therefore indirectly responsible for the creation of the neoliberal world order based on multilateral trade and never ending economic growth.

Unfortunately, some of the principles first used by Bernays to promote capitalism in the United States in peacetime were later adopted by mid-twentieth century totalitarian leaders to exploit the masses in wartime. Hitler and his propaganda czar, Joseph Goebbels, were both familiar with Bernays' philosophy and they adapted it for their nefarious purposes.

OTHER CONSEQUENCES AND VULNERABILITIES OF THE CURRENT WORLD ORDER

There are many other consequences to the current world order beyond rampant consumerism, unbridled economic growth, and looking at the world solely in economic terms (i.e., commodification). Neoliberal globalism has also reduced the strength of local economies while contributing to a concomitant rise of corporate power. In doing so, it widened socioeconomic inequality, among other effects.[191]

The diminishment of local economies is closely related to the devaluation of ecological kinship with the land. Small farms and businesses are more sensitive to their surroundings, and to local ecological issues. They are also inclined to keep a healthy amount of money circulating within the community, which benefits local people instead of large corporations. In the 1970s, British economist E. F. Schumacher coined the phrase "small is beautiful" in support of small farms and local, self-reliant businesses. He sought to counter the rise of large, monocultural agribusinesses that were dominating the market and eclipsing local business.[192]

Neoliberalism has also hastened the commodification of nature and much of what makes life rich and meaningful, turning it all into for-profit business. While the impetus toward commodification and commodities markets is as old as civilization itself, the marketing of real experiences as commodities has exploded since the 1980s. It now affects everything from children's birthday parties to maid services, dating, family reunions, and handyman repairs. All of it is now commodified and sold en masse. This can have a deleterious effect on social cohesion.[193]

Consider, for one, how *Home Advisor* markets their service. In a popular commercial, a homeowner meets his neighbor at the mailbox, and asks him if he knows anyone who can do roof repair. The neighbor replies that he does. But then, before the neighbor can say anything else, the homeowner asks him if he can do a background check, get some additional quotes, research the average price for the job in this area, and book the job within the next two weeks on a specific day of the week. The ad then ends with the tag line, "You can't expect your neighbor to do everything Home Advisor does. Just ask Home Advisor." The ad's message may have some validity; but it directly discourages neighbors from talking to each other, while presenting a false dichotomy. A homeowner could listen to his neighbor *and* do additional research on his own. Neighbors talking to one another promotes social cohesion; the commodification of real experience tends to have the opposite effect.

In fairness, neoliberalism also has a lot of positive effects. A world connected through trade can foster relationships. The thinking is that those who live in interdependent nations will become better acquainted with each other's way of life; in turn, this makes it less likely that those nations will go to war with each other. In his 1999 book, *The Lexus and the Olive Tree*, Thomas Friedman said, "No two countries that both have a McDonald's have ever fought a war against each other."[194] While the McDonald's theory was disproved shortly after the book was published, Friedman's larger point about peace through trade has always been part of the neoliberal global vision. And there is evidence that it is working. A good argument can be made for peace through multilateralism, which is why Trump's policy of decoupling trade from multilateralism is making the world *less safe*. It has already heightened tensions with our enemies and alliances alike. (I return to this topic later).

Capitalist neoliberalism is sometimes considered the root of all evil in the modern age—but this is hyperbole, as worldwide trade has been occurring since the dawn of civilization. However, the dominance of modern neoliberalism is cause for concern. Its sheer scale lends itself to abuse.

At minimum, the once equal marriage of democracy and capitalism has become lopsided, tilting in the direction of large corporations. At maximum, a government originally envisioned as "by the people, for the people" is in danger of becoming (or has already become) a kleptocracy: a government by the wealthy for the wealthy.

Can we get back to a government "of the people, by the people, for the people," or has this already "perished from the earth," as Lincoln insisted it must not? Did the election of Trump signal the end of our republic, or just a choice point? Will America fall into the abyss, or can we seize this opportunity (while there is still time) to create a new order? These are the questions we continue to examine next.

CHAPTER TEN

The Turning Point:
The 2016 Election Amid Changes in the
US Political System and Society

I n late summer of 2016, in the heat of the election campaign, I had a dream.

> *Donald Trump was a window washer, working on scaffolding outside of a tall, New York City skyscraper. He was about three floors from the top of the building. Inside the building, there is a meeting going on. It seems important. From Trump's perspective, he can see what is going on, but cannot hear anything. Then, he pauses, looks down upon the city, becomes frightened by the heights, and passes out, head first, onto the scaffold. His fellow crew members are startled. They huddle up to decide what to do. They are concerned that if "The Donald" were to wake up in that position—with his head over the edge—he would have a heart attack and die. They decide to very slowly lower the scaffolding to the ground. They begin to do so as the dream ends.*

After my dream, Trump won the election, assumed power, and was presumably no longer on the outside looking in. While this dream could represent a great many things, I believe the Trump figure, a window washer, primarily symbolizes the need to see America more clearly. In the dream, he is the man who cleans the apertures we see through, cleansing our perception. In real life, he is transparent and unfiltered, engaging the darker aspects of our collective psyche, effectively pulling back the curtain on the shadow side of America. Politicians are reflections of the larger society. For too long, many of us have had our head in the clouds (where skyscrapers live), blithely unaware of what is going on. Trump has the potential to awaken us to what America really is—its unresolved darkness and its sacred roots—enabling us to see it all, perhaps for the first time, and then urging us to discover what must be changed. It is in this way that Trump is a catalyst for social change, however unwittingly. At the same time, Trump is very dangerous, operating way above his pay grade, both desirous of power and frightened by it. He needs constant monitoring, or both he and the nation could collapse. Trump may not become a monarch or dictator, but the institutions and norms that have long safeguarded us from autocracy are impermanent (like scaffolding), and could break or be taken down. If we do not revitalize our institutions, a true autocrat could follow, or Trump could turn into one himself. This is the turning point for our nation.

HISTORY OF CHECKS AGAINST AUTOCRACY IN THE UNITED STATES

The founding fathers were determined to guard against the imposition of monarchy from outside or within, but over time, changes to the political system and society have made us increasingly vulnerable. The original founding document of the United States—the Articles of Confederation— afforded the best protection against autocracy. It prescribed a strong union between the states, but a weak president, modeled after Native American council government in which the power of the chief was derived from the tribe. A weak executive could not be more different from an all-powerful king. Unfortunately, the Articles, almost directly appropriated from the Great Law of Peace of the Haudenosaunee Confederacy, were ill-suited to Euro-American societies that were based upon financial obligations, such as taxes.

When the Constitution replaced the Articles, the role of the executive branch was greatly strengthened, and the government was given broad authority to tax. The role of the president was greatly strengthened; but the founders remained concerned about future presidents aspiring to be monarchs.

The electoral college was designed to serve as the principal check on potential autocracy. The delegates of the electoral college were the gatekeepers tasked with not allowing an autocratic president to assume power and subvert the system. Under the electoral college system, Alexander Hamilton reasoned that "The process of election affords a moral certainty that the office of president will seldom fall to the lot of any man who is not in an eminent degree endowed with the requisite qualifications; . . . men with talents for low intrigue, and the little arts of popularity" would be weeded out. [195]

However, the founders failed to specify how presidential candidates would be selected; and over time, states adopted laws requiring the electoral college delegates to abide by the popular vote in their state, thereby rendering the gatekeeping function of the electoral college obsolete.

THE POLITICAL PARTIES AS GATEKEEPERS

With electoral college decisions increasingly determined by popular vote in individual states, the responsibility for filtering out unqualified nominees fell to the political parties. For a long time, the party elites held an iron grip on the process. Presidential primaries did not even begin until the 20th century; and when they began, they had no teeth. Party bosses continued to gather in smoke-filled rooms to make the all-important decisions about who would represent the party. The party elites maintained their role as gatekeepers right up until the 1970s.

As unseemly and unfair as this process to eliminate unsuitable presidential candidates may appear today, it worked. For much of American history, demagogues, even popular ones, found no traction within the political parties. From the 1930s through the early 1960s, although many demagogues were popular, including Charles Coughlin, Huey Long, Joseph McCarthy, and George Wallace, none was endorsed by political party elites. None had a serious chance at the presidency. The party heads wielded enormous power to choose the nominee for much of the 20th century.

Then came the 1960s, a pivotal era in American history. The anti-war and civil rights movements brought about great social upheaval, particularly in America's cities. This was also a time of the sexual revolution, in which relationships between the sexes and gender roles began to be reconsidered—if not liberated. Input from Eastern religions exploded, as did experimentation in various forms of body-mind disciplines and consciousness expansion (including recreational drugs). Not coincidentally, the political process also underwent major changes during the 1960s.

In a tumultuous five-year period, between 1963 and 1968, four key political figures—John F. Kennedy, Malcolm X, Martin Luther King Jr., and Robert (Bobby) Kennedy—were all assassinated.

Bobby Kennedy, John Kennedy's younger brother and a US senator, was motivated to join the 1968 presidential race in part because of the unfolding racial tensions in America. A late entry into a race that already included Eugene McCarthy (the first challenger to the incumbent, Lyndon Johnson), Kennedy announced his candidacy only a month before the King assassination and two weeks before Lyndon Johnson, the incumbent, bowed out. Kennedy won the Indiana, Nebraska, and California primaries, and was seemingly riding a wave of popularity to the nomination and presidency. But just after midnight on the day he was declared the winner of the California primary—and only 63 days after MLK was killed—Kennedy was himself assassinated. His death changed the face of politics in ways that reverberate to this day.

It is not certain that Bobby Kennedy would have been the Democratic nominee because the party elites (who held all the power then) favored Hubert Humphrey, the incumbent vice-president. We will never know. We do know that after Kennedy was killed the elites installed Humphrey as the party nominee, even though Humphrey had not competed in any of the primaries. This move backfired on the party, creating a pivotal shift in future politics.

The assassinations had left the country reeling, as had the Vietnam War, so perhaps it is no surprise that the streets outside the 1968 Democratic convention erupted in bloody riots. Then, after Nixon narrowly defeated Humphrey to win the presidency, the base of the Democratic Party was up in arms, incensed at the undemocratic process that had installed Humphrey. The party heads had little choice but to listen.

By the 1972 presidential election, the primary process was much more democratic. George McGovern, who had an integral role in reforming the electoral process, emerged as the Democratic nominee. McGovern ran against the incumbent Richard Nixon on an antiwar platform, calling for the immediate end to the Vietnam War. But McGovern, considered too far left by what Nixon called the "silent majority" of the country, ended up losing in a landslide. Nixon won 49 of 50 states, only to have his second term dominated by the Watergate scandal. Fearing impeachment, Nixon resigned. The size of Nixon's landslide victory, however, convinced Democratic party elites to recalibrate their strategy once again.

This time, the party elites came up with a compromise: They would regain some of their authority by creating a top tier of delegates called *superdelegates*. Superdelegates were party insiders expected to pledge themselves to those candidates whom the elites determined best reflected party values and had the best chance to win in the general election. The idea was to avoid outsiders from hijacking the direction of the party.

This rule change worked as intended for the Democratic Party up until the 2016 election. It was then that the party heads had to consider the possibility of Senator Bernie Sanders—who had never been a member of the Democrat Party—winning the nomination. Sanders was likely seen as a threat to their platform. They may have also reasoned that Sanders, like McGovern, would have been considered too far left by the country, and would have lost in a landslide if he had been the nominee. Since Sanders did not become the nominee, we may never know whether the party elites were right or wrong. In any case, it was not a capricious decision to maintain a bias toward Clinton. When Russia hacked the Democratic Party emails, however, the inner workings of the party were exposed in a way that shocked anyone unfamiliar with the process. Even many Clinton supporters were upset to learn that the deck had been stacked against Sanders because of the establishment party's strong favoritism for Clinton. Consequently, in August of 2018, things shifted again, as the Democratic Party voted to limit the role of superdelegates going forward. Superdelegates will now only play a role if there is a deadlocked convention—which once seemed possible with the large field running in 2020—but otherwise, the will of the people will determine the outcome in the primaries.

History indicates that this latest change may not bode well. Consider what just happened with the Republican Party. While they instituted electoral reforms in the 1970s along with the Democrats, the Republicans never instituted a gatekeeping policy comparable to superdelegates. This opened the door for a candidate such as Trump who was not really a Republican. He was not aligned with many of the stated Republican Party values at the time, such as free (multi-lateral) trade, fiscal conservatism, tough policy on Russia, family values, and so forth. Posing as a populist, Trump hijacked the party. In the past, either the electoral college or the party elites would have short-circuited such an attempt. But this time, even without the support of any Republican power brokers, or any congressional Republicans at all at first, Trump rose to the top. If the Republican Party had the same system of superdelegates as the Democrats had in 2016, Donald Trump would not have been the nominee. He would have fallen short of the requisite number of delegates, and the nomination would have been determined at the convention.

The main point I am making is that party elites were once a line of defense who screened out demagogues. But with their demise, which ironically gives more power to the people, both parties are more vulnerable to an outsider taking power. This means the entire country is more vulnerable to the imposition of an authoritarian populist regime elected through democratic means. Unless something changes, this will continue to be the case even after President Trump departs office.

THE GINGRICH REVOLUTION: THE EROSION OF CIVILITY IN CONGRESS

We inherited from Native America a respectful tone for our political discourse—at least within the halls of Congress and the Oval Office. Campaigns have had their share of mudslinging, to be sure, but almost all presidents—excepting a few cantankerous ones such as Andrew Jackson and Andrew Johnson—have tempered themselves once they assumed office. Donald Trump never did. It is not as if Trump challenged anyone to a dual—as Burr did to Hamilton—but Trump has used his office in confrontational ways, ways that might have provoked a dual if he lived in an earlier era. Trump has attacked people of seemingly unassailable character, such as John McCain and Barack Obama, prompting one to wonder how a person of Trump's own character rose to the presidency. The short answer is that the political climate had already been poisoned. Former Speaker Newt Gingrich is often blamed for that, but there have been others, both inside and outside of Washington, who participated in deliberately degrading the discourse.

It is important to look outside Washington to understand why things shift inside Washington, as successful politicians are only a reflection of the social mood (cultural zeitgeist) of the times. As Daily Beast columnist Michael Tomasky astutely noted, "Politics changes *after* social conditions and expectations change."[196] Gingrich, and later Trump, were responses to what had already changed in the culture. I return to this point later when I discuss making things whole again in part IV of the book, since it is an important aspect of how individuals can effect political change.

It was the social and economic strife of the late 1970s that enabled a resurgence of (Goldwater) conservatism to sweep Ronald Reagan into the presidency. Reagan then proceeded to take down the Fairness Doctrine. Its demise—which eliminated a legal obligation to present the other side—helped trigger culture wars between liberals and conservatives. These culture wars then made it possible, if not inevitable, for an individual such as Gingrich to arise.

Even if Gingrich does not hold sole responsibility for sowing discord, there is still reason to lay some blame at the feet of the former Speaker. Gingrich went to great lengths to personally poison the political well. He began plotting a strategy of partisan combat during the post-Watergate 1970s, a time when the Republican Party was in disarray and seemingly destined to remain a minority party for the foreseeable future. Gingrich had other plans. He implored Republicans to change their ways in a 1978 speech:

> One of the great problems we have in the Republican Party
> is that we don't encourage you to be nasty. . . . We encourage
> you to be neat, obedient, and loyal, and faithful, and all those
> Boy Scout words, which would be great around the campfire
> but are lousy in politics.[197]

The following year, Gingrich was elected to Congress, and he immediately set about blowing up traditional norms of protocol. He took advantage of the newly installed CSPAN cameras to make bombastic speeches that would later be rebroadcast to partisan audiences. He essentially repurposed the tactics of Joseph McCarthy, only this time applying them to the entire Democratic Party. He called the Democrats every name in the book, including *"pro-communist, un-American,* and *tyrannical."*[198]

"His idea," according to Norm Ornstein, a political scientist who knew Gingrich at the time, "was to build toward a national election where people were so disgusted by Washington and the way it was operating that they would throw the ins out and bring the outs in."[199] This would give the minority party the opportunity to make the greatest gains. And, if the end justified the means, it worked.

It took him nearly a decade and a half to subvert the system, but Gingrich prevailed in 1994 in what became known as the Gingrich Revolution. The Republicans took back the House for the first time in 40 years. Gingrich took advantage of several factors: perceived corruption in the Democratic Party resulting from the Keating Five

Savings and Loan scandal of the late 1980s and early 1990s (four of the
five implicated Congressman were Democrats); the 1993 Clinton tax
increase that raised taxes on the top one percent bracket; and general
dysfunction in Congress at the time. For his efforts, he was rewarded
with the position of Speaker of the House. [200]

As Gingrich was rising to power in the 1980s, the book *Chim-*
panzee Politics by primatologist Frans de Waal came out. The book,
which documented the complex rivalries and coalitions governing
chimp communities, confirmed Gingrich's worldview, and it remains
one of his favorite books to this day. The thesis of *Chimpanzee Poli-*
tics was that human political activity was "part of an evolutionary
heritage we share with our close relatives."[201]

Gingrich not only agreed with the conclusions of *Chimpanzee*
Politics; he used the book as justification for his own uncivil behavior.
He and Steve Bannon (the political strategist and chief architect of
Trump's success who followed in Gingrich's footsteps) see themselves
as necessary disruptors. They share the idea that the system, from
time to time, needs to be shaken up to facilitate renewal. Curiously,
Bannon also has a go-to book: *The Fourth Turning* by Strauss and
Howe, which outlines 80-year cycles in American political history and
allows for—even predicts—periodic disruption of the status quo.[202] It
is this ideology that enables Bannon to justify much of Trump's behavior, not viewing it as undermining democracy, but as renewing it.

Gingrich shares a similar worldview to Bannon. He views the
disruption around the world today as a necessary renewal. When
speaking to McKay Coppins of *The Atlantic*, he said, "The old order
is dying . . . almost everywhere you have freedom, you have a very
deep discontent that the system isn't working." Coppins replied, "And
that's a good thing?" to which Gingrich confirms, "It's essential if you
want Western civilization to survive."[203] In that same piece for *The*
Atlantic, Coppins concludes that:

> During his two decades in Congress [Gingrich] pioneered a style
> of partisan combat—replete with name-calling, conspiracy
> theories, and strategic obstructionism—that poisoned

America's political culture and plunged Washington into
permanent dysfunction. . . . and can perhaps be best understood as a grand exercise in *devolution*—an effort to strip
American politics of the civilizing traits it had developed over
time and return it to its most primal essence (italics mine).[204]

While I do not approve of either Gingrich or Bannon's tactics, they
are partly correct about the role of devolution in the broad scope of
history. In fact, I have made a similar argument in these pages. Perhaps
both Gingrich and Bannon have played the role of the black dog to
some degree. I agree that devolution is a natural force that is sometimes necessary to catalyze a further evolution, but I disagree with
Gingrich and Bannon in one important respect: *There is a world of
difference between recognizing and taking advantage of devolution
when it is occurring, and the deliberate planning and implementation of it.* It takes enormous chutzpah to imagine that one can plan
and implement disruption, *and then control the outcome*; yet this
was precisely what Gingrich and Bannon set out to do. In my view, it
is far better to simply recognize disruption when it occurs, and then
take advantage of the situation. As Rahm Emanuel, Obama's former
Chief of Staff, used to like to say, "Never let a good crisis go to waste."

It is not only the Republicans, however, who are responsible for
today's incivility. It takes two to tango. The Democrats had a choice
in how to react to Gingrich, even if he was the principal instigator
of the modern partisan divide. They did not need to respond with
anger and they did not, at first. But the initial lack of combativeness
on the Democrats side was not a moral calculation as much as a political one. The Democrats were in power at the time, and so their plan
was simply to outlast him. They were hoping Gingrich would just go
away. He did not.

Over time, the Democrats were drawn into the fight. The nasty
impeachment battle during the Clinton administration undoubtedly
played a part in provoking a retaliation during the George W. Bush
administration that followed. This time the Democrats drew out their
sharpest knives, relentlessly attacking Bush's integrity and intelligence

and comparing him to *Mad Magazine*'s Alfred E. Neuman, among other barbs. In reality, Bush's closest aides considered him to be highly intelligent with a quick, analytical mind.[205] This is not to say that many of the criticisms of the Bush administration were not justified, but they were also unnecessarily mean-spirited.

In sum, both sides of the aisle had already poisoned the well before Obama and Trump were elected. Obama did his best to navigate the strained difficult political climate with dignity. Senate Majority Leader Mitch McConnell made no such effort, vowing to do everything in his power to not have Obama elected for a second term—then taking the unprecedented step of not holding hearings when Obama nominated Merrick Garland for a Supreme Court vacancy nearly a year before the end of Obama's term. Then came Trump, who teamed up with Majority Leader McConnell to create the most polarized Congress in modern times.

THE 2016 PRESIDENTIAL ELECTION/WRESTING MATCH

The contest between Donald Trump and Hillary Clinton did not resemble any previous election. This matchup was closer to a Wrestle-Mania event between Hulk Hogan and Jesse (The Body) Ventura than a political contest of competing policies, experience, or intelligence. That the election resembled a wrestling match was not a coincidence; Trump had experience in the make-believe wrestling world.[206] Trump used his promotional know-how, coupled with lessons he learned from his mentor, the notorious attorney, Roy Cohn, about how to hype, exaggerate, or simply speak outrageous untruths to grab attention.

The Roy Cohn story is inseparable from the story of Trump. In the 1950s, Cohn made a name for himself as a US Department of Justice prosecutor at the Julius and Ethel Rosenberg espionage trial. He then went on to become the lead prosecutor for Senator Joseph McCarthy and the Permanent Subcommittee on Investigations, pursuing supposed communist sympathizers during a dark period in American political history known for prosecutorial overreach. Cohn's dirty work as McCarthy's henchman led to McCarthy's downfall as

US Senator. But Cohn rebounded to work for many famous clients of dubious reputation over the next three decades, including Mafia bosses Carmine Galante and John Gotti, and then Donald Trump and his father, Fred Trump. (Cohn, incidentally, managed to get Gotti off with a light sentence. But Gotti was later put away for life by then US Assistant Attorney General and later two-term FBI Director, and, most recently, Special Counsel Robert Mueller).

When Cohn aggressively represented the Trumps in a racial discrimination housing suit brought against them, Donald Trump took note of Cohn's "shock and awe" legal style. Cohn frequently used threats and intimidation to get his way, countersuing anyone who dared to sue his clients; and he knew how to plant untruths in the media to twist and control the narrative. Trump's philosophy of "admit nothing, deny everything," comes directly from Cohn. It was Cohn who met a young Roger Stone while they were both working on Richard Nixon's campaign. Cohn tutored Stone in the "dark arts" of politics, and later introduced Stone to Trump. In 1986, just weeks before he died, Cohn was disbarred by the New York Supreme Court for unethical conduct.[207]

In the 2016 election, Trump used everything he had garnered from Cohn, plus his own experience from the related worlds of wrestling, tabloid journalism, and Reality TV to succeed in completely controlling the media narrative. Trump set the terms of engagement. He manipulated the media; they followed his every move, captivated by the latest shiny object he offered for the public's amusement. He made one outrageous statement after the other, and as a result received the most "earned media time" (a euphemism for free publicity) by far, of all the candidates. Trump sucked up all the oxygen in the room. No other candidates could get their message out—neither those in the crowded Republican primary field of 16 other candidates, nor Hillary Clinton during the national campaign.

From the moment he rode down the escalator announcing his candidacy by calling out Mexicans as rapists and murderers, Trump not only survived media criticism—he thrived on it. The more preposterous he acted, the more the media covered him—and the higher he rose in the polls. A significant number of people found him refreshing and authentic even as they were aware of his not being honest. Authenticity (as in not being politically correct) became more important than honesty. This was just one of the oddities of the 2016 election.

None of the rules applied to candidate Trump. One would have thought that no Republican candidate could have survived insulting a bona fide war hero from the Republican Party, but Trump did that to John McCain—and still won the nomination. He insulted the entire Bush family, which included two previous Republican presidents and the presumptive nominee, Jeb Bush, tagging Jeb with the nickname "low energy," a moniker Bush was unable to shake. Trump lied and distorted other candidate's positions, and when media watchdogs tried to point out his inaccuracies, he brazenly called the press "The Enemy of the People" (a phrase that was often invoked in Stalinist Russia). Trump was so successful at stirring up animosity for the press that the journalist Katy Tur, assigned to cover his campaign for the entire 18 months, had to receive Secret Service protection.[208]

Trump was openly sexist toward the only female Republican candidate for president, Carly Fiorina, attacking her looks and barely paid a price. He went on to insult Hillary Clinton in similar, if slightly more indirect ways. He questioned Hillary's "strength and stamina" and whether she "looked presidential"—code for "she is a woman." He was caught on tape essentially admitting to sexual assault, and yet, incredibly, Trump won the majority of the White female vote according to exit polls.[209] I come back to this point when discussing the unique societal perception of Hillary Clinton.

Trump succeeded by giving the media what it most craves: ratings. Les Moonves, then President of CBS, admitted as much when he said, 'Trump is bad for the country, but good for CBS.' Trump also came along during a time when the reputation of CBS and other news organizations had fallen dramatically from the days of Walter Cronkite, America's grandfather of news, who inspired trust. With the advent of 24-hour cable coverage, news programming had willingly changed from conveyor of the public trust to *info-tainment*: a cross between news and entertainment. Trump, groomed on "reality TV," was aware of all of this. He knew exactly what he was doing—because he had been doing it his entire life.

HILLARY CLINTON AND THE CHANGING VIEWS OF WOMEN IN SOCIETY

The 2016 election was an inflection point for attitudes toward women in politics. It was not only Hillary Clinton's campaign that brought this about. Her career has long served as a lightning rod for debates over women and power. It would therefore be a mistake to look at Hillary Clinton only through the lens of the 2016 election. Hillary Clinton became the first woman nominated for president by a major party in part owing to her significant personal achievements, but also because the times had changed.

This is not to say that Clinton was merely a beneficiary of the 20th century women's movement; she was in the forefront of it. When she declared at the United Nations conference on Women in Beijing that "human rights are women's rights, and women's rights are human rights," Clinton had the gravitas to do so because she had already broken many barriers herself.

As a young woman, Clinton attended Wellesley, an all-women's college, where she was valedictorian and the first student ever to give a commencement address (something that caught the attention of *Life* magazine at the time). But this was only the beginning of her breaking barriers. Clinton went on to become one of only 27 women at Yale Law School (out of 235 total students). She was the first woman to be named partner at the prestigious Rose Law firm, the first woman to chair the national board of the Legal Services corporation, the only First Lady to have an office in the West Wing of the White House (where policy is made), and the only former First Lady to be later elected to public office when she served two terms as US senator from New York. Clinton served as Secretary of State during the Obama administration, and, of course, she was the first woman to be nominated by a major party for the presidency, where she went on to win the national popular vote.

By any stretch of the imagination, she has had a phenomenally successful career. Yet somehow Clinton became the definition of a polarizing figure—simultaneously admired and disliked. For over a decade and a half, she was named the most admired woman in America by a Gallup poll, when at the same time an increasing amount of people disliked and distrusted her. How was this possible?

An important clue can be found in the progression of Hillary Clinton's career. As she advanced, she became a litmus test for how successful women were perceived—and more specifically how women's *ambition* was viewed. For many, Clinton was an important public figure and leader, a positive role model and an aspirational example of what women could accomplish. Yet her pursuit of success was often met with resistance—by both men and women. It is a measure of the continuing sexism in society that successful women are sometimes liked less by both men and women, whereas successful men are generally liked more by both men and women. The measure of Clinton's "likeability" was consistently tied to her rise in stature. The evidence is plain to see.

Whenever Clinton was in a position of power, her popularity rose, but when she was seeking a higher position, her popularity dropped. Thus when Hillary Clinton was First Lady she was well-liked, if a bit controversial. When she then decided to run for Senate, her national popularity declined, although she was still appreciated enough in New York to win election. Once Clinton assumed her position, her favorability ratings again rose—and she remained popular throughout the entire time she was in Congress. She was well thought of by her Congressional colleagues, including Republicans, because of her willingness to compromise and work on a bi-partisan basis to get things done. But as soon as she ran for president, her approval ratings sank, particularly her likeability rating. Obama famously said to Clinton in a debate, "You are likeable enough, Hillary," a comment that managed to undermine Clinton while presumably supporting her.

In Obama's defense, he obviously respected Clinton or he would not have later offered her the position of secretary of state. But even as secretary of state, the same dynamic repeated itself. While Clinton held this title, she enjoyed the highest approval ratings of her career. Then as soon as she decided to run for president a second time, her unfavorable rating again rose. The only plausible explanation for this repeated dynamic is that Clinton's ambition (if not all women's ambition) is frowned upon by certain sectors of the population. And this negative perception of ambition is only one of the obstacles faced by women in politics.

WOMEN IN POLITICS

It is impossible to understand either Hillary Clinton or the 2016 US presidential election without examining the obstacles women face in politics; yet, for some reason, many have tried to separate those issues, including Clinton herself. Clinton's own feelings on the subject are telling. In her book, *What Happened*, reflecting on the 2016 election, she wrote that she wished she could have directly proclaimed: "My story is the story of a life shaped by and devoted to the movement for women's liberation" but claims she would have been "jeered, not cheered" if she said that.[210] And she was probably correct, although the times are changing, partly thanks to her.

In the 2016 election, many people reported they would vote for a woman— just not Hillary. Was this really only about Hillary Clinton? It is true that Clinton has been a divisive figure and not the most gifted campaigner (the latter a fact she readily acknowledges). But over the past twenty-plus years, focus groups have consistently reported significant numbers of people who say they "would vote for a woman for president, but just not that woman"—*and that was the case no matter who the potential woman candidate was in the survey*— according to Amanda Hunter, research and communications director at the Barbara Lee Family Foundation, an organization that supports women in politics. [211] Clearly, the reluctance to vote for a female president was not only about Hillary Clinton. Something else was going on. Some of the public continues to have a hard time imagining a woman president.

The way leadership is viewed provides a clue as to why this may be the case. Because relatively few women have been in office, the public perception of leadership tends to be skewed toward qualities of strength, toughness, and valor that are typically associated with masculinity. Women must work harder than men to demonstrate their leadership abilities. Historically, some women leaders have overcompensated for this and embraced policies that were unquestionably tough, pro-war, or pro-establishment: Think Golda Meir or Margaret Thatcher, both of whom were known as "The Iron Lady" in their day. Hillary Clinton was similarly accused of being too hawkish, and perhaps she too was compensating so as not to appear weak.

Perception of leadership style is just one of the many prejudices against women running for office or for women seeking any higher position, elected or otherwise. The likeability issue that plagued Hillary Clinton, for instance, was not unique to her. Women face a double standard around this issue all the time. Male candidates can be disliked, and people still vote for them. Donald Trump was a perfect example of this. In the 2016 election, Trump had an even higher disapproval rating than Clinton, and yet many looked the other way and voted for him. Thus far, this does not seem to be the case for women candidates. At least up to this point, likeability seems a prerequisite for voting for them.

If you are a woman in politics—or at any workplace—you are scrutinized for everything, from your face, body, voice, clothing, and demeanor. When Pat Schroeder withdrew from the 1988 presidential race, she cried when making her announcement. Immediately, she was assailed by both women and men for reinforcing a stereotype, namely, that women are overly emotional and lack composure. Significantly, male politicians used to not be able to show public emotion either. However, in recent years, a curious shift has occurred. It has become acceptable for male politicians to choke up in public, but not so for women. Women are typically berated if they show emotion in public—yet this did not happen with Hillary. When she teared up on the presidential campaign trail, she was not ridiculed; she was praised and gained traction in the polls. Why? I believe it is because Hillary Clinton occupies a unique role in our political history. After so many years of being in the spotlight, the public perception of Clinton was that she always maintained emotional control. Therefore, when Hillary finally showed her feelings, they were welcomed in the same way the emotions of male candidates are today. In the oddest of ways, Clinton again became a trailblazer. She may have helped all candidates, male and female, show more genuine emotion.

HISTORICAL SEXISM AND WOMEN'S PERCEPTION OF HILLARY CLINTON

The way some women view Hillary Clinton is at least partially a reflection of how systemic sexism affects both women and men in our culture. This does not mean that all women are incapable of viewing Clinton for who she is, for what she has accomplished, for mistakes she has made, or for how she comports herself. But the perception of Clinton by some women (and men) has been substantially colored by the societal perception of women in general. Sexism is not only practiced—or perpetrated—by men. Sexist values can be, and often are, internalized by women and then inflicted upon other women. A similar phenomenon occurs with internalized racism. W. E. B. Du Bois, when speaking of African Americans, called this form of internalization "double consciousness."[212] It occurs whenever a class of people are the target of hatred and bigotry sustained over a long period of time. Eventually, the oppressed group begins to see themselves in the same way the oppressor does. This may partially explain why so many women could vote for Trump even though he was frequently openly disrespectful, if not outright misogynistic, toward women. The internalization of sexism or racism is how society perpetuates the existing balance of power, which is why inspiration for change often must come from outside the system.

This goes back to a central theme in America's history: the influence of Native America on almost all aspects of American politics and society. It was mainly through contact with Native American women, for instance, that the 19th century pioneers of the women's movement began to envision another way of being. These pioneers—whom I have dubbed the *founding mothers*—were surrounded by sexism in every aspect of their lives: in their home, government, church, and schools. All these institutions were dominated by men. Even elementary school teachers were mostly male in the mid-19th century, a time when the requisite training to occupy many professions was simply not available for women. Higher education had barely become available for women, and then only on a limited basis, prior to the 1848 Seneca Falls Women's conference. Contrast that with today, when women college graduates outnumber male graduates. Clearly, men must refrain from defining the limits of what women can be or achieve.

There is some reason to believe that the days of men defining women are, if not over, at least on the wane. Women are decreasingly cowed by male definitions of femininity. The proof was in the 2018 congressional election—and not just because an unprecedented number of women won elections; it was because of the diversity of the women. Women of all ages, appearances, and religious groups ran for office—and won. Women campaigned with children in tow. They wore tattoos and piercings; one even wore a hijab.

Of the two Muslim women who won office for the first time in US history, Rashida Tlaib of Michigan and Ilhan Omar of Minnesota, only Omar wears a hijab, and not one that fully covers her face. Since she assumed office, Omar has received far more criticism than Tlaib. This is in part because of controversial remarks Omar made (perceived by some as anti-Semitic), but I strongly suspect it is also because of her appearance. There is a lingering prejudice against Muslim women wearing traditional clothing; many Westerners perceive it as demeaning to women. However, as Matilda Gage and other early suffragists pointed out, Western women have been subject to their own religious (and other) forms of persecution. If one's own oppression is unseen or unacknowledged, it can be projected onto others. This is one reason the #MeToo movement is so important.

It has served to embolden women to speak out regarding their own experiences with sexual assault and abuse, calling out perpetrators by name and confirming what many already knew—that sexual violence and harassment against women is tremendously widespread—and needs to stop.

The founding mothers of America did not have the benefit of a social media campaign, so the full extent of their own oppression only became apparent after encountering Native American women who enjoyed genuine equality in their culture. Native American women occupied an equal position in their society back then. However, largely because of continuing contact with Western governments, the role of Native women in politics has become greatly diminished. That is why it is highly significant—and potentially restorative of original politics—that two Native American women won election to Congress for the first time: Deb Haaland (Laguna Pueblo) of New Mexico and Sharice Davids (Ho-Chunk) from Kansas.[213]

Opportunities for women in politics have changed a lot in the few short years since Clinton's second bid for the presidency. Clinton must have taken some measure of satisfaction at the flock of six qualified women who ran for president during the primaries in 2019. There was even a brief time when about half the field running for president were women (six of the first twelve candidates to declare). Clearly, women were eager to jump into the presidential race this time—an important legacy from the 2016 presidential election. Hillary Clinton may have been a flawed messenger in many ways, but she was a leader in the literal sense. She went first, a bellwether of change. A profound shift has occurred in America. Strong women are emerging, and there may be no more important outcome from the 2016 election.

CHAPTER ELEVEN

The Trickster President: A Necessary Devolution Before Evolution?

Hillary Clinton's failed attempt at the presidency served a purpose in the larger scheme of things. So, too, there is a larger purpose for Donald Trump's presidency.

There is a functional aspect to the dismantling of order, even as it gives birth to temporary chaos. Chaos is never the final step. Chaos is an in-between state, a chrysalis, from which a higher level of complexity—and even beauty—can be born.

Devolution is necessary whenever the current order has become calcified. The old order must be dismantled if something better is to be created. The human tendency, however, is to resist this necessary step. We tend to hang on to what we have, even if we are miserable. So, when the black dog comes, we may not welcome him. We chase him away. If he insists on staying, we try to change, cure, or get rid of him. We have a hard time accepting the black dog for who he is and for the sacred role he plays.

What is happening is that our trickster president creates a whirlwind in which two energies are being simultaneously unleashed. The first is that everything is being shaken up, including policies and social norms. The second is a counter reaction to Trump that has reenergized America's sacred purpose of unity in diversity—and this could have an even greater impact in the long run. The resistance movement began on day one of Trump's presidency when an historic number of women marched on Washington. The Women's March then inspired an historic number of women to run for office, and a record number of women won. These women will continue to serve in office long after

Trump is gone. The public may even vote in a female vice-president because the presumptive Democratic nominee, Joe Biden, has pledged to nominate a woman as his running mate. This may also increase the chance that the women's vote provides the margin that derails Trump from a second term. It is in this manner that devolution ends up being a catalyst for evolution.

Please do not misunderstand me. Things could get a whole lot worse before they get better. This has already occurred with respect to impacts upon the environment and in foreign affairs. Both the assault on our environment and the possibility of a wide-scale war loom large. Trump is unquestionably a dangerous president. The only question is: How dangerous is he?

How Dangerous is the 45th President?

Throughout the tumultuous Trump presidency, many armchair psychologists have felt compelled to diagnose Trump from afar, believing that his actions stem from some sort of mental illness. There was even a book published in 2017 titled *The Dangerous Case of Donald Trump* in which 27 psychiatrists and mental health practitioners felt an obligation to declare Trump psychologically unfit for office.[214] Two years later, it was commonplace for enraged Democratic politicians (and sometimes private citizens) to declare him "unfit for office" and indicate that his mental instability was one of the reasons.

There are problems, of course, with trying to diagnose political leaders from afar, which is why the "Goldwater Rule" advising against diagnosing people without personally evaluating them (more of a guideline than a rule) was put in place after Democratic operatives succeeded in implanting the ultimate fear in the electorate: that presidential candidate Barry Goldwater might blow the world to Kingdom Come.[215]

There are good reasons for the Goldwater rule; any person is much more than their public face. Yet, Trump does seem to fit every conceivable description of narcissism, including an inflated sense of self-importance, need for excessive attention and admiration, and lack of empathy—all of which potentially cause destructive relationships.

It is hard to disagree with the notion that Trump is a narcissist. But how much does that matter? Arguably, most political leaders possess some degree of narcissism, which is in part why they run for public office. It is important to recognize that there is a wide spectrum of narcissism. Not every narcissist is malignant or dangerous. A politician could feel they are special and possess bold visions for the nation and still be emotionally well adjusted. They would not be a great leader, however, if they do not also possess copious amounts of empathy and compassion and be driven to make a genuine difference in people's lives.

An extreme narcissist, on the other hand, would almost certainly be a dangerous leader. And without diagnosing him, there is every indication that President Trump fits the profile of extreme or malignant narcissism. He appears to have become an instrument of the collective national shadow (including the racist, sexist underbelly of America that in recent decades had become socially unacceptable and mostly suppressed or kept out of sight). This is one of the reasons why the Trump phenomenon is dangerous. An extreme narcissist is tantamount to an empty vessel; he or she may lack self-awareness to such a degree that the person becomes possessed by shadow energies. By "possessed," I do not mean possessed by an entity as in the film *The Exorcist*, but rather becoming the personification of archetypal energies, particularly those hidden in our shadows.

A simple way to think of archetypes is this: When stories are repeatedly told, they eventually become part of our collective psyche. These universal stories depict patterns of behavior that have impacted humankind for millennia, and serve as guidelines for how to become more fully human. They teach by providing examples of both what *not to do* as well as what *to do*.

The importance of oral tradition is not only historical. Just after the United States entered WWII, Allen Dulles, America's chief intelligence operative in Switzerland, recruited the famed psychologist Carl Gustav Jung to find out what was going on in Germany at the time—and specifically why the German people seemed to have fallen under Hitler's hypnotic spell. (Jung was known as Agent 488 in the report that later became public).

In his astonishing report, Jung asserted that Hitler was embodying the Norse God Wotan, "the ancient God of Storm and Frenzy," a "personification of psychic force" that much like an extinct volcano being aroused to new activity, was making up for lost time.

At the end of his report, Jung ominously predicted that other personifications of psychic forces may be similarly sleeping in the modern consciousness, soon to be awakened. I submit that something like this has occurred with Donald Trump, except instead of the God of Storm and Frenzy, Trump has become the personification of The Trickster figure. Trump delights in the art of deception, and this has become the guiding narrative of his existence.[216]

In calling Donald Trump a trickster, I am not intending a value judgment as much as an observation. There is a sacred role for tricksters in myth. They normally incite chaos and turmoil, but this forces a corrective response. *They devolve our collective consciousness in order to evolve it.*

The process of devolution tears apart the social fabric so it can be recreated at a higher level of integration. In Trump's case, he does not appear to be a conscious trickster. He may delight in gaslighting liberals concerned with political correctness, but he is not consciously seeking to engender higher consciousness. Nonetheless, he is performing that role. He is the black dog that is unraveling the beautiful rug the woman had been weaving, and even if he has been unconscious of his role, he is still presenting us with an important opportunity. As the social fabric is torn apart for all to see, we can recreate our institutions and values in a more coherent and sustainable way. Be thankful for the black dog. We have an opportunity to reweave a more beautiful rug.

THE TRICKSTER WON THE ELECTION

The presidency was won by a trickster. Donald Trump was not a typical Republican or conservative. He was a completely unconventional candidate with no coherent political philosophy to speak of and little interest in policy details. A modern P. T. Barnum with xenophobic tendencies, Trump promised the impossible (such as no more loss of jobs overseas and building a great wall across our southern border and having Mexico pay for it). Truth was the first casualty of the campaign and civility a close second.

Trickster figures abound in cross-cultural Western mythology and are also integral to many Native American cosmologies and world-views. The trickster figure is not always human, and can often be a coyote, rabbit, fox, or raven, or a combination of shapeshifting forms part animal and part human. In many Native American cosmologies, the trickster is integral to world creation and dissolution. In Navajo cosmology, it is the coyote that interferes with orderly creation, throwing the stars in the sky in the haphazard way they appear today. In Lakota, there is a *heyoka* trickster figure (sacred clown) that acts in a contrarian manner opposite of normal.

According to Hynes and Doty, every trickster figure has several, if not all, of the following six traits:

- Fundamentally ambiguous and anomalous personality
- Deceiver and trick-player
- Shape-shifter or master of disguise
- Situation-inverter
- Messenger and imitator of the gods
- Sacred and lewd bricoleur (jack of all trades).[217]

Clearly Donald Trump has become the trickster figure of modern politics. He lies with impunity, is known to contradict himself within a single sentence, is a situation-inverter who frequently accuses the other of what he does himself, pretends to be a sacred messenger, and has a lewd and bawdy sense of humor. Like a skilled magician, Trump makes himself the principal distraction. The public keeps their eyes on him, while he has something else up his sleeve.

This is not to imply that Trump is a strategic thinker, for there is no discernible pattern to his actions (other than that he fights back whenever criticized). Being unpredictable is something Trump prides himself on, and capricious, unpredictable behavior is the cornerstone of being a trickster. Trump can be mercurial and enjoys keeping people off balance. This does not mean he has a clear strategic plan to do this. This is probably the main reason Special Counsel Mueller's Report exonerated him of criminal conspiracy with Russia during the 2016 election. A criminal conspiracy to defraud the United States requires some sort of strategic agreement between the conspirators, but Trump himself does not seem to know what he will do next.

This constellation of behaviors only makes sense if we see him as the unwitting personification of the trickster figure. The forces of trickster energy move through him; they do not appear to be consciously directed by him. Nonetheless, he has fully assumed the role.

As president of the United States, Trump has enormous power, and as long as he is president, the world is in danger. If President Kennedy wanted the United States to be the tide that lifts all boats, the words and actions of the 45th president could potentially be the tidal wave that breaks everything apart. (I am speaking metaphorically here, but his denial of climate change is also a worldwide concern).

It is not my intent, however, to equate Trump with Hitler, Stalin, or even Putin or Duterte. While Trump uses bellicose language that has fomented violence, he has not wantonly killed political figures that oppose him. [218] Hitler may have been the embodiment of Wotan (the ancient god of Storm and Frenzy). Trump appears to be the personification of somewhat less violent, more mischievous figures such as the Greek god Pan or the Norse god Loki (although that could change). Pan (with the upper body of a man and the legs, hindquarters, and horns of a goat) is the horny god of instant gratification and lusty sexual dalliances. Pan seems appropriate, except that Pan was also a Nature god, and Trump is more a city creature (except while on a manicured golf course). Loki is probably a closer fit. Both Pan and Loki crave shallow pleasures, are sometimes playful, sometimes malicious, and always mischievous and irreverent.[219] Loki, however, is in some ways more dangerous than Pan, because he takes on the entire civilization, bringing it to the brink of destruction before ultimately pulling back, just as Trump has—at least so far.[220]

Both Loki and Pan (the latter being the root of *panic* and *pandemic*), delight in breaking the rules of polite society and causing chaos. Trump, our 45th president, has broken more norms of governing than any president before him, although arguably Andrew Jackson made more substantive changes to the domestic status quo (such as dismantling the Second US Bank). Trump's refusal to play along with the norms of governance is different from Jackson's behavior and sometimes seem more superficial than Jackson's acts. But they are also more numerous and have often involved foreign policy. The destabilization of the world order puts us at greater risk for wide-scale war. It is this disruption of America's place in the world that I turn to next.

Is America Still the Leader of the Free World?

Ever since the end of WWII, whoever occupies the office of president of the United States has been known as the leader of the free world. Yet, under the guise of an "America First" policy, Trump shocked our democratic allies by abdicating this primary role. Trump approached our NATO alliance in the exact opposite manner an American president would be expected to do: praising our enemies and criticizing our allies. These actions are reminiscent of the Lakota *heyoka* sacred clown who acts in a contrarian manner opposite of normal; only the *heyoka* acts this way for the conscious purpose of awakening people to new ways of looking at reality, while Trump does not appear to have any purpose other than aligning with the strong to intimidate the weak.

Nonetheless, at least some of the people seem to be awakening.

Trump has frequently berated our allies, complaining that Europe has taken advantage of the United States, apparently ignoring the fact that in the wake of the 9/11 attacks our European allies spilled blood in Afghanistan and Iraq. (Britain alone lost 450 soldiers in Afghanistan and another 150 in Iraq between 2003 and 2011.)[221] While other presidents, including Obama and George W. Bush, have attempted to persuade our allies to make greater financial contributions to

NATO, Trump's efforts to get them to give more to their defense, while sometimes successful, sound like a Mafia boss demanding money in a protection racket for black-market businesses.[222] This has left our allies not just disconcerted, but also angry.

The straw that broke the proverbial camel's back came in July of 2018 at the NATO summit in Brussels when Trump threatened to pull the US out of the NATO alliance entirely—and then jetted off to meet with Vladimir Putin in Helsinki the very next day. There, Trump stood shoulder to shoulder with Putin and publicly sided with the Russian leader in his denial of interference in the US election, thus rejecting the conclusion of Dan Coates who was the Director of National Intelligence, an office that speaks for seventeen US intelligence agencies.[223] Trump has obsequiously complimented the Russian dictator so often that many people, both liberal and conservative, have wondered just what sort of nefarious partnership they might be engaged in. Trump has also parroted Russian talking points on numerous occasions. One shocking example of this was when he asserted that Leonid Brezhnev of the then-U.S.S.R. was justified in invading Afghanistan in 1979—a comment that prompted the conservative-leaning *Wall Street Journal* to say that "We cannot recall a more absurd misstatement of history by an American President."[224]

Trump's cozy relationship with Putin and other world dictators has induced panic throughout the free world. Why? One simple reason is that the United States and Russia together possess 92 percent of the world's stockpile of nuclear weapons.[225]

DOES THE PRESIDENT HAVE THE POWER TO UNDO THE WORLD ORDER?

No president can accomplish much without the support of their Cabinet officers; Congress; leaders from the military, business, ethnic and religious communities; and a significant percentage (if not the majority) of the American people. The role of Trump's Cabinet officers, and the fraught relationship between them and the president, have been particularly pivotal in the unfolding of the Trump administration.

Several of Trump's initial Cabinet members immediately began assuring world leaders that the United States stood with its allies—that there were adults in the room who would protect the world order. And during the first two years of Trump's term, cooler heads did in fact prevail for the most part. With the exception of the ill-chosen Michael Flynn as National Security Advisor (whom President Obama had personally implored Trump not to select), Trump's key Cabinet positions were occupied by experienced statesmen, including military men such as Secretary of Defense James Mattis and National Security Advisor, H. R. McMaster who replaced Flynn after his record short tenure of 24 days. Trump's first secretary of state, Rex Tillerson, the former CEO of Exxon, can be included among the persons operating on an even keel, even as Tillerson came under criticism for mismanaging the State Department with budget cuts and understaffing.

Trump wanted to act boldly in foreign affairs but soon discovered that US presidents are not omnipotent in such matters. For instance, in 2017 when sparring with Kim Jung Un over who had a "bigger nuclear button," Trump asked his advisors to prepare a pre-emptive military strike option, but they emphatically objected, and for good reason. A pre-emptive military strike would have ensured the deaths of thousands, if not millions, of South Korean, Japanese, and American soldiers and civilians. Trump's order to move a naval fleet to the Korean peninsula was similarly rejected, this time in a curious manner. Defense Secretary James Mattis publicly confirmed Trump's announcement that the fleet was moving toward the Korean peninsula as the fleet continued sailing in the opposite direction to take part in previously scheduled military exercises with Australia in the Indian Ocean.[226]

There were numerous other occasions when Mattis, McMaster, or Tillerson either softened, redirected, or politely ignored Trump's directives. Often they were in the unenviable position of having to do so *after* Trump announced a policy by tweet in the wee hours of the morning without consulting either them or America's allies. Despite regularly waking up to these surprises, Mattis, McMaster, and

Tillerson usually managed to convince Trump to reverse his position after consulting with them. But this was all about to change.

A NEW AND MORE DANGEROUS CABINET

To the alarm of everyone except the most strident of his supporters, President Trump gradually began to replace the stable triumvirate of defense-related Cabinet members with new officers that he deemed more loyal. The two most prominent changes were John Bolton to replace McMaster as National Security Advisor and Mike Pompeo to replace Tillerson as Secretary of State. These new Cabinet officers were known for more hawkish foreign policy positions on both North Korea and Iran. Was Trump, who campaigned on not intervening in foreign wars, changing his stripes?

Again, the trickster kept us guessing. The reason Mattis resigned was Trump's sudden decision to withdraw troops from Syria without notifying him or any of our allies. When Trump tweeted his intent to withdraw troops in 30 days, even dovish members of Congress who might have normally been pleased with this announcement were alarmed by the irregularity of the decision-making process. Mattis made clear in his resignation letter that he did not concur with Trump's disrespectful treatment of allies. When he resigned on December 20, 2018, he gave the president three months' notice, giving him time to find a proper replacement for the critical position of defense secretary (who is in charge of the Army, Marine Corps, Navy, and Air Force). Trump was miffed at the resignation letter and prematurely terminated Mattis at the end of 2018. In doing this, Trump did not have adequate time to confirm a replacement. It took until July of 2019 for Mark Esper, former Vice-President of Government Relations at Raytheon, to be confirmed by Congress to be the next secretary of defense.

The irony of this cascade of events was that the policy to withdraw troops in Syria in 30 days was then changed; it was first changed to months and then back to years, which was the original policy. Thus Trump lost a highly-respected secretary of defense over a mercurial decision that Trump later reversed.

The story does not end there, however. It became clear over time that Trump was pushed against his will into reversing the policy. And in October of 2019, Trump suddenly reverted back to his original decision to withdraw troops from northern Syria. Moreover, this time he apparently gave a green light to Turkish President Erdogan to initiate a military strike on the Kurds (who had been the staunchest allies of the United States against the Islamic State terrorist organization).

An immediate consequence of forcing the Kurds to flee the region was that Russia moved into the region and became the power broker it had not been since the 1970s.[227] An eventual consequence could be the re-constellation of the ISIS caliphate. And perhaps the most devastating consequence could be other allies breaking away from the United States, no longer able to trust Trump's America.

Speaker Pelosi, in trying to explain the action, directly confronted the president, saying, "With you, all roads lead to Putin." But it was not just Democrats who were horrified by Trump's decision. The action to withdraw troops from northern Syria was publicly rebuked by both parties. Senator Mitt Romney dramatically characterized the blunder as a "bloodstain on the annals of American history." Mitch McConnell called it "a grave strategic mistake." The House of Representatives, including 129 Republican congress members, voted their disapproval of the move. The exact result of the decision will play out over time. It is clear, however, that this decision has already changed the dynamics of the Middle East, and may continue to have repercussions for decades to come.

THE CONSEQUENCES OF A TRANSACTIONAL FOREIGN POLICY

In other more normal presidencies, foreign policy is guided by a carefully constructed strategic plan. Then the actual negotiating is left to career diplomats. In the Trump era, we have a personality-driven, transactional foreign policy that changes from moment to moment based on personal whim.

US foreign policy became increasingly erratic as we headed into 2019; yet the new Cabinet largely acquiesced to this state of affairs. Vice-President Pence, who early on was tasked with reassuring allies, began parroting Trump's language. At a February 2019 conference in Poland, the Vice-President urged European allies to join the United States in withdrawing from the Iran nuclear deal and was greeted with a prolonged, stony silence. [228] The notion of US presidents reneging on past commitments was disturbing to allies who have come to expect a certain consistency in US foreign policy regardless of who is president.

Breaking from Past Tradition on Multilateral Agreements

While relations with Iran, North Korea, and Syria present the more immediate threats, the administration's distaste for multilateral trade agreements represents the biggest break from the neoliberal world order of the past three-quarters of a century. During the first two years of the Trump presidency, the administration managed to withdraw from the Trans-Pacific Partnership (TPP); the Paris Climate accords; the Iran Nuclear Deal; the North American Free Trading Agreement (NAFTA); United Nations Educational, Scientific, and Cultural Organization (UNESCO); United Nations Humans Rights Council (UNHRC); and United Nations Relief and Works Agency (UNRWA)—an aid program for Palestinian refugees. Most recently, the Trump administration withdrew from the Arms Trade Treaty (ATT), a treaty negotiated by President Obama designed to keep dangerous weapons out of the hands of human rights abusers. As the country entered 2020, Trump had not withdrawn from NATO or the WTO but had threatened to withdraw from both.

It is almost surprising that at the time of writing this book the president has not withdrawn from the World Trade Organization since foreign trade was one of the signature issues of the Trump campaign—and trade is an issue in which the US president holds enormous power. For instance, a president can unilaterally impose tariffs without Congressional approval. Once the president realized he had sole power to impose tariffs, he insisted upon doing so, to the dismay of Gary Cohn, then Trump's chief economic advisor, who resigned over this decision. Virtually the entire Republican caucus was similarly dismayed. Trump stepped off the tariff cliff all by himself, only to struggle to contain the damage to the US economy ever since.

The worldwide consensus on multilateral free trade following WWII has been fractured. Trump is an outlier who believes America has been taken advantage of by the rest of the free world; he wants to change this by scuttling multilateral cooperation and renegotiating everything from the position of "America First." I further discuss the dangerous ramifications of an "America First" slogan in chapter twelve.

The question I consider next is how much Trump is truly changing the world order. As volatile as events have been, it behooves us to take a sober look at not only how much things have changed, but how much they have stayed the same.

IS THE NEOLIBERAL WORLD ORDER CHANGING AS MUCH AS WE THINK?

Trump supporters love the unorthodox and irreverent approach of the president. The more he bucks established norms, the more they support him. Trump opponents, on the other hand, wonder how he gets away with it and why Congress (especially the Senate) does not do more to stop him.

There is another less considered possibility. The Republican Senate ignores the bombast because Trump has to this point been useful in enacting their agenda. In many respects, Trump has not really changed things as much as one might think. For example, Mitch McConnell's number one priority was to appoint conservative judges. On this point, Trump has capitulated, choosing judges, including two Supreme Court judges, from a preapproved list presented to him by the Heritage Foundation, a conservative think tank. Trump also signed into law a tax cut that benefited the Republican donor class the most. Whatever else Trump has done or threatened to do—no matter how outrageous or disruptive—has apparently been deemed unimportant or worth the trade-off. The Republicans can live with the bluster, the corruption, and even with the policies they strongly disagree with (such as tariffs) that can be reversed in time.

Moreover, Trump has yet to substantially challenge the core of the neoliberal world order, even as he is a destabilizing presence. The core value of the neoliberal world order is the centrality of economics. Monetary concerns are prioritized over all else. Despite his meddling in established multilateral trade policies, Trump wholeheartedly shares the worldview of seeing international relations in financial terms. In fact, he is even more radical in this respect, seeing allies in fundamentally the same way as enemies—by regarding them as competition—not as countries bound together by shared values. To Trump, diplomacy is a series of transactional business opportunities. His primary interest seems to be increasing wealth, which favors the already wealthy, including himself and his family.

If anything, Trump has doubled down on protecting the existing world order when it comes to protecting oil markets, making the United States addiction to oil only stronger. Trump and his son-in-law, Jared Kushner, have catered to the oil barons of the Middle East. Past presidents did this also, just not as openly. In many ways, Trump is not so different from what has come before him. The principal difference between Trump and previous presidents is that Trump makes no attempt to hide his own complicity with immoral leaders. And in Trump's transparency, there is a surprising gift; it makes reality harder to ignore and forces us to ask: *Is this what we really want?*

Despite all of Trump's theatrics, there appeared to be little substantive change to our foreign policy for much of Trump's first term. Iran and China were the biggest changes. Our policy toward Mexico, despite all the bluster, has changed little. The new USMCA agreement replacing NAFTA represented only an incremental improvement. The policy toward Europe, as long as Trump stays in the NATO accord, has not dramatically changed.

Our policy toward North Korea has also not changed that much. Trump is mostly repeating what past presidents have done, trying, albeit in more flamboyant fashion, to entice North Korea to deescalate their nuclear arsenal. Unfortunately North Korea does not appear to be changing anytime soon; and there is not much the United States can do about it.

For a long time it did not appear that official US policy toward Russia had changed either, despite Trump's apparent fealty to Vladimir Putin. That was because Trump's Cabinet officers have pushed back, as had Congress on several occasions. For example, after Special Counsel Mueller indicted thirteen Russian individuals and three companies in the Russian troll farm—and Trump remained (or pretended to be) unconvinced by refusing to speak out against or punish Russia—both the House and Senate voted to impose sanctions against Russia by a veto-proof, near unanimous margin. It took a month and a half for the Trump administration to apply the sanctions, but they finally did so under congressional pressure. Then, in November of 2018, after Russia attacked Ukrainian ships in the Kerch Strait and Trump remained conspicuously silent, the Senate passed a resolution condemning the action by unanimous consent.

In some ways the Trump administration policy toward Russia has been even tougher than that of the Obama administration. Ukraine has been supplied with defensive weapons, something President Obama refused to do.

All of these actions against Russia have taken place with Trump's reluctant assent, or were completely unknown to the president. It was already a highly unusual situation. And then in the summer of 2019 we found out it was even more unusual than we had imagined.

A Shadow US Foreign Policy

In mid-September of 2019, the illusion of continuity in US policy toward Russia and Ukraine suddenly evaporated. It was then we learned that President Trump had been conducting a shadow foreign policy in contradiction to stated US policy. Moreover, this shadow foreign policy was apparently intended to personally benefit the president at the expense of national security.

A whistle-blower stepped forward to claim that "the president of the United States is using the power of his office to solicit interference from a foreign country (Ukraine) in the 2020 US election" . . . and that "this interference includes, among other things, pressuring a foreign country to investigate one of the president's main domestic political rivals" (Vice President Biden, who at the time held a commanding lead in the race for the Democratic nomination). [229] The whistle-blower named Rudy Giuliani, the one-time mayor of New York, as a "central figure" in the plot and also said that Attorney General Barr "appears to be involved as well."

Multiple US officials had informed the whistle-blower that they were deeply concerned about "Mr. Giuliani's circumvention of national security decision-making processes to engage with Ukrainian officials." These same officials claimed that any meeting or phone call with Ukraine would be dependent upon the Ukrainian President Zelenskyy's willingness to "play ball" with Trump's demand for Ukraine to investigate Vice President Biden and his son, Hunter Biden, who was on the board of directors of Burisma, a Ukrainian energy company.

Further, the whistle-blower learned that the Office of Management and Budget (OMB) had issued instructions to suspend military aid to Ukraine already appropriated by Congress unless the new Ukrainian president agreed to their demands. Perhaps most significantly, the whistle-blower reported that President Trump held a phone conversation with President Zelenskyy on July 25, 2019, in which he directly asked the Ukrainian president to take actions that would benefit President Trump in the 2020 election. Finally, the whistle-blower asserted that there were "approximately a dozen officials who listened to the phone call" and that multiple sources confirmed that "senior White House officials had intervened to 'lock down' all records of the phone call, especially the word-for-word transcript of the call."[230]

Recognizing the gravity of the situation, Speaker Pelosi threw her weight behind an impeachment probe for the first time. (Pelosi had been steadfastly resisting calls for impeachment of the president until then). President Trump countered by insisting the phone call was "perfect" and in a show of bravado took the extraordinary step of releasing a summary of the phone call (incorrectly referred to by the president as an exact transcript, when it was a partial transcript at best).

THE IMPEACHMENT INQUIRY AND THE QUID PRO "THOUGH"

At the time impeachment hearings began in September of 2019, the facts of the whistle-blower complaint and the (partial) transcript of the July 25th Trump phone call with Zelenskyy were not in dispute. Moreover, President Trump had produced no exculpatory evidence. This did not stop President Trump and his allies from repeatedly calling for the whistle-blower himself (or herself) to testify or to call Hunter Biden to be a witness.

Thus, the impeachment inquiry unfolded in the inverse order of how one might expect. The smoking gun had come first, voluntarily provided by the president. Trump had essentially confessed by releasing the partial transcript of the July 25th call with President Zelenskyy of Ukraine on September 25th, one day after Speaker Pelosi announced she would support an inquiry and one day before a redacted version of the whistle-blower complaint was released. Then, one week later, in broad daylight on the south lawn of the White House, Trump publicly invited China to interfere in our elections by also investigating the Bidens. It might seem that Trump was oblivious to what had just occurred, but I would contend he knew exactly what he was doing.

In true trickster fashion, Trump was publicly admitting to self-incriminating evidence and then counting on inverting the situation to be in his favor. He was essentially saying: I am doing this in plain sight; therefore it cannot be wrong. The incriminating evidence in the July 25th phone call was also there for all to see, in black and white. President Zelenskyy asked for funds for javelin missiles, and President Trump began his reply by saying "*I would like you to do us a favor though* . . ." Trump then went on to ask the Ukrainian president to investigate "Crowdstrike" (referring to a debunked conspiracy theory that implicates Ukraine, not Russia, as the origin of the 2016 cyberattacks on the Democratic National Committee). Both the attempt to divert blame from Russia to Ukraine (for the 2016 election) and the ask to investigate the Bidens were clearly intended to personally help President Trump's electoral prospects. These actions had no relation to stated US national security policy. I therefore playfully refer to this exchange as a *"quid pro though."*

The impeachment inquiry took place in the House Intelligence committee, chaired by Representative Adam Schiff. Over a dozen career officials testified, including former Ambassador to Ukraine, Marie Yovanovitch; National Security Advisors Fiona Hill and Lieutenant Colonel Alexander Vindman; top US diplomat to Ukraine William B. Taylor; Deputy Assistant Secretary of State George Kent; and US Ambassador to the European Union, Gordon Sondland. All of them corroborated the whistle-blower's report and President Trump's own partial transcript of his phone call with President Zelenskyy. Many of them were alarmed that partisan politics was put ahead of national security.

Despite an increasing flood of incriminating evidence, the White House did not admit to any wrongdoing. In fact, they continued to act in (seeming) defiance of reality. Two months after the impeachment probe began, Rudy Giuliani was again back in Ukraine. And after continuing to deny an Oval Office meeting for President Zelenskyy, Trump brazenly met with Russian Foreign Minister Sergey Lavrov in the Oval office. Trump met with Foreign Minister Lavrov on December 10, 2019, the same day Articles of Impeachment were announced. (Trump had previously met with Foreign Minister Lavrov in the Oval Office the day after firing FBI Director Comey).

ARTICLES OF IMPEACHMENT

The House of Representatives ultimately elected to pursue a narrow path, authoring only two Articles of Impeachment: Abuse of Power and Obstruction of Congress, and making the Articles short and easily understandable. The Articles were largely restricted to the events that unfolded in Ukraine that prompted the impeachment inquiry. They made a clear and concise argument that focused on preventing the president from committing future abuses of power rather than revisiting the events surrounding interference into the 2016 election as outlined in the Mueller Report.

While the evidence justifying impeachment and removal of Trump seemed overwhelming, Trump's trickster abilities to control the narrative were equally effective with his followers. Thus the country remained divided on party lines at the conclusion of the impeachment hearings in the House. "It was as if truth itself were on trial," said Peter Baker of the *New York Times*.[231] The country has seemingly lost the ability to discern truth from fiction. The muddling of truth and fiction is what a trickster wants. A similar level of distortion of facts and disingenuous legal arguments ensued in the Senate trial, ultimately leading to Trump's acquittal.

All Democrats voted to convict in the impeachment trial. In addition, Mitt Romney—a devout Mormon and the standard-bearer of a different era of Republican politics—courageously broke with his party and also voted to convict. Choking up with emotion, Romney made an historic address that cited the oath he took before God to be an impartial juror. He went on to say that the president was ". . . guilty of an appalling abuse of public trust,"[232] and then specified exactly why the case against the president was so conclusive. History will look favorably upon Romney's principled decision.

THE THREAT OF WAR: THE ULTIMATE DISTRACTION

As 2020 began, and President Trump was facing an imminent impeachment trial in the Senate, he suddenly authorized an assassination strike against Iranian General Qassem Soleimani, leader of the Quds force of the Islamic Revolutionary Guard. Soleimani had long been considered an enemy of the United States. But he was also a state leader, considered to be the second most powerful man in Iran (next to Supreme Leader Ayatollah Khamenei).

This action, and the entire policy toward Iran, was the most controversial and precarious of the Trump administration to date.

In my view, the US withdrawal from the Iran nuclear agreement and the subsequent maximum pressure campaign against Iran has been a spectacular failure. Let's review the facts.

The Iran nuclear agreement was secured during the Obama administration and agreed to and signed by all five permanent members of the UN Security Council (US, UK, Russia, France, and China), plus the entire European Union. It ensured that Iran would not manufacture nuclear weapons for 15 years. Mattis and McMaster had previously dissuaded the president from pulling out of The Joint Comprehensive Plan of Action known as the "Iran Nuclear Deal." Once they were no longer around to stop him, Trump announced that the United States would withdraw from the deal. This step was taken on May 8, 2018, despite incontrovertible evidence that Iran had *not* violated the terms of the accord. None of the other parties to the deal withdrew; nor did Europe support sanctions. The Trump administration imposed sanctions on Iran anyway. The United States became the isolated party who had violated an international agreement while all other parties remained in good faith.[233]

In the meantime, the United States reimposed severe sanctions against Iran. This only served to increase tensions. Then, in defiance of the sanctions imposed upon them, Iran sent three missile-laden boats to the Gulf of Oman in the spring of 2019. Iran's Islamic Revolutionary Guard Corps then shot down a US surveillance drone on June 20, 2019. On that same day, Trump announced a retaliatory strike after consultation with secretary of state Mike Pompeo and national security advisor John Bolton. Pompeo and Bolton recommended not one, but three retaliatory strikes, which would have resulted in approximately 150 casualties and could have led to an indefinite military escalation. Trump agreed to the plan and approximately 10,000 sailors and airmen deployed for the mission while White House lawyers prepared papers justifying the military strike by citing the president's Article II powers.[234]

A mere ten minutes before launch time, Trump suddenly told the Pentagon to call off the attack. He later claimed that he had been just informed of the number of casualties that would have been the result, but this explanation does not seem credible since the rate of projected casualties is routinely discussed early in the planning process of any proposed military strike. This entire incident was a clear manifestation of a Loki-like energy—coming as close as possible to the brink of destruction before pulling back.

Then, on January 3, 2020, President Trump, without informing Congress or our allies, authorized the assassination strike against General Soleimani. Soleimani was once an ally of the United States, fighting against the Taliban after the 9/11 attacks. Since the invasion of Iraq, Soleimani has been considered an enemy of the United States. But neither Bush nor Obama dared to assassinate the state leader for fear of military retaliation that could escalate into a larger war.

The same day Soleimani was killed, Iranian president Hassan Rouhani declared, "The great nation of Iran will take revenge for this heinous crime." Then, two days later, Iran announced that they would abandon all limits on uranium enrichment, signaling the de facto end of the nuclear pact. The following day, Iraq voted to evict all American forces from their country and the United States voluntarily suspended attacks against the terrorist organization ISIS for fear of reprisal. Thus the assassination strike made an already precarious situation much more volatile. Soleimani's killing was reminiscent of the assassination of Austria's Archduke Ferdinand that led to WWI.[235] An action like this made the possibility of wide-scale war in the Middle East more likely.

True to form, Trump justified the assassination as a way of preventing a war, not starting one. He claimed he would only go to war with Iran if they resumed building nuclear weapons. But if that was the case, why pull out of the nuclear deal in the first place?

THE NEED FOR RETHINKING OUR REPUBLIC

Donald Trump, a trickster president who routinely lies to the American public, has repeatedly taken the country to the verge of a wide-scale war. Even before this event, Trump had threatened nuclear war against North Korea. He has consistently displayed significant authoritarian tendencies and been shown to be profoundly unstable. If he were to remain commander-in-chief during an all-out war, anything could happen. This is a choice point of paramount importance for our nation and the world.

It is truly concerning that the country has enabled a president like Trump—exactly the kind of man our founding fathers warned us about—to infiltrate the most powerful position in the society. Hamilton, while he favored a strong executive, also cautioned:

> When a man unprincipled in private life[,] desperate in his fortune, bold in his temper . . . take[s] every opportunity of embarrassing the General Government & bringing it under suspicion – to flatter and fall in with all the nonsense of the zealots of the day – It may justly be suspected that his object is to throw things into confusion that he may 'ride the storm and direct the whirlwind.'[236]

Hamilton's warning is apropos. Trump is a trickster who delights in sowing confusion and riding the whirlwind. He has misdirected the masses through a steady stream of lies and distortions. While Trump appears to have no grand strategy, he uses practices that have previously undermined democracies and given rise to dictatorships, including sowing doubt about the integrity of our elections and government institutions. The republic itself is now at stake.

At the same time, as I continue to emphasize, Trump's transparent vanity has served as a window into government the likes of which we have never seen, revealing a lot of what previously remained hidden. This too can be dangerous if the secrets of government are exposed to foreign powers with ill intentions who then manipulate our president for their purposes. But it is also potentially a blessing because it allows us to reconsider how things ought to work.

Benjamin Franklin, when asked what the Constitutional convention had just given birth to—a republic or a monarchy—famously replied, "A republic, if you can keep it."[237] Franklin's admonition is often repeated these days, and with good reason. Indeed, we are at a pivotal crossroads. Trump survived impeachment, but if he were to win a second term of office, the question then becomes: Can the republic survive?

In the end, *We the People* will play a pivotal role in determining whether the 45th president is removed in the coming election or simply through the end of a second term in office. In any case, it is prudent to take a good, hard look at the Trump presidency and rethink our republic going forward. We must come to terms with what direction we are now headed. Are we headed toward a fascist America or a sacred America? This is the question we consider next.

CHAPTER TWELVE

Fascist America or Sacred America?

I have said that America is on an inexorable path toward realizing its original sacred purpose of unity in diversity. I believe America—the place and nation—will return to that sacred purpose again. I admit to another possibility, however: one in which America rejects its destiny and devolves in the opposite direction so far it cannot right the ship. The devolved state of unitive consciousness is uniformity. America could become a fascist state. In truth, both possibilities have been in play ever since we broke away from monarchy and began our experimental path forward. Today, a fascist America seems more possible than ever before; yet, at the same time, the seeds of a sacred America are still present.

The word "fascist" requires some definition, as it has been wrongly applied to any government with even a whiff of authoritarianism. Fascism is an extreme form of authoritarianism, which is why all fascism is authoritarian, but not all authoritarian regimes are fascist. An authoritarian leader may go unchallenged, but there are still social and economic institutions that exist outside of government control. The most succinct definition of fascism was provided by Benito Mussolini, the Italian leader who coined the term in 1919. He simply said fascism is: "Everything within the state, nothing outside the state, nothing against the state." Fascism is "all embracing," he said in the *Doctrine on Fascism*.[238] He further clarified that the fascist state is "a synthesis . . . inclusive of all values [which] interprets, develops, and potentiates the whole life of a people. . . . Outside of it no human or spiritual values can exist, much less have value."[239]

For our purposes, fascism is a devolved mode of unitive consciousness in which a radically unified, ultra-national consciousness is
obtained by individuals through an undifferentiated identity with
the state. The state is everything. This is opposed to a representational republic in which national identity is composed of a cultural
mosaic (unity in diversity). Fascism, because it is all-encompassing,
is equivalent to totalitarianism and closely related to ancient monarchies (but not the modern hybrid monarchy/parliamentary system of
the United Kingdom).

A fascist state and a representational republic may seem like opposites, but both seek national unity. And curiously, both seek power
through strength in numbers—a similarity that is worth closer exam-
ination. The 20th century word "fascism" is derived from the ancient
Latin *fasces* meaning a bundle of rods tied around an ax as shown in
the drawing below. The symbol itself is even older, originally from
ancient Greece (Crete), and believed to be one of the oldest Hellenic
symbols period.[240]

The members of a fascist movement therefore conceive of themselves as a tightly wound bundle of people—a group of ultra-nationals—who figuratively chop down whatever stands in the way of their ideology. Compare this with the Great American Seal, which depicts an eagle holding in its talon the 13 arrows symbolizing the joining of the thirteen colonies. The contrast is not as stark as one might think. Both symbols imply strength in numbers. In fact, the symbol of a perched eagle clutching the *fasces*—shown here next to the drawing of the Great Seal of the United States—was a large insignia worn on the cap of 20th century Italian fascist uniforms.

The key difference is that a fascist regime represents a radical reduction of diversity into an undifferentiated oneness; whereas a republic, even as it is dependent upon strength in numbers, retains the notion of diversity of individuals. Moreover, a fascist state implies a purity of nationality, often expressed in a singular purpose or race. *E pluribus unum* (out of the many, one) describes the formation of the political entity called the United States; however, the American states were independent political bodies before *and after* they were joined in union. The states continued to retain local sovereignty over whatever was not under federal jurisdiction.

Great Seal of the United States

Italian fascist symbol on the cap of Italian uniforms in the 1930s under Mussolini

Unsettling as this might be, both "united states" and "fascist states" are means of achieving strength through unity. Both are expressions of Unitive Consciousness.

A republic distinguishes itself from an authoritarian state by its acknowledgment that it emerges from and depends upon individual citizens. The word "republic" comes from the French *république*, the Latin *respublica*, and from *Res,* meaning entity or concern + *publicus* or "concern of the people." The United States Constitution proclaims to represent "We the People," a magnificent intention, but not one that guaranteed long-term success. The founders were very concerned that the republic would lapse into either monarchy or anarchy. If a leader with authoritarian tendencies were permitted to reach the presidency and consolidate power, the republic could collapse. Is Donald Trump that figure? At minimum, it gives us pause to consider the possibility.

MUSSOLINI AND TRUMP

As already pointed out, Trump and Hitler are scarcely comparable. However, there are closer similarities between Trump and Mussolini. Mussolini had a gift for theatre, as does Trump. Mussolini was known for putting on a show while exploiting dissatisfaction among the working class. They both promised to fundamentally change the political culture. Mussolini campaigned on the phrase: *drenare la palude*, which translates as "drain the swamp." Trump adopted the same pledge. But Mussolini moved more aggressively to keep his pledge, firing 35,000 civil servants at the outset, while Trump's strongest action so far has been to issue executive orders to make it easier to discipline or fire federal employees.

Perhaps the most striking similarity between Mussolini and Trump is their extreme self-confidence that approaches almost cartoonish levels. Mussolini, like Trump, relied on his instincts even in the face of contradictory information. He once told a gathering of intellectuals, "Only one person in Italy is infallible." On another occasion he said, "Often I would like to be wrong, but so far it has never happened."[241] Compare this with Trump, who spoke of his own "great and unmatched wisdom."[242] Such displays of overconfidence are always suspect.

Mussolini likely suffered from what has been called the Kruger–Dunning effect, and perhaps Trump does as well. This syndrome applies to people who tend to hold an overly favorable opinion of their own abilities. Not only do such people reach faulty conclusions; their incompetence also prevents them from seeing the errors in their judgment. At the same time, this kind of leader's steadfast self-confidence often comes across to others as charismatic. It is this force of personality that brought them a following in the first place, and it also helps them retain it. With both Mussolini and Trump, there was a tendency among party elites to believe they could manipulate them—that they could be employed as a "useful idiot." But people like Trump and Mussolini are often underestimated. They are too unpredictable to be easily manipulated.

THE IMPORTANCE OF NATIVE AMERICAN INFLUENCE ON AVOIDING AUTOCRACY

Many people think fascism is not possible in America because they are secure in their belief that the United States is the paramount example of freedom and equality for the world. They are convinced that our constitutional system of checks and balances provides a firewall of protection. But the Constitution does not, in and of itself, provide failsafe checks against the abuse of power. We see the proof of this in the fact that other countries have essentially copied the US Constitution only to incur different results. For example, two-thirds of the text from the 1853 Constitution of Argentina was taken directly from the US Constitution—but this did not stop rigged elections in the late 19th century, military coups in the 1930s and 1940s, and the subsequent populist autocracy of Peron.[243]

It is not the US Constitution and its systems of checks and balances that has protected us, at least not solely. Something else—an unwritten set of agreements we inherited from Native America—has been safeguarding our freedoms. Our system depends upon a climate of respectful engagement between the branches of government, and it was Native America that first instilled the notion of respectful Congressional protocol.

It is ironic, in the face of the genocide inflicted upon Native America, that one of the most significant and enduring contributions Native America has made to the United States has been its influence on American political protocol. The original politics of Native America provided a superb example of inclusive, dialogic consensus government. This influenced the founding fathers in their sincere, if ultimately futile, attempt to avoid factions and political parties altogether. But the efforts of the founders did not go for naught.

It was Native American influence on the founding fathers that provided the inspiration for the overall impetus to grow into an inclusive, harmonious society. While America has yet to fully realize this vision, we have generally maintained—compared with our mother country and most of Europe and the world—a more harmonious political body. This climate of respectful engagement has been the major reason that the United States has thus far avoided a fascist takeover. Unfortunately, this climate no longer exists.

In May of 2019, when Trump announced he was exercising an unprecedented form of broad presidential authority to refuse to honor *any and all subpoenas* relating to the Mueller Report, both House Judiciary Chairman Nadler and Speaker Pelosi declared that we had entered a constitutional crisis. But this was never a constitutional crisis in a legal sense. *We were in a crisis of protocol*—and still are— in which the tacit rules of engagement have been run roughshod over by a power-hungry executive in league with a powerful Majority Leader in the Senate. This became painfully obvious during the Trump impeachment trial in the Senate. John Bolton, the author of the book *The Room Where it Happened*, made it clear that he was a first-hand witness willing to testify. Despite the fact that 75 percent of the American people wanted witnesses, according to polls, Majority Leader McConnell successfully prevented any additional witnesses from coming forward. McConnell's actions went against all norms of fairness and common sense. A trial without witnesses and documents is not a trial. But that is what occurred in the Trump Senate impeachment trial. It is no longer hyperbole to say that we are perilously close to losing our republic. At minimum, it was an indicator of two other possibilities:

1. The abdication of Senate responsibility could permanently harm the separation of powers between Congress and the executive branch going forward.

2. The legal counsel for the president, certain powerful senators—and even possibly the Attorney General of the United States—apparently had a corrupt motive in covering up evidence. If the latter is true, look for more abuses in the criminal justice system going forward, and for continuing revelations to surface in the coming months and years. This is a time of great unveiling.

We have fallen a long way from the vision of our founding fathers, who entrusted the ability to try impeachment to the Senate because they considered them to be the more impartial, wise, and deliberative body (similar to the Mohawk and Seneca "Older Brothers"). During the trial, Chief Justice Roberts admonished both sides for failing to remember they are arguing before "the world's greatest deliberative body." Roberts' characterization was a throwback to an era that was no longer the case (if it ever was). The Senate has become a partisan shell of its former self. The checks and balances of the Constitution are no longer providing a safeguard, and really never were. It is *not* the Constitution that will save us. We can save ourselves only if we agree to once again play by the unwritten rules of the game.

THE UNWRITTEN RULES OF DEMOCRACY

The only thing that has kept America from lapsing into tyranny is an informal set of what might be called "gentlemen's agreements." These are agreements to play by the rules of the game, to not deny the legitimacy of one's political opponents, to discourage civil unrest, and to protect and whenever possible to increase civil liberties.[244] Excepting the Civil War era and the past thirty or so years leading up to the Trump administration, we have generally adhered to these rules. As a result, we were successful in intercepting any opportunity for authoritarianism to take root, at least, until now.

Few realize, let alone acknowledge, that the original source of these gentlemen's agreements were Native American political leaders. This began with a delegation of 21 respected Iroquois elders who attended the month-long independence planning meeting organized by the Continental Congress in 1776. It was these elders who suggested important protocol changes that were adopted at the inaugural meeting of the Continental Congress. These practices mirrored the respectful listening that characterized Native council gatherings, and they set the tone for future American government protocol.

There was, however, a shadow side to Congressional congeniality in the early years of the republic because the civility within the congressional body masked the fact that these "gentlemen's agreements" were just that—only among men. Women were excluded from participation, something that was entirely the doing of the founding fathers.

Despite the absence of participation from women and people of color, the American republic still held enough of the Native spirit for the seed of inclusivity to later unfold. Native influence permeated our founders' vision (and the founding documents they composed), setting a tone of respectful engagement that helped prevent autocratic leaders from taking power. The importance of this cannot be overstated. The most important course correction we can do now is to recover respectful listening. This does not mean we have to all agree, but we must listen to our political opponents and be open to new ways of thinking.

ELEMENTS OF DYING DEMOCRACIES

So how dangerous are Trump's trickster ways to our democracy? How close to authoritarianism are we? According to Stephen Levitzky and Daniel Ziblatt, the authors of *How Democracies Die*, four key indicators of authoritarian behavior are:

1. *Rejection of (or weak commitment to) the democratic rules of the game.* This would include threatening to not accept the results of an election, or to cancel them altogether; suspending or violating the Constitution; and considering extra-constitutional means of seizing power, such as military coups, violent insurrections, and so forth.

2. *Denial of the legitimacy of one's political opponents,* including claiming that rivals represent an existential threat (or should be jailed) and are committing treasonous acts.

3. *Toleration or encouragement of violence,* including tacitly endorsing violence on the part of their supporters by refusing to unequivocally condemn it; maintaining ties to armed gangs or militia, or any other organizations that engage in illicit violence.

4. *Readiness to curtail civil liberties of opponents, including the media,* by supporting laws or policies that restrict civil liberties, such as the expansion of libel laws, and threatening to restrict or take legal action against critics and/or the media.

All the items on Levitzky and Ziblatt's list have already occurred in the Trump administration. This is cause for great concern.

I would, however, add a few more items to the above list of symptoms of a dying democracy. The first is *erosion of truth.* There has been a dramatic decay in truth-telling under the Trump administration that could have dire consequences for our future. The second is the disturbing usage of the term "America First" because of its association with white nationalism. The third is the rise of the surveillance state (something that has been occurring in America for some time, but especially since 9/11).

EROSION OF TRUTH

Abraham Lincoln was fond of asking this riddle: "If you call a sheep's tail a leg, how many legs will a sheep have?" Most people would answer "five," to which Lincoln would reply, "Wrong. A sheep has four legs. Even if you call a tail a leg, it is still a tail."[246] The above anecdote is an example of why Lincoln was a great leader. He wanted the people to see the truth. An authoritarian leader, on the other hand, seeks to manipulate the people with falsehoods. Truth is the first casualty of any authoritarian regime.

When society is functioning well, there is no opening for an authoritarian figure to emerge. There must be discontent for an autocrat to gain a foothold. An authoritarian leader takes advantage of the existing cracks in the social order to garner, and then consolidate, power over the masses. The first thing the autocrat does is to create a false narrative, pretending that the problems in a society are larger than they are. Then they offer themselves as the solution. Both are a lie.

If the leader starts out lying and lies long enough, people start to believe it—and the bigger the lie the better, according to Nazi leaders Hitler and Goebbels. In Nazi Germany the primary lie was that international Jewry was the secret world power that started WWI against an innocent, besieged Germany—a war the Germans lost. Thus Hitler's first Big Lie was to accuse the international Jewish community of perpetrating a Big Lie against Germany. This was a classic case of trickster politics: projecting onto the other what you yourself are doing, no matter how absurd the claim. A joke circulated after WWI in which an anti-Semitic man tells another man, "The Jews caused the war." The man replies, "Yes, the Jews and the bicyclists." "Why the bicyclists?" asks the anti-Semite. "Why the Jews?" is the reply.[247]

Unfortunately, the falsehoods of Hitler and Goebbels were no joke and their lies were believed by enough people for Hitler to consolidate power. Like many false or misleading narratives, Hitler's claims were based on partial and outdated facts that were distorted and then repurposed to lend a semblance of plausibility to his argument. His assertion of undue Jewish influence in Europe that harmed Germany was false, but there was a time when Jews did have access to the levers of power because they had found a niche as bankers of the state. In truth, Jewish influence on society had been on the wane for quite some time before Hitler took power. It was the *decline of Jewry* that precipitated the rise of anti-Semitism, according to Hannah Arendt, in her classic book *The Origins of Totalitarianism*. In Arendt's words, "Anti-Semitism reached its climax when Jews had similarly lost their public functions and their influence, and were left with nothing but their wealth."[248] Thus, Hitler was able to exploit a weakness in the social order from which to fabricate lies about the Jews.

Donald Trump began creating his narrative in a similar manner. During his 2015 campaign he exploited old wounds that once had some basis in truth, but this was no longer the case. Trump depicted the country as reeling from crime, when in fact general crime within the US in 2015 was at historic lows (less than half of its peak in the 1990s, a period immediately before the 9/11 attack). Capitalizing on the wound of 9/11, Trump claimed that the country was being invaded by out-of-control waves of violent immigrants, either Mexicans or Muslims, when studies show that illegal immigration was lower in 2017 than at any time since 1971, and violent crime is less likely to be committed by immigrants than US-born citizens.[249]

Since Trump took office, an actual humanitarian crisis has erupted at our southern border, as legal asylum claims, mainly from Guatemala, Honduras, and El Salvador, have skyrocketed; but the administration has consistently misrepresented this as an illegal border crossing crisis when US and international law permits refugees to apply for political asylum. Instead of attempting to increase the capacity to process asylum seekers, the Trump administration has treated the asylum seekers as if they were criminals. They have been locked in cages in unsanitary conditions for extended periods of time, with children often separated from their parents. The administration has consistently distorted the truth, successfully convincing many that we are being invaded by caravans of illegal aliens, not legal asylum seekers. While reasonable people can discuss reforming asylum laws, it is misleading to characterize these existing laws as protecting illegals. These sorts of lies, as journalist Masha Gessen pointed out, were told for the same reason Vladimir Putin lies: "to assert power over truth itself."[250]

AMERICA FIRST AND WHITE NATIONALISM

Trump's blunt style of "America First" has sought to reject refugees and asylum seekers from Black and Brown countries. Trump has also used "America First" as a justification for renegotiating existing trade deals to maximize benefit to the United States. Trump supporters see him as standing up for America's interests as no other president has, particularly with China, and they like his bold, uncompromising attitude. Even critics of the administration have occasionally given Trump some credit for at least attempting to confront China for deceptive trade policies, including theft of intellectual property rights.

There is an historical problem associated with the phrase *America First*, however. The last time the phrase was used was by an organization called the America First Committee, begun in 1940 in an effort to keep America out of WWII. The committee grew rapidly to 800,000 members, but was disbanded a few days after Pearl Harbor was attacked. The America First Committee was composed of pacifists, isolationists, and anti-Semitic Nazi sympathizers, a bit reminiscent of the Know-Nothing Party from the previous century.

Historically, white nationalism has played a significant role in movements that envision America in isolation from the world. While Trump may or may not be a racist at heart, he has undeniably taken on the language of white nationalism in an attempt to gain or maintain support from working class whites. In one case, this resulted in his being formally censured by the House of Representatives for saying that four freshmen congresswomen of color should "go back to the countries they came from." He was referring to Representatives Omar, Ocasio-Cortez, Talib, and Pressley. All four Congresswomen are US citizens, and three of the four were born in the US. (Omar is a naturalized citizen, originally a refugee from Somalia).

Significantly, avowed white nationalists have confirmed that Trump is speaking their language, even as they do not consider him a true white nationalist (because, for one, he permits Blacks and Jews to join Mar-a-Lago, his private club in Palm Beach, Florida). In 2015, as the presidential campaign was just beginning, Derek Black, the godson of the KKK Grand wizard David Duke, said this: "He (Trump) speaks our language when it's useful to him, even if he doesn't really believe it." At the time Black made that statement, he was a young man being groomed for a leadership role in the white nationalist movement. Black later renounced his white nationalist ideology after being exposed to alternative viewpoints from people who did not judge him. This remarkable story of transformation is chronicled in a book by Eli Saslow called *Rising Out of Hatred: The Awakening of a Former White Nationalist.*

White nationalism is, by definition, the idea that people of color are not welcome in the country, that nonwhites are somehow less American. Many Americans, not just white nationalists, mistakenly believe that the United States was, originally, a White, European country. After all, it was a British colony, and its founding fathers were White. But this view is not the whole truth. It ignores the critical contribution of Native America to the founding of the United States, a contribution I have sought to honor throughout this book.

I cannot emphasize enough that the notion of *a White America— that America was a nation created entirely by White Europeans*—is now, and has always been, a falsehood.[252]

The United States of America was formed through a hybrid of European and Native American values. The most sacred principles of liberty and equality were inspired by, if not directly appropriated from, the original politics of America's Indigenous Peoples.

THE RISE OF SURVEILLANCE IN AMERICA

I pointed out earlier that Putin's coming to power in the late 1990s represented the resurgence of authoritarianism in Russia. It also represented the rise of the surveillance state. Surveillance, however, has also been on the rise in the United States. Beginning with the Cold War and especially after 9/11, America has increasingly emphasized surveillance, including of our own citizens. The most important development in the wake of 9/11 was the creation of the Homeland Security Department, which required a massive reallocation of resources. Homeland Security employs over 200,00 people and manages more than twenty-two intelligence agencies with corresponding missions. The primary mission of Homeland Security is to protect the American people from terrorist threats, but the mission has spilled over into securing our borders and conducting domestic surveillance (in coordination with other intelligence agencies). Surveillance of one's own citizens is antithetical to a free society and reminiscent of "Big Brother is watching you" from Orwell's classic book *1984*.

Within two months of 9/11, the Patriot Act was signed, suspending many of the civil liberties of our citizens in a trade-off for greater security. Many citizens, still paralyzed with fear, readily accepted this—and the details of the law received scant publicity. The Patriot Act provided for the indefinite detention of immigrants, gave permission to search a home or business without the owner or occupant's consent or knowledge, and expanded the access of law enforcement agencies to business records. It also permitted the FBI to search telephone, email, and financial records without a court order. Some, although not most, of the Patriot Act provisions have been rescinded after court challenges to their constitutionality. The Patriot Act was originally slated to sunset in 2005, but never has. It has continued to be renewed right up until the present day. The question then becomes: Is the increase in domestic surveillance a welcome mat for an authoritarian leader to emerge?

THE SURVEILLANCE STATE IN THE TRUMP ERA

Unlike Mussolini or Hitler, Trump has been unsuccessful in molding US intelligence agencies into corrupt agents of his will. This has not been for a lack of trying. Trump has done his best to dismantle the US intelligence apparatus. Trump has repeatedly insulted and attacked the FBI, CIA, and Homeland Security. He accuses the intelligence agencies of having a covert agenda—of representing the interests of the so-called *deep state*. Trump openly distrusts the conclusions of his intelligence agencies and accuses them of plotting to remove him from office. His continual accusations against the intelligence agencies, sowing doubts about the integrity of our own government, are precisely what Hamilton warned about.

Trump's disparagement of his own intelligence agencies clearly derives from an instinct for self-protection. His main motivation is to remain in power, and to accomplish that, he must sow doubt about the agencies that are investigating him.

There is a partial truth to Trump's suspicions—and not just because they may genuinely suspect him of wrongdoing—or because the December 2019 Inspector General's report on the origins of the Russia investigation, while finding no political bias against Trump, did find "significant inaccuracies and omissions"[253] on the part of the FBI.

It is true that in the past, intelligence agencies have committed significant abuses of power, particularly when it comes to domestic surveillance. The string of abuses from long-term FBI Director J. Edgar Hoover were legendary. Hoover worked with six different presidents from 1924 to 1972, and with the exception of President Kennedy, whose brother Robert served as attorney general, Hoover maintained close relations with all of them—and in hindsight, too close. His departure led to changes in FBI protocol that included a ten-year term limit for future FBI Directors.

Donald Trump was the first president since Hoover to attempt to establish a personal relationship with his FBI Director, going so far as to ask for personal loyalty according to former FBI Director James Comey's contemporaneous notes. This was later corroborated by other witnesses in the Mueller report. It is therefore doubtful that Trump was ever truly concerned about the abuse of power by his intelligence agencies—and far more likely that he simply wished to be in control of it. Nonetheless, the unfiltered quality of Trump's speech serves a purpose in unveiling aspects of US government that normally would be closed to outsiders.

As paradoxical as it may seem, *Trump is both the worst liar of any American president and a truth teller who reveals what no other president would dare speak of.* This is all part of his bag of tricks. The upside to this behavior is that it offers an opportunity to observe a part of America that would normally remain hidden. Trump is an apocalyptic president in both the modern and archaic senses of the word: He has the potential to be destructive and dangerous, and he also has the propensity to reveal or unveil.

The Bush and Obama administrations before him, like all normal US presidencies, operated in a completely opposite manner. They aggressively protected government secrets. During Obama's tenure, whistle-blowers Edward Snowden and Chelsea Manning came forward to expose the excesses of the surveillance state. Although they claimed to do so for patriotic reasons, the Obama administration aggressively pursued charges against them for stealing and leaking classified information. Obama eventually commuted Manning's sentence, but Snowden remains exiled abroad, accused of more serious crimes.

Ironically, *Trump himself is a whistle-blower,* only he does so without any discrimination. He takes in various conspiracy theories and turns them into material he can use to rile up his base. He has never stopped insinuating that Hillary Clinton has committed crimes. He regularly accuses various opponents of committing treasonous acts. In his mind, it is treasonous to disagree with him. This behavior smacks of totalitarianism, because Trump is equating his person with the state. Alan Dershowitz, legal counsel to the president, had the temerity to imply that this was an acceptable position to take during the Senate impeachment trial. Dershowitz argued that it was okay for the president to pursue help for his own reelection with foreign governments provided he believes his election is in the national interest. It was truly stunning to hear this "legal argument" spoken on the floor of the United States Senate.

In sum, Donald Trump's behavior as president is, at minimum, a flirtation with authoritarianism, if not fascism. At the same time, Trump is a revealer of what is, which gives us a unique opportunity to reassess and change. We are at a precarious moment in our nation's history. But there is still hope for a return to a sacred America.

THE COVID-19 PANDEMIC: ITS EFFECTS AND LESSONS

As I was completing this book, the coronavirus (COVID-19) began its exponential explosion into a worldwide pandemic. In the first half of March, confirmed cases in the United States jumped from 15 to over 15,000, resulting in more than 250 deaths. Italy and Spain both exceeded 1,000 fatalities in March, and by March 20th Italy's death toll was greater than the number who died in China where the outbreak originated. To save lives, a dramatic reduction in economic activity was instituted. After the health crisis passes, the world will still be suffering from the economic fallout.

At first President Trump tried to assure the nation by announcing it might go away soon. This calmed no one. On March 18, the stock market plummeted to lower levels than its closing on January 19, 2017, the day before Trump took office. With the economy in free fall, Trump's chance of reelection seemed unlikely. His cause was not helped by his administration's decision in 2018 to disband the National Security Council's pandemic response team established by the Obama administration. Instead, Trump relegated management of disease outbreaks to lower levels of the bureaucracy. This decision—compounded by his inexplicable refusal of World Health Organization test kits for COVID-19—proved to be fatal errors.

The president also kept changing his stories. After initially downplaying the crisis, he later claimed he knew early that it would be a serious epidemic in the United States. Of course, Trump's various stories in his trickster playbook had worked before because he himself had been the principal agent of chaos. Now, the tables were turned. The president who wielded fear to achieve his own ends was in danger of being upended by something more fearsome: a tiny virus.

The coronavirus also brought into stark relief many of the themes of the Trump presidency. Trump had long fed off the anxieties of the White working class. Therefore it was not surprising when Trump turned the virus into an immigrant, labeling it the "Chinese virus." This became the enemy in a way that all fascist governments require an enemy, real or imagined. If Trump succeeds in uniting the country against a supposed foreign virus, he could win re-election after all.

The flaw in this logic is that viruses do not discriminate. They do not care about nationality, race, or ethnicity. A virus has a simple goal: to reproduce in a host body. If the host immune system is strong, the infectious agent is overcome. If the immune system is weak, the malignant organism can kill by transforming the host body for its own purposes.

In the end, COVID-19 is a change agent. It impacts not only health, but the political and economic environments. When the environment changes, an organism has to adapt. If we survive the disease, we come out stronger. In a similar manner, the country must do more than survive the Trump administration; we need to learn from this and change. We must rethink everything, from the economics of the neoliberal world order to our looming ecological challenges.

Modern virulent viruses such as swine flu, Ebola, and SARS (Severe Acute Respiratory Syndrome) of which COVID-19 is part of, come about due to the dominant way human beings interact with nature. The human species has diminished animal habitats all over the world. It is because of this that humans are increasingly becoming infected with animal pathogens. The only solution for this is to rethink how we interact with the more-than-human world. An original politics that includes nature in our planning, not one that simply dominates her, is imperative.

PART FOUR

❖

Return to Wholeness

"Is it possible that humanity will love life enough to save it?"[254]

—E. O. WILSON
Biophilia Hypothesis

"Whether we and our politicians know it or not, Nature is party to all our deals and decisions, and she has more votes, a longer memory, and a sterner sense of justice than we do."[255]

—WENDELL BERRY
Text from Berry's endorsement of
Charles E. Little's book *The Dying of Trees*

"We ought to recognize that our greatest battle is not with one another but with our pain, our problems, and our flaws. To be hurt, yet forgive. To do wrong, but forgive yourself. To depart from this world leaving only love. This is the reason you walk."[256]

—WAB KINEW
The Reason You Walk

CHAPTER THIRTEEN

Making America Sacred Again:
First Steps

D olores Lewis Garcia and Emma Lewis Mitchell of Acoma Pueblo learned how to make traditional pottery from their mother, the renowned Acoma potter, Lucy Lewis. To make a new pot, they always begin with shards of old pots. This is the traditional way of honoring the ancestors, of bringing the sacred energies of the past into the present.

I find this process amazing—and inspirational—in so many respects. The fragmented shards are repurposed, creating a new whole, and the new pot joins the past and present in an original creation of timeless beauty.

This is a metaphor for what I mean by original politics: ancient wisdom repurposed for today, creating a new wholeness. The shards represent today's fragmented society, cut off from what is most needed—perennial wisdom—in this time of chaos and strife. Our task now is to re-collect how to put our fragmented society back together. We need to make a new pot, a beautiful pot expansive enough to include not only many diverse people, but also all the animals, plants, and minerals of this land. We need to re-constellate this nation from its disparate parts: from all the different colors, religions, ethnic backgrounds, political parties and beliefs. We need to, once again, from the many, make one, and this time not leave anyone out. All men, all women, all people, and all life are created equal. Humanity and nature, including all the elements: earth, air, fire, and water must come together in harmony.

Pottery is a beautiful art form because in the process of its creation, it brings together the whole of life. It takes all the elements—earthen clay, water, air, and fire—to make a pot, and then, according to Dolores and Emma, it is not just a pot but a living being. They say that every pot they make has a spirit. America has a spirit too, and it is one in need of rekindling.

THE NECESSITY OF DIALOGUE

The main reason we are divided in America is not only polarization *between* the parties, or fragmentation *within* the parties; but because of how we think. We think in partial fragments, not in contextual wholes. We have become a fragmented society, as the physicist David Bohm observed, because of the way we think.[257]

No place in the society is more fragmented than the political arena. The game of politics is played in a way that tends to limit perception and narrow our consciousness. Pundits describe competing candidates as running in one or the other lane (of appeal) as if they are on a horse track. Any candidate who speaks from a broader, more inclusive platform is at risk of being dismissed for having no core values.

I often hear people say they avoid politics, but this is impossible. Life is politics. You cannot avoid it or escape it. Politics brings people of different perspectives together; and therein lies the opportunity for growth. The learning curve in politics, as in life, requires listening to those with whom we disagree.

It is not enough to bring people together, however, if we do not listen with open hearts. The problem with much of modern communication is that it just perpetuates existing views. Moreover, in most conversations, at least half of our attention is devoted to thinking of what we are going to say in return; and we respond with our own agenda. In political debate, this is even worse. Participants only listen for the purpose of countering, discrediting, defeating, or exposing a weakness in their opponents.

Dialogue circles, on the other hand, are a wholly different way of communicating. The most important thing in dialogue is listening.

Participants listen for the sake of understanding, not to ready a reply. Because the quality of listening in dialogue is so much better, dialogue does not simply perpetuate the already existing view of the participants.

A good dialogue circle has the potential to make real changes in how the mind works. If you listen to another for the purpose of understanding, there is always a possibility that you will be moved to change your view.

Moreover, a dialogue circle mimics the inclusiveness of nature. A circle is, by its very nature, whole. It is also inherently egalitarian. There is no hierarchy; nobody has their back to anyone else and everyone can see each other's face. In the circle of nature, everything is related, even as there is an infinitely wide array of expression. A dialogue circle is inherently inclusive of diverse points of view; every point of view is welcome.

In Native American council settings or similar talking circles, the speaker holds a staff, feather, or other sacred object, and while holding that, holds the floor. It is understood that the speaker will not be interrupted. Council circles are the reason that rules of no interruption still apply on the congressional floor, even without a talking staff. When off the congressional floor, however, incivility has become the norm.

During the testy, 35-day government shutdown that began right before Christmas 2018, Senator Susan Collins courageously decided to use a talking stick during informal bipartisan meetings held in her office, hoping to alleviate tensions. While these meetings were successful in building consensus, the senators clearly have a learning curve with respect to participating in talking circles. Senator Collins tried to make clear that the person holding the staff has the floor, but at one point in the proceedings, one senator rudely interrupted another. This prompted the senator holding the talking stick to "forcefully deliver" it to the person who interrupted, flinging it with such velocity that it missed its target and ended up damaging a glass elephant on one of Senator Collins' office shelves. It is interesting that an elephant was damaged since this is the symbol of the Republican Party. Those who are without sin should cast the first talking stick at glass elephants? In any case, Senator Collins apparently kept her composure (and perhaps sense of humor) and switched from a talking stick to a rubber ball.[258]

While we cannot expect Congress to regularly meet in dialogue circles, there is nothing stopping ordinary citizens from doing so. In my experience, dialogue circles provide a means for expanding thinking beyond pre-conceived notions, ideas, biases, and prejudices. Moreover, participation in dialogue circles is often healing. The experience of listening fully to everyone in the circle, and of being fully heard in return, is rare in modern life. A dialogue circle evokes the ancient, archetypal mode of story-telling by the fire—the oldest way humankind communicated—which formed the basis of coherent community for millennia. It was the beginning of original politics. It also could serve to renew our path back toward wholeness.

RETURN TO WHOLENESS

Part IV of this book is called "Return to Wholeness." The modern English "health" came from the Old English "haelp," which is also the origin of "being whole, sound, or well." To be whole is to be healed. Thus, I offer this final part in service of healing. To return to wholeness, however, we must reclaim our past and make a frank reassessment of where we are today. That requires us to start at the bottom, accepting and including the unpleasant truths of our past, just as a traditional potter begins by gathering the cow dung they will eventually use to fire the pot.

We know that the nation is divided. But why? What are the underlying issues that brought us to today? One of the issues we have discussed is the exclusion of women from the political process, but we have yet to address other ramifications and consequences of patriarchy. The legacy of patriarchy has been an attempt to control and conquer, rather than to harmonize with nature. This has produced great innovation but has also produced a host of ecological problems.

And unfortunately, the shadow side of patriarchy has been the dual subjugation of women and nature. We are not only at war with each other and with other nations; we are at war with the earth. It is our war mentality that most needs to change.

THE NEED FOR PEACE

The United States currently faces a situation not dissimilar to that of the Iroquois before Peacemaker arrived. The nations that would eventually throw down their weapons, unite, and become the great Haudenosaunee Confederacy had not yet come to terms with their war-like nature, just as America has not yet done. We have to face this truth: The political nation of America was formed through an act of war, rebelling against our mother country; and we have been engaged in one war or another for much of our history ever since, including nonstop military action in the Middle East since 9/11.

Clearly we have yet to recover from the wounds inflicted upon our psyche by a foreign attack on our soil in 2001, the first since Pearl Harbor. While the tragic loss of 3,000 lives was more than ample reason to feel shock, horror, and grief, it is also true that we over-reacted in our military response. We met one day's violent outburst with two decades of war in Afghanistan and Iraq. The result has been 500,000 deaths, approximately half of that toll coming from civilian casualties; 2,500 American soldiers were killed and 20,000 American warriors came home wounded, with countless cases of post-traumatic stress.

The beating of the war drums that led to the Gulf War was nothing new, of course; nor was it unique to America. Governments everywhere have always employed the mechanisms of fear and hatred toward the enemy in order to garner support for war efforts. It is the only way to get soldiers to willingly kill; and the only way the public supports military action.

FEAR AND VIOLENCE

America's destiny is to embrace unity in diversity, but there is much resistance to that sacred purpose today, in part because our government is fomenting fear and division. The root cause of war is fear. Fear separates. It contracts our hearts and sends our brains into a fight-or-flight response. It limits our ability to think rationally. Fear makes us reactive, and it can also make us susceptible to manipulation and misinformation, a hallmark of war propaganda.

Trump's rhetoric has clearly fomented acts of violence, serving to divide us. However, our vulnerability to fear preceded him; he merely identified something that was already there in our cultural psyche and effectively exploited it. Before Trump, there were Americans who feared Muslim terrorism and immigrants. Trump fanned the flames that already existed.

After 9/11, many Americans were caught up in a fight-or-flight response; we could not think clearly, and thus conflated radical terrorism with the religion of Islam. Islam, as George W. Bush understood, is at its core a religion of peace—as distinct from radicalized terrorism as white nationalism is from mainstream Christianity. *Salaam* (the Arabic word for peace) and Islam are related words. Muslims came to America more than a century before the first Protestants, and today make up more than one percent of the American population. Approximately 80 percent of all Muslims living in the United States are US citizens, and more than 50 percent of American Muslims were born in the US.[259] While we have not quite repeated our error of rounding up fellow citizens into internment camps, as we did with Japanese Americans during World War II, we have made American Muslims feel unwelcome in their own country.

We got caught up in a fear reaction that focused our attention on foreign terrorism. This single-minded focus resulted in a drop-off of attention to other potential sources of terrorism, particularly domestic terror perpetrated by white supremacist organizations.[260] Our inattention to white supremacist terror may have been the worst consequence of the two-decade push to eradicate radical Islamic terrorism. In the immediate aftermath of 9/11, the FBI reallocated enormous resources to combating radical Islamic terrorism. But in 2019 FBI Director Wray acknowledged that white supremacist killings now account for the majority of mass killings in America.[262]

White supremacism has, of course, long been a part of America, from our slave-owning past to the creation of the KKK and the implementation of Jim Crow segregationist laws immediately following the emancipation of the slaves. The civil rights legislation of the 1960s did not end white nationalism; it just pushed it into the shadows. It reemerged out of the shadows when Barack Obama was elected president, and President Trump has given cover for white nationalism to come out in the open even more. One gets a feeling that things are now coming to a head. In one horrible weekend in August 2019, just one week after FBI Director Wray issued his warning, there were two consecutive mass killings linked to white supremacist manifestos in El Paso, Texas, and Dayton, Ohio.

America appears to be intractably locked in fear and conflict. But it is not. As the saying goes, the darkest hour is right before the dawn. The elements of transformation are on the horizon.

A Transformation of Consciousness Begins with Restoration of Respect

The opposite of fear is love. Two candidates in the 2020 presidential race talked openly about love—Marianne Williamson and Cory Booker. Booker dubbed his campaign the "Lead with Love Tour." Williamson has long spoken about the need for love in politics and even wrote a book about it called *A Politics of Love*.[263]

Both are right that love is what is needed in politics today. Love is the antidote to fear; only love can rejoin what fear has separated. Fear contracts and closes the heart. Love expands it. To manifest our potential, we must move from fear to love. The capacity for love is neither liberal nor conservative; both Democrats and Republicans would benefit from creating a more loving atmosphere.

However, neither Booker nor Williamson got any traction in the polls. It could be that they are ahead of their time, a harbinger of a better form of politics we are not ready for. It is also probable that we cannot talk productively about love without reestablishing a foundation of respect in our current politics. It makes no sense to add a new floor if the foundation of a house is breaking apart. That is the situation our country is in now. We need to reestablish a foundation of respect first and foremost.

In chapters that follow, I seek to expand our worldview, opening up a new (original) definition of politics that is beyond the current limited definition. In this chapter, I begin modestly, with baby steps for how to restore respectful relations between the parties and then build upon that. I call these baby steps because they can be accomplished without transforming the Western neoliberal worldview. In fact, all these steps depend upon our remembering or restoring something lost, rather than creating something anew. The steps are:

- Return to Regular Order in Congress
- Reintegration of Liberal and Conservative Philosophies as Two Aspects of One Whole
- Reconfiguration of Democratic and Republican Parties
- Recognition of the Shadow Side of Conservatism and Liberalism

So, let us address each of these baby steps in turn. Then we can talk more productively about love.

RETURN TO REGULAR ORDER IN CONGRESS

We can begin with the restoration of regular order in Congress, something that in his dying months John McCain implored Congress to do. Politics without regular order is equivalent to a potter without clay. Regular order is the clay from which a harmonious whole can be shaped.

To use a more common political metaphor, regular order is the process by which the sausage is made. It is how a bill becomes law. It is first assigned to committee(s) where it undergoes deliberation, public hearings, and/or debate before amendments are proposed; then it comes to the floor for a vote. Significantly, regular order gives the minority party a forum to contribute. The acceptance of input from all sources is essential to unity in diversity.

The idea of allowing for minority input came into American politics from Native America. In a Native-American talking circle, all input is welcome. Franklin, Washington, and other founding fathers either participated in these or observed the way council circles operated. What makes a Native talking circle sacred is the quality of listening. Today, however, the breakdown of regular order has been detrimental to both listening and the overall democratic process.

Over the past quarter-century, the majority party has increasingly bullied the minority party in Congress. They do this by not opening bills for discussion or preventing bills from coming to the floor. There are still some bipartisan issues that have been passed, such as criminal justice reform (one of the few bipartisan achievements of the Trump era); but the most difficult issues with the most far-reaching consequences are not being tackled. This would include measures to address the curbing of perpetual war and rampant gun violence, as well as climate change and a host of critical ecological issues that have a profound effect on future generations. For all these reasons, regular order and mutual respect must be restored.

Both sides are responsible for this erosion of the legislative process. The most common way to get around regular order is the reconciliation process—which cannot be filibustered, requires only a simple majority, and allows for a limited amount of amendments. Reconciliation was used by the Democrats to pass Obamacare in the first place (after they lost a supermajority of the Senate).[264] In retaliation, Republicans abandoned regular order in their failed effort to repeal Obamacare. Instead of a normal legislative process of public hearings and committee deliberation, the Republicans used a task force that kept secret the contents of the bill until it came for a vote.[265] McCain, who had made an emotional speech decrying the abandonment of regular order just days before, cast the deciding vote against repealing Obamacare.

Ultimately, the restoration of respectful relations in Congress will require a moral act of courage from the Majority Party Leader of the Senate and/or the Speaker of the House. He or she must willingly give up a measure of power to the minority party if they are to reverse the trend of the past quarter-century.

Reintegration of Liberalism and Conservativism as Two Aspects of One Whole

When functioning properly, liberal and conservative philosophies are two aspects of one whole. For much of the modern era, Democrats have tended to be more liberal and push for rapid change, while Republicans have tended to be more conservative and tap on the brakes, seeking stability. It is in this way that liberals and conservatives can be a healthy complement to each other, as Thomas Paine and Edmund Burke were.

Both liberal and conservative philosophies are necessary for balance. Without liberal progressives pushing for change, Congress would lapse into inertia, doing little or nothing to help the country address social ills or keep up with the times. And without conservatives tapping the brakes, liberals might enact too much change too rapidly. Both liberals and conservatives must recognize that the other philosophy complements their own. They must respect their counterpart, welcoming input from the opposition party. This kind of thinking—respecting opposites as complementarities—is integral to Native American philosophies, particularly medicine wheel teachings that promote wholeness and balance.

Reconfiguration of Democratic and Republican Parties

It is also true that liberal and conservative philosophies have diverged a long way from the centuries-old prototypes of Thomas Paine and Edmund Burke. While this divergence occurred long before Trump took office, the Republican Party has now become the party of Trump. Only a small faction of the party bears any resemblance to the conservative ideology of the past. Principled conservatives have been fleeing the party, and a new version of the party could be gestating. Democrats are a bit more coherent under Speaker Pelosi, but they too are showing signs of fracture. Thus we no longer have a dance of opposites in Congress. We have a *dance of fragments*.

Political psychologist Karen Stenner has identified three distinct factions in the modern Republican Party. The first she calls status-quo conservatism and the second, laissez-faire conservatism. Status-quo conservatives would be comparable to the European conservatism of Edmund Burke I outlined in Chapter 5. This form of conservatism seeks to conserve traditions, and that can include conserving the environment. American conservativism has mostly gravitated toward Stenner's second classification: laissez-faire conservativism, which gives primacy to market forces regardless of the impact upon the environment.

Stenner has also identified a controversial third category, which she calls "conservative authoritarianism." She claims that a certain percentage of American conservatives now favor obedience and conformity over freedom and difference.[266] In light of how many Republicans have fallen in line with Trump, she could be right about this—but I am not comfortable assigning a tendency of authoritarianism to Republicans alone. I believe that people of any political affiliation are subject to authoritarianism's lure under certain circumstances.

Democrats have also become fragmented of late, although Democrats are notoriously difficult to organize into categories. This tendency is what prompted Will Rogers to famously quip: "I am not a member of any organized party. I am a Democrat." The fact that Speaker Pelosi, for the most part, manages to keep the disparate parts of the party together on critical issues is remarkable. Only a few Democrats did not vote to proceed with impeachment, when previously many moderates were opposed to proceeding, although there is increasing tension between the far-left liberal progressive wing that supports Medicare for All and the Green New Deal (an economic stimulus plan to address climate change and income inequality) and the more moderate wing that favors a strengthening of Obamacare with a mix of private health insurance and a public option. The liberal progressive wing of the party gets all the media attention while the conservative Blue Dog wing of the party is considered a vanishing breed. But the Blue Dog Democrats actually outnumber the Democrat Socialists by a significant margin. There are roughly 25 remaining Blue Dog members in the Democratic caucus compared to a handful of Democratic Socialists (technically, Bernie Sanders is an Independent).

The question now becomes: How can these fragmented parts come together to create a more harmonious whole? Can the parties reconfigure themselves, and in so doing rediscover how to cooperate on a bi-partisan basis on the most important and challenging issues of the times? I am particularly concerned about climate change and other pressing ecological issues that cannot be put off any longer.

As recently as the Nixon administration, there was bipartisan cooperation on environmental issues, resulting in the establishment of the EPA and the Clean Air and Clean Water Acts. Now, despite the toxic water in Flint, a similar crisis in Newark, and increased air pollution everywhere due to wildfires (particularly in the Western states), Congress has not intervened in a meaningful way. Bipartisan dialogue, let alone compromise, will not occur until civility and regular order is restored; that is the first order of business. But there is something more: If we are to meet our ecological challenges, liberals and conservatives alike must acknowledge their respective roles in creating our despoiled environment, and adjust accordingly. I turn to this subject next.

SHADOW SIDE OF CONSERVATISM AND LIBERALISM

Both parties share responsibility for our current climate crisis because of their shadow sides. The shadow side of conservatism is protecting the interests of the wealthy, even if the wealthy are industry titans engaged in mass pollution of the environment. The shadow side of liberalism is its nearly unconditional support for scientific and technological progress. Some of my liberal readers may object, wondering, "What is wrong with supporting science?" Science has unquestionably improved the standard of living for people. But science has also resulted in dramatic degradation of our environment, dating back to the push for progress in the Industrial Revolution. Ironically, it is the liberal progressive mentality that has contributed most to the destruction of our environment. Recently, however, it has been liberals (in America) who are trying to clean up the environment—over the objections of conservatives.

Conservatives claim that liberals reflexively rely too much on government regulation to protect us from ourselves. There is some truth in this claim. Government regulation has an important role to play, but regulation cannot be the panacea for all our problems. As individuals and as a society, we must make different, more responsible choices with respect to the environment.

Arguably, it is conservatives who are best suited to protect the environment. The proper domain of conservatives ought to be to *conserve*—and this should first and foremost include the environment. Nothing could be more important. Moreover, an argument can be made that it is a long-standing conservative ethic that encourages individuals to take responsibility—and that old ethic can be repurposed, like an old pottery shard, into making the environment whole again.

Conservatives could—and should—lead on this issue to spur a much-needed change in consciousness. The reason American conservatives do not champion the preservation of the environment, as increasingly green conservatives in Europe do, is explained in part by history. American and European conservatism evolved in different directions. This is not surprising, because their lands and histories are so different. American conservatism is based upon rugged individualism, risk-taking, and free enterprise—a philosophy that evolved in accord with an unimaginably wide continent of abundant resources. The vastness of America is what prompted Jefferson to promulgate the mythos of individual pioneers spreading out across the land to find and tend to their own little plots. This Jeffersonian ideal was only reinforced by Lincoln's Homestead Act and is thus deeply inculcated into the American psyche.

America was the land of opportunity, and Europeans flocked here to take advantage of her seemingly limitless natural resources. In a

land of such plenty, conservatism evolved in a way that did not prior-
itize caring for the natural environment. Hence American conservatism favors market solutions. Europe, on the other hand, produced a
conservatism with more of an ecological consciousness—especially
recently. Europeans who did not flee, but stayed in their homelands,
have a longer history of connection with their land. They appear to
have a more developed sense of place, perhaps in part because the
land mass is smaller and therefore is perceived as more precious.[267]

Today, America must face the fact that we are no longer a wilderness of unlimited potential. The continent has now been largely
settled, and we are approaching an environmental crisis point similar
to what Europe already went through. It was never a viable strategy
to recklessly pillage the land and pollute the water, air, and earth that
we humans (and other animals and plants) depend upon to live. But
now we really must change, or die. Inaction is no longer an option.
This is where I see the greatest potential for change: It is time—past
time—for American conservatism to reset and become more like
European conservatism. If this were to occur, commonality could be
found between conservatives and liberals on critical ecological issues,
as happened as recently as the 1970s.

Both the Republican and Democratic Parties must restructure.
And they must find a way to work together again on climate change
and other critical ecological issues. This is only the beginning of a
much larger process that must occur. Ultimately, politics and the
neoliberal worldview itself will have to be completely re-thought. We
must realign human action with that of the natural world. This will
require rethinking the role of the human and our relationship with
nature, from the ground up (literally). We must entirely rethink the
concept of economic growth, decoupling it from well-being, for there
is so much more to life than economic progress. At present, we are
so addicted to economic growth that even ecological ventures, such
as the Green New Deal, are pitched as economic stimulants. This is
because robust economic growth covers all sins, or so it seems. But

ultimately maximum growth is a mirage. The economy cannot grow infinitely on a finite planet.

In the coming chapters, I explore a different approach in which we reorient our thinking about what it means to be human in integral relationship with the natural world. If we are to change the way we live, let alone the neoliberal world order, we have to change the way we think. We need to change our worldview before we can change our way of life.

CHAPTER FOURTEEN

The Dream of Mother Earth:
A Turtle Island Renaissance

From this point through the conclusion of *Original Politics*, I am asking the reader to consider a new definition of what is politics. Specifically, I am asking the reader to reposition politics as a bridge between the human and more-than-human natural world. To do so also completes a circle back to the beginning of the book, because it helps to bridge the past with the present and future of the land and nation.

Ever since Aristotle defined politics as of the city (the *polis*), a politics that takes account of factors beyond the human realm has been unheard of in the West. However, for our ancient Western forebears, the opposite was true. Our ancestors sought to align all their actions with nature because they had learned this was imperative for physical survival. It is time for us to relearn the same lesson.

To be frank, the political divide between the left and right is no longer the biggest challenge America faces. It is the divide between corporate interests and the interests of living organisms that should concern us most.[269] The biosphere continues to be divided into profit opportunities; nature is being commodified. As Buffy Saint Marie sang, "Got Mother Nature on a luncheon plate. They carve her up and call it real estate."[270] Placed in this context, the differences between the Republican and Democratic Parties are not as large as they may appear: Both parties are for unlimited economic growth; both are subject to enormous pressure from corporate special interests. And the interests of Mother Earth have been lost in the shuffle.

Native people believe that Mother Earth is alive, and many believe that she dreams. What, then, is the Dream of Mother Earth? I imagine her dream is to manifest what is truly best for *all* of life, not just humanity—and what is best for long-term health and well-being, not short-term profit. She would want her atmosphere intact, serving its purpose of softening warmth and light. She would want her water to be pure and running free; she would want fertile, uncontaminated soils for diverse, healthy crops and trees to grow; and she would want clean air for all her creatures to breathe.

The dream of Mother Earth was once the lodestar of what I have been calling original politics. Human beings once subordinated their will to something larger; they devised their politics based on the vision of what Mother Earth wanted to happen. We Americans are fortunate that a vestige of this ancient way still existed on this continent when the United States was being formed. It was this spirit of original politics, still connected with nature, that influenced Franklin, Jefferson, and other founding fathers to design a modern government based upon natural, unalienable, human rights. Original politics is therefore embedded in the American spirit. Even if it seems obsolete, it is not.

We must return to some version of original politics if we are to confront our looming ecological crises. The North American continent known as Turtle Island by our ancestors is urging us to awaken. The entire earth is urging us to awaken. And the people are awakening—however slowly. Increasingly, human nature is seen not as separate from but co-joined with Earth's nature.

The land retains the energy of what came before. Memories, held in specific sites across this great land, are arising in the modern psyche. Some of these sites have long been sacred places of prayer and ceremony, and these have begun speaking to us again, awakening us to our full potential. But not all of the memories held in the land are pleasant. Some sites contain memories of unresolved pain and violence, and these are calling us to face the truth of our history, such as the 1864 Sand Creek massacre in Colorado. Significantly, when the Arapahoe and Cheyenne were evacuated to reservations in Wyoming and Oklahoma after the massacre, White farmers and ranchers moved into the area of Littleton, Colorado. I do not find it coincidental that this then became the site of the tragic mass shooting at Columbine.[271] If we are to stop the cycle of violence in America, we must make a sincere effort to reconcile with Native American tribes. President Obama began this process in earnest during his administration. That was a very good thing, but needs to continue.

To come to terms with our past and reclaim shadow parts of our national psyche requires a process of truth and reconciliation. After the slaves were freed, or after civil rights legislation ended segregation, the United States did not hold a truth and reconciliation process as was done in South Africa after apartheid. A restorative justice process was used in South Africa, intended to heal victim and perpetrator alike.[272] A similar process can still be held for Native America. During the Reagan administration, Congress took a positive step when acknowledging "the contribution made by the Iroquois Confederacy and other Indian Nations to the formation and development of the United States." The Obama administration took more significant steps toward compensating Indian nations for broken treaties, at least financially. But so much more needs to be done. It is never too late to hold a truth and reconciliation process. If done correctly, the dialogue could not only be profoundly healing; it could offer guidance for how to heal the nation as a whole.

Return to Humility

To be whole again requires humility because we as humans can never totally comprehend or understand wholeness. Wholeness is ineffable and unknowable because wholeness is All There Is. The ancients had a humble phrase to represent this totality. They called it The Great Mystery—a clear acknowledgment of their inability to know it all. Ancient Jews had a similar intent when invoking the Hebrew name for God. YHWH was intentionally written without vowels because the name was too holy to be spoken. Our modern words—Yahweh, God, or Creator—do not hold quite the same power, for they are the exoteric representations of esoteric, unknowable truths.

There is no equivalent expression of wholeness in our Western scientific lexicon, though perhaps the closest parallel might be the Higgs boson, sometimes known as the "God Particle" because it is believed that all elementary particles arise out of the Higgs energy field, where they are given mass. But even the Higgs field, thought to exist everywhere, falls short of the ancient concepts of wholeness. Other scientific notions of wholeness, such as a *Theory of Everything*, or TOE, are fitting only in the sense of knowing one's toe and confusing it for the whole body. We will never know everything, so why pretend otherwise? It is human arrogance that has taken us to the precipice of destruction. It is time, therefore, for a different approach.

STANCE, NOT STRATEGY

My goal herein is not to provide a neat summary of logical arguments, nor to posit final answers, but instead, to speak from my heart. Many of the political problems we face are caused by an excess of rational thought and not enough heart. As I speak from my heart, I am speaking to a better future, but not trying to precisely predict what that future will be or when it will come—for that would be foolish. I am instead recommending a shift in direction—the change I believe is necessary for the next generations of humanity to thrive together with all other species on Earth.

We must begin by acknowledging the gravity of the present situation. While we do not even know how many species there are on this planet, we do know that the current rate of species loss is rapidly increasing, at a rate approximately 1000 to 10,000 times faster than normal. The need for a course correction is obvious. Exactly how to do it is not. But we can make an important start by shifting away from using our human intelligence to dominate the rest of creation and can instead follow nature's intelligence. The planet does not revolve around humanity, much as we might imagine it does. Everything contributes to the whole. Everything has a right to exist.

I have pointed out that politicians can be narcissists. Ultimately, however, our politicians are but a reflection of ourselves. Their consciousness reflects our own. In the same way, our government also mirrors what We, the People have allowed to be done to our environment. As our water, air, and soil have eroded, so have our systems of government. This is why I believe *We, the People* have more power than we realize. When we change, so will our external circumstances.

Where, then, do we go from here? Do we go back to normal, whatever that is? Or do we redesign the world order in a more equitable way, whatever that is? The second option seems better, but may not be currently feasible. Our systems are now collapsing. We are in too much tumult to effectively redesign the world order. If this is so, then what? How we deal with this present state of affairs is critical. Perhaps there is another, more creative way to address our situation— by dancing with the chaos, understanding that it is transitory—that this, too, shall pass. I wholeheartedly agree with Nora Bateson, who proposed that "the practice of stance, not strategy, is next." She goes on to explain:

> While the tendency is to contemplate replacement forms of order, it may be more appropriate now to consider how to prepare to be in chaos more creatively. Re-envisioning order is pre-emptive, and in a sense, off-topic. Systems as we know them are in transformation. Ecological, economic, political, and cultural diagrams are washing off the page. Like martial arts masters, to be in this transformation calls for increasing sensitivity and responsiveness within the momentum and chaos of this era. So, the question now is not 'what is better than democracy?' but 'how can . . . [we] adjust to everything we know as normal melting into new opportunities to be better humans?'[273]

REMEMBERING WHAT IT IS TO BE HUMAN

Bateson's words are wise. Now is not the time to try to replace chaos with some sort of order, for that would be premature. I believe we are being called to relearn how to move with the flux of nature, a dynamic flux we have been vainly trying to control. Now is *not* the time for humanity to reassert control over nature, but to remember what it means to be human, humbly finding our place within the circle of all beings.

An original politics requires us to radically redefine what it means to be human—not by our differences *from* the rest of creation—but by our interdependence. Original politics no longer separates the future of humanity from the future of the earth. We humans are a microcosm of the macrocosm, embedded in the Great Mystery, dependent upon and related to all of creation. We can never prevail in forging a pathway for humanity that is separate and independent of nature; so, we should simply cease trying.

The ancients knew how interconnected we were with the elements and considered it a great blessing. They knew that none of us could be alive without the warmth and light of the sun; the sacred breath given out by the trees (which we humans and other mammals return to them); the living soil we stand upon; the water in the clouds, under the earth, in the rivers, streams, lakes, and oceans—and the living water in our own veins. Our health and well-being is now, and always has been, dependent upon the health of nature. We must recalibrate our needs with the needs of nature if we are to survive and thrive together. We must realign our destiny with that of the earth, and stop trying to usurp nature for human purposes.

The ancients had a concept of action for the greater good. But, ever since Socrates, the greater good has been redefined in terms of what is good for humanity alone. This is why we came to see politics as a strictly human venture. But it is this kind of human-centered thinking that has gotten us into so much trouble. We have abstracted the human experience from the whole, and because of that, we have upset the balance. Therefore, the most important change we can now make is to *give up the idea of politics as a solely human enterprise.*

Giving up on the idea of politics as a strictly human venture—separate from nature—will not solve everything; in fact, it will not solve anything at first. It is not a solution, but it may well open up solutions we otherwise could not have imagined while clinging to our current worldview. What makes me say this? *Because a worldview that has elevated the human as separate and transcendent from the natural world is the root cause of all the seemingly intractable ecological crises we now face.*

We will never solve water pollution while maintaining an attitude that we are the ruler of water and that water is a resource for us to manipulate. The words *solve* and *solution* are water metaphors; they come from water. Water is the universal solvent. She knows how to purify herself if we let her. We can help water by giving her our respect, by showing our appreciation for her as our relative—and water is a very close relative. Our bodies are mostly water, approximately 90 percent at birth and 70 percent as adults. When we honor water, we honor ourselves, and when we despoil water for profit, it only ends up hurting us. We are doomed as a species if we continue to think human problems only impact humans, and problems in nature only impact nature. We are inextricably interconnected with all life, and must remember how to practice a form of politics that includes all. I have been calling this practice *original politics*; but it is only original in the sense of being *so old it is new again.* It is what the ancients knew, and we would be wise to learn from them.

A TURTLE ISLAND RENAISSANCE

The symbol of the Italian Renaissance was the Roman god Janus, the god of doorways, who looked backward and forward. January, the first month of each year, is derived from Janus for the same reason. The early Renaissance thinkers were not trying to come up with something new, but were instead looking back to the classical philosophies of the ancient world to recover the wisdom that was appropriate for their times. We must do the same thing today.

We are on the cusp of a Turtle Island Renaissance, which like the European Renaissance before it, will look backward to go forward. Native Americans could, and perhaps should, have an important role to play in this emergence, as they have long been stewards of the perennial wisdom of this land. For a Turtle Island Renaissance to be impactful, however, it will require a significant portion of the population to awaken to an intimate connection with the land. The message—the dream—of Mother Earth must be heard by more, if not all of us, if we are to make a substantive change.

When I speak of a Turtle Island Renaissance, I am referring to a revival of Indigenous wisdom and also a revival of modern Native American cultures. The negative impacts of colonization upon Native peoples were undeniable and devastating—and these populations still suffer these effects, both through historical trauma and ongoing government policies. The colonists introduced numerous infectious diseases into the indigenous populations that had no immunity for those diseases, including smallpox, bubonic plague, chickenpox, scarlet fever, and tuberculosis. The colonists went on to force Native populations to accept Western education and the English language, and they tried to impose mainstream cultural and religious (particularly Christian) values. Native American people were relocated to reservations; and outright genocide was committed for much of the 19th century. Colonization wiped out 90 percent of the Native populations on this continent. For the survivors, the historical trauma has been real and lasting.

At the same time, Native American culture has been remarkably resilient. Their traditional ways have continued, even though many traditional tribal ceremonies had to go underground for some time. Nonetheless, these ceremonies continue, and are conducted for the benefit of all peoples and all our relations that share the planet. A Turtle Island Renaissance would support, not suppress, these ceremonies.

A Turtle Island Renaissance would also mean that non-Natives, in their own way, would engage in ceremonies that reconnect with the land. Western culture has its own ceremonial traditions, even if most of them have been forgotten or relegated to secret societies. The Essenes, Gnostics, Rosicrucians, Kabbalists, Basques, and Celts all practiced some form of direct communion with divine, universal intelligence. But listening to nature does not have to be esoteric. Anyone can go out into the wild (or their backyard), learn how to quiet their internal chatter, and listen. Nancy Maryboy (Navajo/Cherokee), simply calls this, "going to the natures."[274] If you go to the natures with an open heart, she (Nature) will reveal herself to you. It is this stance of open-heartedness that I am advocating.

Earlier, I explored how Western culture moved away from immersion in nature in favor of objective distance—and pointed out that neither worldview has a corner on the truth. Western and Native ways of knowing are two distinct ways of being in the world. It is important to remember that any worldview enables our ability to see certain aspects of reality, while disabling our ability to see others. A Native worldview is more immersive and participatory; a Western worldview is more detached, seeking greater objectivity. In the immersive worldview, knowledge is obtained through a reciprocal relationship with Nature; in the objective worldview, data is collected through trial and error and scientific experimentation. The latter method is said to be more reliable and reproducible, but both ways of interacting with nature are *science* in the original meaning of the word, which is from the Latin *scientia*, meaning simply *to know*.

Native educator Gregory Cajete (Santa Clara Pueblo) wrote a book called *Native Science*, in which he outlines the creative, participatory process of Indigenous knowledge, demonstrating how it is an equally valid way to learn. Blackfoot elder and educator, Leroy Little Bear, wrote the foreword to the book. Little Bear and Cajete were both participants in groundbreaking, formal science dialogues that brought together Western-trained physicists and Native American elders. David Bohm, the physicist and author of *Wholeness and the Implicate Order*, participated in the inaugural dialogue, held in 1992. These dialogues, originally sponsored by the Fetzer Institute, continued for the better part of three decades. The organization I founded, SEED, sponsored the last 13 of these dialogues under the name *Language of Spirit*, with Little Bear as moderator.[275]

The *Language of Spirit* dialogues were a microcosm of what has been happening in the United States for the past two-and-a-half centuries. This country has been a test-lab for the intersection of Western science and Indigenous ways of knowing. It is not a coincidence that the last century has produced a mode of science that has come full circle, returning to a more participatory way of knowing familiar to Native America. Relativity, quantum, and chaos theory are all predicated upon a radically interconnected world. The modern ecological movement, ignited by Rachel Carson's 1962 book *Silent Spring* that illuminated the dangers of introducing harmful chemicals into the food chain, similarly educated Americans to how the natural world is radically interconnected. I do not find it a coincidence that all of these theories were initially envisioned here, on Turtle Island. They are the harbingers of a Turtle Island Renaissance. They are also the harbingers of an original politics that is not cut off from the larger circle of life.

COMING BACK FULL CIRCLE

The Greek geometrician Euclid imagined that straight, parallel lines would never meet, no matter how far they were extended in either direction. This idea formed the basis for the Western scientific conception of space, until Einstein. Euclid was not entirely correct, of course, because there is no such thing as a perfectly straight line on a curved planet. In a similar way, a renaissance of thought is always possible because divergent lines of thought extending across a curved planet eventually cross. Western leading-edge science has come full circle; it has come back to Native American wisdom, and at just the right time—if we are to avert an ecological collapse.

In invoking collapse, I do not wish to alarm the readers. In fact, in the next chapter, I discuss climate change, but I promise not to lecture or alarm. I have too much respect for my readers. You do not need another person imparting fear of looming destruction. The truth is that we can only be alarmed for so long; our brains are wired that way. We process fear in our amygdala, the ancient, reptilian emotional center of the brain. Our amygdala shocks us into attention, giving us a shot of adrenaline. But our brains cannot sustain the jolt.

The organ that can best sustain emotion is the heart, not the brain, and it is to our hearts we must now turn, allowing them to open, even in the face of fear. The heart can sustain love of nature's beauty, and that will motivate us to restore our ecosystems to health. It is the heart that will allow us to beat with the pulse of Mother Earth. It is love, not fear, that has the greatest capacity to produce lasting change in the world. But it is not just love of humanity we need to rekindle; it is love for all life on Earth.

CHAPTER FIFTEEN

Biophilia: Love of Life and Nature in the Face of Climate Change

Ahummingbird hovering over a trumpet vine flower is heavenly, as is a sunflower turning with the sun, seemingly following his father. But no less miraculous is the lowly dung beetle, who steers his dung in the right direction by following the stars; or the earthworm, named after her mother, faithfully burrowing her tunnels, loosening and aerating the soil to enable plants to access water more easily. So much of life is profoundly mysterious. How does an acorn turn into a mighty oak? Or a human embryo into Abraham Lincoln? There is a hidden order in Nature—a divine plan we cannot see.

Mother Nature's love runs deep; she makes it possible for every organism to flourish. A tree and a human baby are both born out of a dark, damp, womb and grow up toward the light. The lifespan of a tree may be longer, but its development and that of a human baby are similar. A tree progresses from seed to root, bud, fruit, and back to seed again; just as we humans are born, grow, mature, decline, and die. The fruit of a person's life is, hopefully, wisdom. When a person dies, they leave behind the fruition of their words and deeds—the seed thoughts that may sprout in a future generation. To realize this is to glimpse a tiny part of the Great Mystery and to understand that human beings are part of a much larger unfolding than we can possibly fathom.

Humanity is blessed to live on an abundant and resilient planet, with warmth, light, air, water, food, and materials for shelter—everything we need to survive and thrive. Why, then, do we cross Mother Nature, biting the hand that feeds us? We persist in going against natural rhythms: building on cliffsides and floodplains, damming rivers, clear-cutting forests, growing monocultures, and a myriad of other ill-advised behaviors that affect watersheds, spawning habitats, the quality of our air and soil, and biodiversity. We are ignoring nature, the true source of our abundance, and instead pay homage to artificial substitutes: money, oil, material possessions, prestige, and the like. We drill offshore, searching for a pot of black gold to fuel our material desires and risk the despoiling of waters and all that live there to make our fortune—even as our bodies ourselves are made of, and dependent upon, clean water.

We do all these things because we have accepted the myth of human linear progress, the central organizing story of Western humanity in the past millennium. The idea that humanity must continually progress justifies our subjugation of the wilderness and domestication of the planet. We, and by "we," I mean only mainstream Western culture, have roundly rejected an earlier story—one of nature as a sacred hoop of wholeness—and instead adopted a story of nature as raw material to be shaped by human hands, serving human progress distinct from nature's progress.

The story of human linear progress does not easily lend itself to gratitude. We no longer give thanks for the gift of being alive and for the elements that sustain us, or at least not as often as we used to. We take our existence for granted; take from Mother Earth without thinking of making an offering in return, show no concern for her replenishment, nor do we offer her our gratitude.

Our human vision of life has become increasingly narrow and limited. Our political, economic, and social concerns are largely human-centric, and sometimes even narrower than that: focused on a tiny smartphone or a slightly larger computer screen (on which this book was written). Joyous immersion in nature is becoming relatively rare. While nearly everyone feels exhilarated when rafting down a wild, rushing river or when glimpsing a majestic eagle soaring above, much of the natural world is ignored or dismissed as irrelevant or boring and sometimes feared or even hated. We routinely kill predators that threaten our pets and livestock, such as wolves and coyotes, and then wonder why the deer are overpopulated; we exterminate insects that invade our crops or houses, never considering that wasps, ants, flies, and even mosquitoes and midges are pollinators; and we attack bacteria and other micro-organisms that live in our soil, depleting it of its vitality.

Ever since we committed to large-scale monocultural farms, we have been conducting an all-out war on our soils. A healthy handful of soil is home to about ten billion bacterial micro-organisms, one million fungi, and scores of insects, nematode worms, and other larger creatures.[276] We honor the eagle, displayed on the Great Seal of the United States, but we ignore the earthworm and other burrowing and crawling ones—that is, when we don't kill them.

The living soil is a good metaphor for cultivating a fertile mind open to growth of new ideas. Make your mind "like compost," wrote the poet Gary Snyder, the "new stuff goes on top . . . turn it over, turn it over . . . wait and water down from the dark bottom . . . turn it, turn it inside out, let it spread through . . . watch it sprout. A mind like compost."[277]

Large scale monocultural farming does the opposite, repurposing living soil for business. Poisonous pesticides are poured into the earth in an attempt to subdue the bugs that could eat up profits; then, we add back fertilizers and amendments to recreate a semblance of what we took away. But soil is our friend, not our enemy. It is not necessary to trick soil into repeatedly producing the same crop. Healthy soils do not need to be plowed or fertilized other than through natural means. A semi-permanent ground cover and mulch will protect them from weeds and build the soil. Instead of sowing seeds in spring, we could sow them in autumn, directly in the field where they would have naturally fallen.

These techniques were all employed by Masanobu Fukuoka, author of *One Straw Revolution*. Fukuoka's approach was considered radical because he advocated what he called "do-nothing" farming. (In actuality, there is plenty of work to do using Fukuoka's methods, but significantly less than either traditional or chemical farming methods.) Fukuoka and his followers produce yields roughly equal to either traditional or chemical farming, but the difference is in the soil. In Fukuoka's method, the soil improves every season; whereas in traditional farming, the soil remains about the same, and in chemical farming the soil becomes depleted and lifeless after a short time.

Fukuoka based his method on nature. Only in our modern age could copying nature be considered revolutionary. It is revolutionary merely in the sense of making a circle (revolution) back to wisdom.

THE EFFECT OF SOIL ON CLIMATE CHANGE

The depletion of our soils, leading to massive amounts of erosion (over 1.5 billion metric tons per year), is a primary reason for drought and increasing temperature. It is also a primary cause of climate change, but you would never know it if you googled "soil erosion effect on climate change," as Charles Eisenstein, author of *Climate: A New Story*, did. All Eisenstein found, as I did when doing the same, were pages and pages of the opposite: *the effect of climate change on soil erosion*. This is because climate change has become the "mother of all causes," according to much of the modern ecological movement. Further, we have fixated on a singular metric: carbon emissions, designating this as the singular root cause of climate change, when it is far from it.

Eisenstein likened our fixation on a singular cause to a war mentality, the same mentality that identifies a single enemy, and then sets out to eliminate them. We do the same thing with bacterial germs, believing they are solely responsible for disease, despite the fact that most people exposed to germs do not get sick. The desire to avoid contact with bacteria at all costs (overly relying on anti-bacterial soaps, antibiotics, and the like) ends up weakening a person's immune system.[278]

I wholeheartedly agree with Eisenstein, who noted that we have long maintained a war mentality with respect to many aspects of life. This has resulted in a succession of metaphoric wars: War on Poverty, War on Cancer, War on Drugs, War on Terror, War on

Hunger, and now the War on Climate Change.[279] Our war mentality is an outgrowth of a history of perpetual war mentioned earlier. It is also a subset of the story of linear progress I have been outlining: the separation of the real into the abstract in an attempt to study, manipulate, and ultimately conquer nature—a story that deadens us to the living world around us.

Climate science is being sold to the public as settled science. But even if there is a high degree of consensus, the subject is immensely complex. And so, while the data for climate science is real, there has also been an oversimplification of the problem in service of making it suitable for public consumption. Further, our scientific findings are not as infallible or set in stone as we have been led to believe. Contrary to common parlance, scientific theories do not *prove* hypotheses. Theories are not facts as much as *they explain facts*. A solid theory is supported by a considerable body of evidence, but still open to revision and change.

Climate scientists include much more than quantitative measures of carbon emissions in their calculations. They consider deforestation, drought, soil erosion, and biodiversity, among other complex factors. While climate scientists are doing this, I wonder how many are examining all these measures from the perspective of interconnection with each other, with human beings, and with every other living creature on the planet. Like compost, it is time for many of us to turn over our thinking on climate change, and perhaps turn over a new leaf in the process.

None of what I am saying here should be construed as a denial of climate change. Clearly, the natural world is on the verge of ecological collapse. But climate change is not the cause. *Climate change is the result.*

Climate change is the result of years of careless manipulation of the environment, something that could only have occurred because we have severed our emotional connection to the land. We have stopped loving and caring for places in the way we used to do. Instead of caring for the land, we reduced land into an economic resource to be pillaged.

The despoiling of the elements of life is the cause of climate change, not the other way around. Even if we are successful in reducing the increase in temperature on the planet, that will not be enough if we do not address all of the other factors that gave rise to climate change.[280] Soil erosion, contaminated groundwater, and weakened watersheds (from the damming of rivers) are some of the many contributing factors we should be focusing on.

Underlying the despoliation of Earth is the thinking that prompted it in the first place. Western mainstream thought has a sense of entitlement. We believe it is okay to take from the earth as we see fit. Economic progress is our number one priority. Such is the legacy of the neoliberal world order. But Earth is not our personal playground; this planet does not exist to serve human needs alone.

It is time for a radically different approach—a course correction to our thinking that considers all of nature in our decision-making processes. It is time, as I have been saying, for a new definition of humanity—one not based on our supposed separation from nature, but rather on our relationship with the rest of creation. This will facilitate a more harmonious and peaceful life for all. If we start respecting the natural world again, it will resume speaking to us. It is in this manner that we may fall in love with Nature again, and that love is what can save us. Our love of life and affinity with other creatures is the definition of *biophilia* coined by E. O. Wilson. A resurgence of biophilia is what is most needed now.

THE POLITICS OF CLIMATE CHANGE

With the 2020 election around the corner, the political debate on climate change is heating up—but it's mostly a lot of hot air. That's not a joke; it's two. But, seriously, there is a lot of hyperbole on both sides of the climate change issue, and precious little communication, let alone intelligent discourse, between them. Climate science deniers (including President Trump) cynically suggest climate change is a hoax. I doubt they really believe that, but that position allows them to continue business as usual. On the other hand, politicians, activists, and almost all reputable scientists have been exhorting immediate and urgent action, asserting that climate change is the existential crisis of our time. While I have far more sympathy for the latter position, there are problems and blind spots with it too.

I have already made a case for climate change being caused not just by one factor, carbon emissions, but multiple factors. I mentioned soil erosion, contaminated groundwater, and weakened watersheds due to damming of rivers; but I could easily have named a dozen more: the decimation of the Amazon rainforest; destruction of animal and fish habitats; a near annihilation of bees, butterflies, insects, and other pollinators from pesticides in industrial agriculture, among others. While serious climate scientists are doing their best to take all this into account, the political discourse is not so nuanced. Instead, we hear one message over and over again: that we are facing an existential crisis of global warming due to human-made carbon emissions. Period. The question then becomes limited to: How can humanity reduce our output of carbon emissions?

This is a start, but in my view, much too narrow an inquiry. Much of the political discourse focuses on the question of what extent humans cause climate change. But this question is tied to a worldview of humanity as separate from nature. A more interesting question is: *What can climate change teach us?*

One of the things climate change can teach us is to recognize the radical interrelatedness of all nature. Nature is a nonlinear flux—not a billiard table of cause and effects, but an orchestra playing together. It takes careful observation to understand the natural world because it is composed of so many relationships, and relationships upon relationships, all occurring simultaneously.

If any one of us were to make an in-depth study of climate change, we would learn a great deal about life. And while we would undoubtedly still conclude that we are in a climate crisis, we would also see that we are in an even more urgent and multifaceted ecological crisis. Every living being on this earth is connected in a sacred hoop of interdependence. With each spoke of the wheel we lose, we draw closer to ecological collapse. The real crisis we are in is a *worldview crisis*. We are in crisis because our worldview leaves us out of the sacred hoop.

We are also in a *values crisis*. We are in a values crisis because our worldview of separation has led us to *devalue* the sacred elements of life: water, air, and soil, that we, and all creatures, depend upon to survive and thrive. In 1985, the Haudenosaunee elder Oren Lyons participated in a United Nations forum with some esteemed company: The Dalai Lama, Mother Teresa, Senator Al Gore, and Mikhail Gorbachev, to name a few. They came to consensus on one point, which they succinctly encapsulated in four words: *Value Change for Survival*. If humankind, and much of the remaining biodiversity of life, is to survive, we must change our values to honor Nature more than money; otherwise, we will not survive. It is a Cree Indian proverb that says:

> Only when the last tree has been cut down, the last fish been caught, and the last stream poisoned, will we realize we cannot eat money. [281]

It seems clear that the political dialogue in Washington around climate change will never amount to much until we change our values. Climate change could one day be a unifying issue, and needs to be. But for the moment, it only divides us, in large part because we see climate and nature in a peculiarly limited way.

HUMANS ARE THE CLIMATE

We humans are an inextricable part of the Sacred Hoop of life, whether we realize it or not. Humans, like all mammals, breathe in oxygen and breathe out carbon dioxide. We receive oxygen from trees and phytoplankton; they receive our carbon dioxide in return. Trees, phytoplankton, and certain microorganisms in soil make energy through photosynthesis, the process of capturing sunlight and using it to convert water, carbon dioxide, and minerals into oxygen (released into the air) and glucose (stored for food). The seemingly opposite, but deeply reciprocal processes of respiration and photosynthesis sustain all life on the planet. Humans are in a literal *conspiracy* (to conspire means to breathe together) with all life on the planet.

There is no real separation between us and the climate. We *are* the climate. We are made of light, air, water, and earth. We are the microcosm of the macrocosm. We are the weather. The weather and climate move in cycles, and so do we.

Since climate is part of us, we cannot overcome climate change with force. We must instead learn to gracefully move with it. We need to accept it, work with it, unfold with it. In the end, climate change is not our enemy, but our teacher.

REMEMBERING HOW TO TALK WITH THE ELEMENTS

Modern science perfunctorily dismisses the idea that Native peoples, or any human, can communicate with, and thus affect, the weather. It rejects the idea that ceremonial acts of communication with the natural world, such as rain or corn dances, could have any efficacy. The Western worldview precludes the possibility of our interacting with the elements because it renounces the idea that the constituents of life are themselves alive. The reason is understandable, but is it correct?

During the earthquakes and subsequent tsunamis that struck Indonesia, the Indigenous peoples who lived there survived at a far greater rate than those who were non-Indigenous peoples. These *Pribumi*—meaning "first to be on the soil"—were living in remote islands with no communication to the outside world—that is, no electronic (human-media) interface. Yet, when disaster was about to strike, the Pribumi knew it was coming, and sought higher ground. Non-Indigenous people did not, and thousands died.

The reason given stunned Western researchers. The Pribumi claimed they survived because they communicate directly with the elements. This includes wave patterns, but also large animals, such as whales and dolphins, and small animals, such as ants, the latter being closely attuned to the vibration of the earth.

I have personally known many Indigenous people who communicate with the elements. They believe they can, and so they do. On one occasion, about ten years ago, my wife and I attended a deer dance at Taos Pueblo. It was held on Christmas Day, which happened to be very cold and clear, with not a cloud in the sky. We waited for the dance to begin for about two hours. All of a sudden, a single cloud appeared in the unmistakable shape of deer antlers. At that exact moment, the dancers came out, and the deer dance began. I said to my wife, "Now, that is power!" Those that believe they can, do. Those that believe they cannot, cannot. Belief systems are powerful things. If we believe we are separate from nature, then we are. But that does not mean it is so, or that it must remain that way. When it comes to climate science, we in the West should not be so quick to think we are the most advanced researchers. It could be that we have forgotten more climate science than we have learned.

THE LUNGS OF MOTHER EARTH

What would happen if we adopted a worldview that saw the entire planet as a living organism? This would not only be an Indigenous viewpoint, by the way. The ancient Greeks called the earth Gaia, their name for the primordial mother goddess. There are as many names for Mother Earth as there are tribes: Pachamama, Seynekun, Akna, It-Bunoo, Papatunanuku, Papa, are just a few of them. If we saw the entire planet as alive, we might hesitate before damming rivers, which we would see as Mother Earth's ventricles. We might hesitate before cutting down trees, which we would see as cutting off Mother Earth's breath.

To Indigenous peoples, the rainforests are the *Lungs of Mother Earth*. In the last century, we have cut down roughly half the world's rainforests, half of the Mother's lungs. In the past forty years alone, we have cut down one billion hectares of rainforest, about the size of Europe.

When rainforest is chopped down, carbon is emitted into the atmosphere. It is estimated that deforestation accounts for 15 percent of global greenhouse gas emissions. While I do not wish to minimize the impact of that on global warming, my immediate visceral reaction is concern for the jaguars, monkeys, frogs, birds, and sloths that have just lost their habitat—and my next lament is for the reduction in the oxygen supply. Without trees, we would all be wearing gas masks all the time, because trees act as a giant filter for air contaminants, trapping pollutants in the stomata of their leaves. Moreover, trees have a relationship with the photosynthetic bacteria in the soil, and the phytoplankton in the ocean that also produces oxygen. Without the trees, the microorganisms in the soil and the phytoplankton would die too, along with much of life on earth.

THE HEART OF MOTHER EARTH

If the rainforests are the lungs of the earth, the Sierra Nevada de Santa Marta mountains of Columbia—the tallest coastal mountain range on the planet—are the *Heart of Mother Earth*. Indigenous Peoples who live there (Arhuaco, Kogi, Wiwa, and Kankuamo) think so, anyway, and with good reason. A human heart is the central source for the blood that circulates throughout the body, carried by a series of arteries, veins, and capillaries. The Sierra Nevada de Santa Marta mountains are the source of 35 free-flowing, major rivers and over 200 tributaries. These rivers and streams can be likened to Mother Earth's arteries and veins, facilitating the flow of water around the globe.

Unfortunately, the Sierra Nevada de Santa Marta area is now being encroached upon, bulldozed at the base in the Gaira River basin to build roads for the exploitation that will follow unless enough people with influence intervene. Tribal elders are convinced that this proposed development will interfere with the energy grid of the planet. If we adopt the view of the planet as a living organism, it is easy to see how this would be true. For this reason, we must protect these sacred sites, and the Indigenous people who live there.

REFAMILIARIZING OURSELVES WITH NATURE

I hold dear a vision of the world in which humanity treats all of nature with love and respect, as we do our family. Here in New Mexico, my family consists of not only my human and animal relations, but also the rocky mountains and alpine forests; a few precious rivers flowing into wide open valleys, including the rift valley that formed the deep gorge of the Rio Grande; the powerful confluence of the Rio Grande and Red River in the area known as Wild Rivers (now called Del Norte National Monument); Mount Taylor, sacred mountain to the Navajo and the lava fields it gave birth to, along with numerous buttes, some volcanic, that stand like warriors, surrounding and protecting her; the red rocks of the Jemez mountains and the vast Valles Caldera, home to many elk herds, bear, and mountain lion; the Gila river, the last free-flowing (undammed) river in the state, meandering through the homeland of the great Apache chief Geronimo, which, perhaps not coincidentally, became the homeland for the great naturalist, Aldo Leopold, shortly after Geronimo's passing.

I have lived in New Mexico a quarter-century, and my state never fails to surprise me. While mostly arid, we are sometimes blessed with a good rainy season. When that happens, wildflowers suddenly pop out of nowhere—pleasing outbursts of sunflowers, Indian paintbrush, black-eyed Susans, morning glories, yucca and prickly pear flowers, and the jimson weed that Georgia O'Keeffe made famous.

In the high desert, the interrelationship between water and mountains is evident to all with eyes to see. The mountains that look over the wide expanses of valleys protect and nourish them by attracting clouds that then bring the much-needed rains to the parched earth. For millennia, the Indigenous peoples who live here have honored the relation between mountains and rivers, as have people all over the world.

THE DUSTY WORLD OF HUMAN AFFAIRS

The ancient Chinese believed we could understand the whole of nature by closely observing the relationship between mountains and waters. They used the Chinese compound character 山水 (*shan-shui*) to depict that relationship. It is still used today to describe landscape paintings. Gary Snyder explains why:

> There are several surviving large Chinese horizontal hand-scrolls from pre-modern eras with titles something like

"Mountains and Rivers Without End." Some of them move through the four seasons and seem to picture the whole world. Mountains and waters is a way to refer to the totality of the processes of nature. . . . As such, it goes well beyond dichotomies of purity and pollution, natural and artificial. The whole, with its rivers and valleys, obviously includes farms, fields, villages, cities, and the (once comparatively small) dusty world of human affairs.[282]

"The dusty world of human affairs" is what we have come to call politics. The ancient Chinese understood what Native Americans have long understood—that the world of nature and the world of human affairs are inseparable. If we are to create an original politics of love and respect, we must first love and respect the natural world.

CHAPTER SIXTEEN

From Politics to Love:
A Journey From Fragmentation
to Wholeness

L earning to appreciate the biodiversity in nature is the best preparation I can think of for loving and respecting the diversity of
humankind. The human race is composed of different colors of
people who originally came from different lands. The people of these
lands developed religious ceremonies, cultural practices, political
beliefs, and various other forms of unique local knowledge in keeping with their particular territories. All of these ways of living are
valid and should be respected. The five colors of humanity: black, red,
yellow, brown, and white are linked together, as five fingers make up
one hand. We are all five-fingered ones. We are one race of humanity, connected to all creatures on the planet through the five elements:
light, air, water, earth, and spirit. We are all related.

Because we are all related, our lives are interdependent with all
other species. The human race may be unique, however, in imagining that our consciousness—and our sense of agency—is something
that we alone possess, independent from the rest of creation. But
this simply is not so. Our human evolution occurs in concert with
the evolution of nature. Everything, from our inspiration, energy,
creativity, healing, sense of beauty, connection and belonging, and
all our emotions—including love— originate from and are involved
with the natural world. Even love is originally a property of nature,
which is how love renews itself. The spiritual activist and author,
James O'Dea, expressed this eloquently:

> Breathe into your heart so that it opens and empties. Do not
> try to keep it full all of the time. Let it empty. Let it fill. You
> will discover as you do so that you do not have to invent love
> or gratitude, because they are natural forces in a universe that
> could not exist without them.[283]

What a powerful realization—that love and gratitude originate in the natural world! It makes sense, because there is nothing human that did not come from nature, and nothing in nature that is not within us to some degree. We may attempt to outwit, outsmart, or transcend nature, but we cannot. We can never step outside that boundary because it extends to infinity. There is simply no place to transcend to—no place beyond Nature. Even the heavenly realm, whatever or wherever that might be, would in my view still be part of the natural world. The ancient Chinese spoke of human beings as a bridge between earth and heaven. And indeed, we humans are two-legged; we stand upright between earth and sky.

Our two-leggedness leaves us vulnerable in certain respects; a four-legged has surer footing on ice and snow, for instance—but, in another way, our two-leggedness is our greatest gift, because it gives us the ability to bridge the realms of earth and sky. While reaching for the sky, however, we must remain rooted in the earth. Mother Earth is our foundation and support. We must always remember her and take care of her, and insist our politicians do the same, or vote them out.

A Politics That Includes Nature

Gary Snyder began his poem, *Tomorrow's Song*, by saying: "The USA had lost its mandate" … because it "never gave the mountains and rivers, trees and animals, a vote."[284] The idea of including the rights of nature in politics—of giving the mountains, rivers, trees, and animals a vote—is a thought that has been, until now, dismissed as romantic fantasy. This is starting to change, however. Beginning forty years ago, charters have been adopted proclaiming that humans have a moral responsibility not to inflict damage upon other species.

UNESCO adopted the Universal Declaration of Animal Rights back in 1978, and in the past two decades we have seen adoption of The Universal Charter on the Rights of Other Species (2000) and the Universal Declaration on Animal Welfare (2007). Then, perhaps most significantly, in 2015 the country of New Zealand signed into law the Animal Welfare Amendment Bill recognizing animals as sentient beings, and in 2017 New Zealand granted legal personhood to the Whanganui River and all its tributaries, upon petition from the Maori, who now serve as one of the legal guardians of the river in concert with the New Zealand government. The movement to include the rights of elements of nature that are not animals or even plants into our politics and laws, as farfetched as it may seem, is becoming a reality.

I am not suggesting we put a ballot box in front of mountains, rivers, and trees, expecting them to vote; but we might want to consider what we are doing *for them*, and hopefully not just *to them*, in everything we do. We must speak for those that cannot speak for themselves.

What I just wrote sounds right, but actually requires amendment. *The mountains and rivers do speak. We need to remember how to hear them.* Otherwise, it would be meaningless or worse to speak for them.

How, then, do we speak to mountains and rivers? The only thing I know is to go to the things in nature and ask. Ask with humility and an open heart. And then listen. You may get an answer directly, or indirectly. As Jesus is said to have counseled, "Ask and it shall be given to you; seek and ye shall find; knock, and it shall be opened unto you. For every one that asks receives. . . ."[285]

In my own experience, if I open my heart to Mother Nature, she lets me in. There are many avenues for opening the heart. A long time ago, a wise woman advised me to surround myself with the sound of running water—that I would find inner peace if I did. I found this to be good advice, and I have followed it ever since. The movement of water is key to my sense of peace and healing. Why? I believe it is because water speaks the language of the heart.

I feel most alive in the presence of free-flowing rivers, in places like the Sierra Nevada de Santa Marta mountains of Colombia. I believe undammed rivers can open the human heart, and that dammed rivers close off our hearts. One of the most important restorations we can do on planet Earth is to undam the rivers. This would literally be a watershed moment, because it would restore watersheds and all life that surrounds them.

A Politics Based on Natural Cycles

Effective political action must be grounded in what is already unfolding in nature. It is the wise politician who recognizes this, who goes with the tide, never against it. It is through this lens that I have looked at American history, viewing political action in terms of cyclic, natural forces.

We do not typically recognize political cycles in the same way we do financial cycles, weather patterns, and the like; but there are patterns to political change. In this book, I have used a circular model to trace the history of America: from an initial conception created by an encounter of opposite worldviews—in this case, of Western Europe and Native America—followed by a pregnancy period in which both cultures added genetic material to create a new, hybrid country. I chronicled how the original peoples and land of America gave rise to what was to become the United States of America, implanting the seed thought that we should unite the states (then colonies); and, once united, gave birth to a new country through separation from our mother (country).

This was followed by our initial attempt to establish a separate identity—a singular *unitive consciousness*—which, for the founding fathers, meant no political parties or factions (although that did not prove sustainable). Because unitive consciousness could not be contained in one body, it eventually split, amoeba-like, into two separate life forms: the Democratic and Republican Parties. Increasing conflict between the parties over the expansion of slavery into new territories led to our nation's bloodiest war between North and South.

This was followed by a post-Civil War reconciliation that established a creative, if tenuous, partnership between the parties—a *dance of the opposites* with each party reacting to what the other party was doing. This led over the next century to the parties surreptitiously switching places on the dance floor vis-à-vis their Civil War positions. And all of this took us, finally, to the current era of Maximum Diversity. To be clear, we are not just in Maximum Diversity. We are in the degraded (devolved) mode of it. Because we are in devolved mode, cooperation and regular order has ground to a halt, and chaos and disruption (with the threat of authoritarian government) is on the rise. There are also hopeful signs of rebirth, most prominently led by a resurgence of women in politics—in keeping with a seed that was planted by Native American women in the 19th century.

I wholeheartedly believe that the direction of the nation will eventually conform with *what Nature wants to happen*: a Return to Wholeness through unity in diversity—the evolved mode of Unitive Consciousness. Yet, clearly, we are today far from such a goal.

In the run-up to the 2020 presidential election, our society appears to be coming apart. The coronavirus epidemic has interrupted life as we knew it, and large sectors of the economy have been placed on hold. In the past, national tragedies often brought the country together. But this crisis, like the impeachment trial and the upcoming election, is being viewed through a highly partisan lens. The need for reconciliation and healing is urgent.

Traditional Indigenous philosophies recognize that human health and healing is dependent upon a healthy relationship with the natural world. According to Native educator Gregory Cajete, Native healers recognize that "disease was always caused by improper relationship to the natural world, spirit world, community, and/or to one's own spirit and soul."[286] Having a healthy relationship with the natural world means including nature in our decision-making processes. It requires a shift from thinking of humans as superior and transcendent to nature; and instead, seeing humans as an integral part of the whole—interdependent, and ultimately inseparable from nature. In this view, human and nature are one. If we apply this view to politics, everything shifts in a healthy way.

WE ARE ALL ONE

When the East Indian sage Ramana Maharshi was asked, "How should we treat others?" he replied, "There are no others." This is, on the deepest level, true. What we see as other is only a projection of what we have rejected in ourselves. We may feel repelled by certain ideas and perspectives, but we are unwittingly dancing with them, as shadow dances with light, always remaining connected. We suffer to the extent that our thoughts and perspectives feel separate from others and from Nature—and we are healed to the extent we perceive them as emanating from the same source.

The wide variation of political views, acted out on the stage of life, are ultimately different expressions of one whole. They mimic the enormous biodiversity of life here on Earth. Everything on Earth, from the earthworm, to the eagle, mushroom, slug, flapping fish, or sunflower, are all nourished by the same sun, atmosphere, waters, and soil. People with different political views may seem different, or act different, but your thoughts and theirs emanate from the same well of consciousness. There is far more that connects us than separates us. It is important to always keep that in mind.

Once we recognize the truth of how we are all connected, it becomes easier to stand back and look again at people with whom we disagree on one thing or another, including politics. The etymology of the word respect is to "look again." It is a simple concept. If our first impulse is to judge, dismiss, or denigrate the other individual, look again. Everywhere we look is the face of our teacher. We can learn from everyone, even if the only thing we learn is what is a bad example.[287]

Respect is, ultimately, not about judging. To respect someone is to make an effort to understand them—to realize that they too are sacred, an equal part of creation. Vive la différence, as the French say. We are all in the dance of life together.

Moreover, the people who irritate us the most can be our greatest teachers. This includes any politician you might find irritating. If you are a laissez-faire conservative who believes in the authority of free markets, you might be irritated by Senator Sanders or Representative Ocasio-Cortez. But look again. They were elected at this time for a reason. The same is true for Donald Trump. He can be a teacher, too, and not only because of providing what is a bad example. There is something we can learn from the fact that Trump became president at this time.

And so, if he (or any other politician) irritates you, consider it an opportunity to explore: What is it about him (or her) that irritates you? Is it something within you that you believe you have rejected, only to project upon another?

Psychological projection occurs whenever we are uncomfortable seeing in another an aspect of ourselves we think we have overcome, but really have not. If we have totally overcome a fault within ourselves, the other person would not bother us. We would maintain poise and equanimity. This is, of course, very hard to do. Everyone I know has some rough edges yet to be polished. I know I do.

I would be dishonest if I said that Donald Trump does not irritate me on occasion. Okay, frequently. But some of what I see as his negative characteristics (vanity, inflated sense of self-importance, insecurity) are things I have struggled with as a fellow human being. If I had completely overcome these characteristics, I would not be bothered by Trump. He may or may not be an extreme example of these faults. In a way, it does not matter. I need to stand back and look at the man again.

If I give him the benefit of the doubt, I see someone who is, in his own mind, trying to do the right thing. I believe he takes care of himself first and foremost. But even in this, he thinks he is doing the right thing—that everyone, and every country, should look out for themselves first. It could be that he is a complete con-man, and that he has no love for our country, or for anything other than himself and his family, as the man on the Amtrak train told me years ago. Perhaps that man was correct—and clearly there is increasing evidence to suggest he was. However, I do not know for certain. I sense Trump does care, at least to some degree, but simply does not know how to do the job. He is in over his head. He wasn't wrong, however, when he said that past presidents have tried and failed to negotiate with North Korea. He wasn't wrong when he said other presidents have let China take advantage of the United States. He does not know how to change this any better than his predecessors, and unfortunately most of his attempts have only made matters worse. But I still give him some credit for recognizing that a new approach was needed, at least in these two examples given.

In the end, I believe Trump desperately wants to be perceived as successful, if for no other reason than to satisfy his ego. I do not believe that will occur—the majority of historians will almost certainly judge him as one of the worst (if not the worst) and most corrupt presidents. But to the extent that he is trying to succeed, I support his efforts to try. He is probably genuinely hurt by all the negativity thrown at him, and the only way he knows how to deal with it is to strike back. His very name saddles him with that behavioral predilection. He has to be the one who trumps. When someone criticizes him, he is incapable of letting it go. I pray that the president finds peace of mind; that he overcomes his insecurities, does not react to every criticism, and learns to live in a balanced, harmonious way. I support his personal growth, and if that makes me a Trump supporter, then so be it. I am a Trump supporter, if only in that sense.

I could not disagree more with Trump when it comes to his ecological policies, America First policies, or his opposition to asylum seekers fleeing embattled countries. Nothing is more important to me than protecting the environment, having peace between nations, and for America to be a beacon of hope for those in need. I am still moved today, as I was when a child, by the Emma Lazarus poem inscribed upon the Statue of Liberty in New York Harbor: "Give me your tired, your poor, your huddled masses, yearning to breathe free." To me, the Statue of Liberty represents the soul of America and its sacred purpose: to bring all the world's peoples together on one soil and to be a model of unity in diversity. Trump appears to believe the opposite. His family immigrated here not long ago; but now he, and others, want to lock the door behind them.

The Trump administration is trying to end the idea of America as a refuge for immigrants, particularly immigrants of color. They are not only trying to end illegal immigration; they are trying to curtail legal immigration and asylum laws as well. This goes against the sacred purpose of America, and will not succeed. Policies of hate will not prevail, but I do not hate Trump or his strategist Stephen Miller or former strategist Bannon for being the architects of these misguided policies. To hate one that hates makes no sense. To dehumanize one that dehumanizes also makes no sense.

Instead, I am oddly grateful for Trump the trickster, because he has been playing a sacred role in America's unfolding, even as he does not know it. It could be that Donald Trump is the only person who could have played this part. All the painful experiences we are now enduring, from the white nationalist violence, to the kids locked in cages on the southern border, are playing a role in our national awakening. We are awakening to the true sacred purpose of America. And Donald Trump is helping us awaken, however unwittingly.

On a mystical level, Ramana Maharshi is correct. There are no others. Donald Trump is us. Mitch McConnell is us. Nancy Pelosi is us. All of our elected officials are reflections of us. We the people voted them in. They have a role to play in the bigger picture. And so do we. The very least we owe these elected officials is the same respect and compassion every human being deserves. Some may represent the worst of America, but that is a part of America we apparently need to see.

After our 45th president is gone, the nation must not simply go back to normal, but instead aspire to a higher purpose in keeping with the original vision of unity in diversity inculcated by Native America. We must seize this moment, during the Trump presidency and its aftermath, to uncover the deeper truths about America. It is possible to appreciate why America has been a beacon of hope and light—and also acknowledge the shadowy past our country has yet to overcome. To transform our future, we must integrate the lessons from our past. This is our opportunity to do so. It is time to reexamine our values and institutions, preserving what is worth preserving, while enlarging and expanding our original vision as necessary.

One of the ways our original vision has expanded is the inclusion of women in leadership positions throughout society. This includes politics, where there has been a powerful reemergence of feminine leadership. Because we are better served with a balance between the feminine and masculine, we must support the resurgence of the feminine. The drawbacks of an unbalanced patriarchal society have been exposed. If we are to assume a leadership role in addressing the ecological challenges the planet now faces, we must honor women and Mother Earth as the sacred life-givers they are.

Ultimately, we must move, as individuals, and as a country, from a conditioned normal state to our true natural state, reuniting and realigning our political action with the powerful cycles of nature.[288] This is how a new form of original politics will emerge that is not limited by the narrowness of selfish vision.

AND IN THE END, LOVE IS ALL YOU NEED

The 1960s was another divisive time in our nation's history, a time of the Civil Rights movement and the Vietnam War, and also a time when something else was stirring: the psychedelic summer of love in the Haight-Ashbury district of San Francisco and the Woodstock Festival in upstate New York. I was unaware of Woodstock when it happened. I was only 14-years-old at the time and away on a family vacation in Europe. But I ended up living in Woodstock less than a decade later and went into the music business.

One of the pivotal events of the 1960s was the March on Selma that led to the passage of the Voting Rights Act in 1965. Less than 50 years later, the Supreme Court gutted the Voting Rights Act while Barack Obama was our president. Chief Justice Roberts, in announcing his decision, justified it by saying, "Our country has changed." He was not alone; many felt we were living in a post-racial age, demonstrated by our newly elected Black president. Not many saw the backlash that was already happening, a backlash that was at least partly responsible for the rise of Trump.

The 60s were a tumultuous time between the races, not unlike today. The politics of the time were also divisive. President Nixon came under threat of impeachment, and was eventually forced to resign. There was much chaos and strife at the time, but there was also the seeding of something hopeful: a consciousness of peace and love.

The 50th anniversary of Woodstock is now in the rearview mirror. The Woodstock generation is growing old. But something special was born then that never died. There was a certain freeing of the soul. The young men grew their hair long; the hippies returned to the land, living in communes.

Some of the most famous communes ended up locating in New Mexico—the Hog Farm, New Buffalo, and the Lama Foundation, among them. Later, when I myself moved to New Mexico, I wondered why there were so many communes here, a place where Native American culture is still strong. Was that a coincidence? Many Native Americans noticed that the hippies seemed to be imitating them, growing their hair long and living off the land. I don't believe it was a coincidence or a conscious imitation; it was something else. I think the hippies were tuning into the spirit of the land, even if they were not fully conscious of it. I believe it heralded the re-emergence of ancestral spirits—that it marked the beginning of a Turtle Island Renaissance. It was a nascent attempt to live in peace and harmony with each other and the land. It was the spirit of original politics knocking, waiting to be let back in.

REMEMBERING THE VISION OF MARTIN LUTHER KING JR. AND ROBERT KENNEDY

In thinking of the 1960s and how it mirrors today, I am drawn to memories of Martin Luther King Jr. and Robert Kennedy. The two are forever linked through the history of the Civil Rights Movement.

Both men were dedicated to peace and social justice through non-violence, and both were tragically assassinated. But what they stood for did not die.

Martin Luther King was a harbinger of sacred or original politics, a much larger figure than the Civil Rights Movement. His statement that "Injustice anywhere is a threat to justice everywhere," from a letter written in a Birmingham jail cell defending non-violent resistance to racism, was widely published and became known worldwide.[289] His rhetorical question: "Why should we love our enemies?" was answered in a way that served to awaken consciousness. "Returning hate for hate multiplies hate, " he began, "adding deeper darkness to a night already devoid of stars. Darkness cannot drive out darkness; only light can do that. Hate cannot drive out hate; only love can do that."[290] Martin Luther King's vision stretched far beyond the era he lived in. He may have realized that when he proclaimed the day before he was killed: "I've been to the mountaintop . . . I've seen the Promised Land. I may not get there with you. But I want you to know tonight, that we, as a people, will get to the Promised Land."[291]

The assassination of King on April 4, 1968, ignited race riots across the country, with the notable exception of Indianapolis, Indiana. It was there that Bobby Kennedy (in an era before 24/7 news coverage) stood in the back of a flat-bed truck in an African American community and delivered the news of King's untimely death. In a moving speech delivered straight from the heart, Kennedy appealed to the better angels of the grief-stricken crowd. He called for love and compassion, not vengeance, in response to the news.

Kennedy's impromptu speech remains an excellent example of what I have been saying all along—about making politics—and America—sacred again. He said,

> Ladies and Gentlemen: I'm only going to talk to you just for a minute or so this evening. Because . . . I have some very sad news for all of you, and for all of our fellow citizens and people who love peace all over the world. And that is: Martin Luther King was shot and killed tonight in Memphis, Tennessee.

Kennedy went on to say the following:

Martin Luther King dedicated his life to love and to justice between fellow human beings. He died in the cause of that effort. In this difficult day, and this difficult time for the United States, it is perhaps well to ask what kind of a nation we are and what direction we want to move in. For those of you who are black, considering that evidently there were white people who were responsible, you can be filled with bitterness, hatred, and a desire for revenge. We can move in that direction as a country, in greater polarization, or we can make an effort, as King did, to understand, comprehend, and replace that violence, that stain of bloodshed that has crossed our land, with an effort to understand, with compassion and love.

For those of you who are black and are tempted to be filled with hatred toward all white people, I would only say that I can feel in my own heart the same kind of feeling; I had a member of my own family killed, and he was killed by a white man. But we have to make an effort in the United States, an effort to understand—to get beyond, these difficult times. . . . What we need in the United States is not division. What we need in the United States is not hatred. What we need in the United States is not violence and lawlessness, but love, and wisdom, and compassion toward one another . . . a feeling of justice toward those that still suffer in our country, whether they be white, or whether they be black. We can do well in this country. . . . Let's say a prayer for our country and a prayer for our people. Thank you very much.[292]

From Original Politics to Original Love

Original Politics was written because the oldest form of politics in America is the newest form of politics we need today. The most important thing we can do now in politics is to listen to all points of view with an open mind and heart, realizing that everyone has something to contribute to the whole. We are all in this together:

all the people, and all the plants and animals, soil, water, light, and air.

Native Americans originally conducted their council government with the understanding that their actions were nested in the larger whole of the natural world. The people understood that the most intelligent way to live was in accord with natural rhythms of their land—to be in harmony with what Nature wants to happen.

Native American politics is still here in America, not only because Native Americans are still here, but because the spirit of that original politics is forever recorded in the land. The land retains the memory of all that happened before. It was the land that originally spoke through Native Americans and informed their languages and ways of life. The land is still speaking to us now, if only we could hear her. If we remember how to love nature, we can remember how to love each other. Love of nature is the most "original" form of love there is. To truly love humanity, we must have love, respect, and compassion for all there is—every tree, every flower, and every person, regardless of their race, gender, ethnicity, or political persuasion. The best connective tissue of all is love, because love is of the heart; the heart is of water; and it is the waters of the world that give us life. Love is a life-giver that dissolves fear and includes difference. Love is where hate comes to be transformed; it was through love that the Peacemaker persuaded Tadadaho to accept peace. "Peace is not the absence of conflict," counseled Muscogee elder Marcellus Bearheart. "Peace is the resolution of conflict with love."[293]

In the spirit of Martin Luther King Jr., Robert F. Kennedy, and all the ancestors, both Native and non-Native, who have worked for peace, I say a prayer for our country, our people, and for all humanity and all our relations. May we resolve conflict with love. May we treat each other with love and respect from this day forward. May we make America, and all of Mother Earth, sacred again.

Acknowledgments

Iam grateful to all the ancestors who whisper inspiration in my ear, including Grandfather Leon Secatero, Dan Moonhawk Alford, Tobasonakwut Kinew, Paula Gunn Allen, Angeles Arrien, Jerry Honawa, José Villa, and my parents, Joan Parry and Juan Paricio Parry. I give thanks to the inspiration that comes from every source: human, plant, animal, and mineral, light, air, water, earth, and spirit. I am eternally grateful to my wife, Tomoko, and to all those who love and support me, including family and friends, but also to those that have challenged me in various ways, including politicians and previous business associates, for they have helped make me a kinder and more patient person.

Thank you to my agent Bill Gladstone and to Kenzi Sugihara and everyone at SelectBooks for understanding, believing in, and supporting the project. Great thanks to my editors JoAnne O'Brien-Levin and Nancy Sugihara for enabling my thoughts to be expressed in the clearest possible way, and to all those that read whole or partial drafts of the manuscript: Harlan McKosato, Oren Lyons, Stephen Sachs (Muqit), James O'Dea, Bruce Johansen, Sally Roesch Wagner, Ohki Simine Forest, Betty Booth Donohoe, Bill Pfeiffer, Jeffrey Mishlove, Dave Zuckerman, Kennedy Braden, Denise Ames, Jurgen Kremer, Susan Kaiulani Stanton, Michael Two Bears Andrews, Martin Chesler, Tom Polgar, Marlene Simon, Paula Bandy, and Joanna Harcourt Smith. Thank you Alfonso Montuori for opening my eyes to the fact that fascism is also a form of unitive consciousness; and to Carole Rominger for similarly awakening me to the original meaning of apocalypse as a revelation or unveiling. Thank you to Leroy Little Bear, Nancy Maryboy, David Begay, Lee Nichol, and everyone from the SEED dialogues. Thank you to the Taos IONS group for the many scintillating dialogues on the metaphysics of politics and to the Gebser conference folks for the same. Thanks to the folks who joined in a dinner conversation on the Amtrak train years ago. And finally, thanks to Donald Trump for helping reveal the collective shadow of this nation and for his role, however unwitting, of catalyzing a national awakening of our nation's sacred purpose.

Endnotes

Front Matter

1. https://www.onondaganation.org/culture/wampum/george-washington-belt/

2. "Standing Rock" refers to the Dakota Access Pipeline protests that began in early 2016 on the Standing Rock Sioux Indian reservation in North Dakota. Many in the Standing Rock tribe and surrounding communities considered the pipeline and its intended crossing beneath the Missouri River to constitute a threat to the region's drinking water, as well as to the water supply used to irrigate surrounding farmlands. The construction was also seen as a direct threat to ancient burial grounds and cultural sites of historic importance.

3. Faulkner, William. *Requiem for A Nun.* (New York: Random House, 1951), Act 1, Scene 3, p. 73.

4. https://en.wikipedia.org/wiki/Seven_generation_sustainability

Part One: Unitive Consciousness

5. Neihardt, John, *Black Elk Speaks: The Life Story of a Holy Man of the Oglala Sioux.* Told through John Neihardt (Flaming Rainbow). New York. Pocket Books, 1932, p. 164.

6. Kripalani, Krishna. *All Men Are Brothers: Life and Thoughts of Mahatma Gandhi As Told in His Own Words.* Lausanne. UNESCO Publishing. 1958, p. 169.

7. Little Bear, Leroy; Boldt, Menno; and Long, Anthony J. *Pathways to Self-Determination: Canadian Indians and the Canadian State.* Toronto University of Toronto Press. 1984, p. 21.

8. This detail (that Jikonsahseh was asked to help select the men to set up the Grand Council) is not always included in written Peacemaker stories; however, what is included is that Jikonsahseh is named Clan Mother, and it is a historical fact that the Clan Mothers were given the responsibility of appointing the male chiefs, which I detail in Chapter Seven of the book.

9. This story was culled from multiple sources, but mainly from the Smithsonian Museum of the American Indian website. https://americanindian.si.edu/sites/1/files/pdf/education/HaudenosauneeGuide.pdf.

Chapter 1: Original Unitive Consciousness

10. Bragdon, Kathleen Joan. 1996. *Native People of Southern New England, 1500–1650.* Norman. University of Oklahoma Press, p. 29.

11. Pratt, Scott L. 2002. *Native Pragmatism: Rethinking the Roots of American Philosophy*. Bloomington and Indianapolis. University of Indiana Press, p. 88.

12. Sharon O'Brien, American Indian Tribal Government (Norman: University of Oklahoma Press, 1989), p. 37. See Debo p. 19–First Voyage–"A Gentle People" the text of Christopher Columbus first voyage to American in the year 1492 is available on line at http://www.fordham.edu/halsall/source/columbus1.html.

13. The Kogi and Arhuaco Indigenous peoples of Colombia speak of Western society in this manner, as their younger brothers that need guidance.

14. Cajete, Gregory. *Native Science: Natural Laws of Interdependence* (Santa Fe: Clear Light, 2000, p. 95.

15. Dan Moonhawk Alford, a linguist, wrote of his favorite word for Great Spirit (a translation from the Cherokee). in http://hilgart.org/enformy/isss-da3.htm.

16. Private conversation with Leon Secatero, Head Man of the Canoncito Band of Navajo, who was a dear elder to many, including me.

17. Begay, David, & Maryboy, Nancy Cottrell. (1999). Nanit`a Sa` ah Naaghai Nanit`a Bik`eh Hozhoon [Living the order: Dynamic cosmic process of Diné cosmology]. *Dissertation Abstracts International*, 60(05), 1596A. (UMI No. 9930321), p. 312.

18. Thompson, Frank Charles, Ed. The Holy Bible Genesis 1–2. B.B. Kirkbride Bible Co. Indianapolis, 1964, p. 1.

19. Native American wisdom also impacted the Renaissance after first contact, because Native philosophy made its way back across the pond to Europe, and influenced Renaissance thinkers.

20. Da Vinci, Leonardo. (1941). *The Notebooks of Leonardo da Vinci*. (Arranged, Rendered into English, and Introduced by Edward McCurdy). (Garden City, NY: Garden City Publishing) p. 654.

21. Underwood, Paula. *A Native American Worldview. Hawk and Eagle: Both are Singing*. Noetic Sciences Review, Summer, Petaluma. 1990.

22. I was unable to verify this quote frequently attributed to Einstein; thus, I am only saying Einstein purportedly said this.

23. Morley, Julie. *Future Sacred*. Inner Traditions, Rochester, Vt. 2019, p. 2.

Chapter 2: The Seeds of a Uniquely American Character

24. Sachs, Stephen and Johansen, Bruce; Haas, Ein; Donohue, Betty Booth; Grinde, Donald A. Jr. and York, Jonathan, et al. *Honoring the Circle: Ongoing Learning from American Indians on Politics and Society. Vol 1: The Impact of American Indians on Western Society Until 1800*. Cardiff, CA. Waterside Productions, Forthcoming, 2020.

25. Philbrick, Nathaniel *Mayflower: A Story of Courage, Community, and War*. New York, Penguin, 2006.

26. Sachs, Stephen and Johansen, Bruce; Haas, Ein; Donohue, Betty Booth; Grinde, Donald A. Jr. and York, Jonathan, et al. *Honoring the Circle: Ongoing Learning from*

American Indians on Politics and Society. Vol 1: The Impact of American Indians on Western Society Until 1800. Cardiff, CA. Waterside Productions, Forthcoming, 2020.

27. The name Massasoit means "grand sachem." The pilgrims only called Massasoit by his title but he did have another name he was called by his people, and that was Ousamequin.

28. Some sources say Tisquantum was in Europe as short a period as six years. The important point is he lived in Europe long enough to become fluent in English.

29. Johansen, Bruce E. *Forgotten Founders: Benjamin Franklin, The Iroquois, and the Rationale for the American Revolution.* St. Louis, New Blankets, 2016, p. 151. Franklin said, "No European who has tasted Savage life can afterwards bear to live in our societies."

30. Sachs, Stephen and Johansen, Bruce; Haas, Ein; Donohue, Betty Booth; Grinde, Donald A. Jr. and York, Jonathan, et al. *Honoring the Circle: Ongoing Learning from American Indians on Politics and Society. Vol 1: The Impact of American Indians on Western Society Until 1800.* Cardiff, CA. Waterside Productions, Forthcoming, 2020.

31. Other Indian tribes, such as the Pequot, did not enjoy such a long peace. The Pequot war of 1636 was between the Pequot, the Plymouth and Massachusetts Bay Colony, and their Indian allies of the Wampanoag and Naragansett tribes.

32. Philbrick, Nathaniel *Mayflower: A Story of Courage, Community, and War.* New York, Penguin, 2006, p. 99 Philbrick. Full treaty was as follows:

    1. That neither he nor any of his should injure or do hurt to any of our people.

    2. And if any of his did hurt to any of ours, he should send the offender, that we might punish him.

    3. That if any of our tools are taken away when our people were at work, he should cause them to be restored, and if ours did any harm to any of his, we would do the like to him.

    4. If any did unjustly war against him, we would aid him; if any did war against us, he should aid us.

    5. He should send to his neighbor confederates, to certify them of this, that they might not wrong us, but might be likewise comprised in the conditions of peace.

    6. That when their men came to us, they should leave their bows and arrows behind them, as we should do our pieces when we came to them.

33. Relations between the Pequot and the colonists deteriorated far quicker, and resulted in a devastating war that nearly wiped out the Pequot tribe. In that war, the strong relationship between the Pilgrims and Wampanoag resulted in an alliance against the Pequots.

34. Pequot venture is now struggling after falling into debt during the 2008 recession, but initially, it was remarkably successful.

35. MaGee, Maureen and Lieberman, Bruce. "What Schools Teach About Thanksgiving." *San Diego Union Tribune.* November 25, 2009.

36. Pilgrim Hall Museum. Source: Winslow, Edward. Writing in Mourt's Relation and Bradford, William. Source: Of Plymouth Plantation. http://www.pilgrimhall.org/pdf/TG_What_Happened_in_1621.pdf.

37. Marlow, Connie Baxter and Cameron, Andrew. *The First Fifty Years: Freedom and Friendship at Plymouth Plantation.* A Cameron Baxter Film Project. https://first50yrs.wordpress.com/about/

38. https://en.wikipedia.org/wiki/Mayflower_Compact#cite_note.

39. Pratt, Scott L. 2002. *Native Pragmatism: Rethinking the Roots of American Philosophy.* Bloomington and Indianapolis. University of Indiana Press, p. 88.

40. Parry, Glenn Aparicio. *Original Thinking: A Radical ReVisioning of Time, Humanity, and Nature* (Berkeley: North Atlantic, 2015).

41. Weatherford, Jack. *Indian Givers* (Fawcett Books. New York 1988), pp. 121–122.

42. Johansen, Bruce E. *Forgotten Founders: Benjamin Franklin, The Iroquois, and the Rationale for the American Revolution* (St Louis: New Blankets, 2016), p. 53. Johansen notes that perhaps the most absurd account was from Frenchman Joseph Francois Lafitau, who compared the Iroquois to the Romans (something others did too) in a pictorial that showed he never actually attended a council meeting. He depicted the Iroquois council wearing white, toga-like garments and sandals, with short, curly, hair.

43. Sachs, Stephen and Johansen, Bruce; Haas, Ein; Donohue, Betty Booth; Grinde, Donald A. Jr. and York, Jonathan, et al. *Honoring the Circle: Ongoing Learning from American Indians on Politics and Society.* Vol 1: *The Impact of American Indians on Western Society Until 1800* (Cardiff, CA: Waterside Productions), Forthcoming, 2020.

44. Sachs, Stephen and Johansen, Bruce; Haas, Ein; Donohue, Betty Booth; Grinde, Donald A. Jr. and York, Jonathan, et al. *Honoring the Circle: Ongoing Learning from American Indians on Politics and Society.* Vol 1: *The Impact of American Indians on Western Society Until 1800* Cardiff, CA: Waterside Productions), Forthcoming, 2020.

45. Sachs, Stephen and Johansen, Bruce; Haas, Ein; Donohue, Betty Booth; Grinde, Donald A. Jr. and York, Jonathan, et al. *Honoring the Circle: Ongoing Learning from American Indians on Politics and Society.* Vol 1: *The Impact of American Indians on Western Society Until 1800* (Cardiff, CA: Waterside Productions), Forthcoming, 2020.

46. Aristotle. *Politics.* Translation: Jowel, Benjamin. (Kitchener: Batoshe Books, 1999).

47. Williams, Roger. *Key Into the Language of America* Bedford: Applewood), Originally Published in London by Gregory Dexter in 1643.

48. Alford, Dan Moonhawk. "The Secret Life of Language," In *The Great Whorf Hypothesis Hoax: Sin, Suffering and Redemption in Academe* (draft, chap. 7, 2002). Retrieved August 2, 2008, from http://www.enformy.com/dma-Chap7.htm.

49. Pratt, Scott L. 2002. *Native Pragmatism: Rethinking the Roots of American Philosophy* (Bloomington and Indianapolis: University of Indiana Press), pp. 100–102.

50. Sachs, Stephen and Johansen, Bruce; Haas, Ein; Donohue, Betty Booth; Grinde, Donald A. Jr. and York, Jonathan, et al. *Honoring the Circle: Ongoing Learning from American Indians on Politics and Society.* Vol 1: *The Impact of American Indians on Western Society Until 1800.* Cardiff, CA. Waterside Productions, Forthcoming, 2020.

51. Johansen, Bruce E. *Forgotten Founders: Benjamin Franklin, The Iroquois, and the Rationale for the American Revolution* (St. Louis: New Blankets, 2016) p. 46. In addition to Franklin, William Johnson was also a trusted friend, mediator, and advisor to the Six Nations.

52. Different than the modern version of "town hall" as binding decisions were made in town meetings.

Chapter 3: Native American Influence on the Founding of the United States

53. Sachs, Stephen and Johansen, Bruce; Haas, Ein; Donohue, Betty Booth; Grinde, Donald A. Jr. and York, Jonathan, et al. *Honoring the Circle: Ongoing Learning from American Indians on Politics and Society.* Vol 1: *The Impact of American Indians on Western Society Until 1800* (Cardiff, CA: Waterside Productions), Forthcoming, 2020.

54. Sachs, Stephen and Johansen, Bruce; Haas, Ein; Donohue, Betty Booth; Grinde, Donald A. Jr. and York, Jonathan, et al. *Honoring the Circle: Ongoing Learning from American Indians on Politics and Society.* Vol 1: *The Impact of American Indians on Western Society Until 1800* (Cardiff, CA: Waterside Productions), Forthcoming, 2020.

55. Ellis, Joseph. *American Sphinx.* (New York: Doubleday. 1998), p. 119.

56. Sachs, Stephen and Johansen, Bruce; Haas, Ein; Donohue, Betty Booth; Grinde, Donald A. Jr. and York, Jonathan, et al. *Honoring the Circle: Ongoing Learning from American Indians on Politics and Society.* Vol 1: *The Impact of American Indians on Western Society Until 1800.* (Cardiff, CA: Waterside Productions), Forthcoming, 2020.

57. Sachs, Stephen and Johansen, Bruce; Haas, Ein; Donohue, Betty Booth; Grinde, Donald A. Jr. and York, Jonathan, et al. *Honoring the Circle: Ongoing Learning from American Indians on Politics and Society.* Vol 1: *The Impact of American Indians on Western Society Until 1800* (Cardiff, CA: Waterside Productions, Forthcoming, 2020.

58. Ibid.

59. Carl Van Doren and Julian P. Boys, Eds., (1938). Indian Treaties Printed by Benjamin Franklin 1736-1762). Philadelphia: Historical Society of Pennsylvania, 1938, p. 75, italics added.

60. Rollins, James. *The Death Colony* (New York: Harper Collins, 2011). The accuracy of this story is not completely accepted, and thus I characterize it as legend. The author says the story is historically accurate, but it appears in a novel. Because the story is strikingly similar to the details of the Peacemaker story, and Chief Canassatego obviously knew that story, he could have reenacted it, or simply told Franklin the story. In either case, it was this that moved Franklin to include its depiction on the Great Seal of the United States.

61. Albert H. Smyth, Ed. (1905–1907). *The Writings of Benjamin Franklin* (New York: Macmillan, 1905–1907) Vol. III, p. 42.

62. http://www.abrahamlincolnonline.org/lincoln/speeches/gettysburg.htm.

63. Sachs, Stephen and Johansen, Bruce; Haas, Ein; Donohue, Betty Booth; Grinde, Donald A. Jr. and York, Jonathan, et al. *Honoring the Circle: Ongoing Learning from American Indians on Politics and Society. Vol 1: The Impact of American Indians on Western Society Until 1800.* (Cardiff, CA: Waterside Productions), Forthcoming, 2020.

64. Grinde, Donald A. Jr. *The Iroquois and the Development of the American Government. Historical Reflections*, Volume 21, No. 2. The Scholarship of Cultural Contact: Decolonizing American History. Spring 1995, pp. 301–318.

65. Freedman, Russell and Malone, Peter. *The Boston Tea Party.* (New York: Holiday House, 2013).

66. Grinde, Donald A. Jr., "Iroquoian Political Concept and the Genesis of American Government." In *Indian Roots of American Democracy.* Editor José Barreiro. (Ithaca. Akwe:Kon Press, Cornell University, 1992), p. 50.

67. Sachs, Stephen and Johansen, Bruce; Haas, Ein; Donohue, Betty Booth; Grinde, Donald A. Jr. and York, Jonathan, et al. *Honoring the Circle: Ongoing Learning from American Indians on Politics and Society. Vol 1: The Impact of American Indians on Western Society Until 1800* (Cardiff, CA: Waterside Productions), Forthcoming, 2020.

68. Grinde, Donald A. Jr., "Iroquoian Political Concept and the Genesis of American Government." In *Indian Roots of American Democracy.* Editor José Barreiro. (Ithaca: Akwe:Kon Press, Cornell University, 1992), pp. 47–60.

69. Johansen, Bruce E., *Forgotten Founders: Benjamin Franklin, The Iroquois, and the Rationale for the American Revolution* (St. Louis: New Blankets, 2016), p. 135.

70. While the "Indian Wars" can be said to have begun in the 17th century, it was not until the 19th century under Andrew Jackson and the Indian Removal Act that the United States sustained a century-long campaign that aimed at cultural genocide.

71. Underwood, Paula. *Franklin Listens When I Speak: Tellings of the Friendship between Benjamin Franklin and Skekandoah, An Oneida Chief* (San Anselmo, CA: A Tribe of Two Press), p. 44.

72. Grinde, Donald A. Jr., "Iroquoian Political Concept and the Genesis of American Government." In *Indian Roots of American Democracy.* Editor José Barreiro. (Ithaca: Akwe:Kon Press, Cornell University, 1992), p. 50.

73. Addison, Kenneth. *We Hold These Truths to be Self-Evident. An Interdisciplinary Analysi of the Roots of Racism and Slavery in America.* (Lanham: University Press of America, 2009), p. 90.

74. Sachs, Stephen. *Honoring the Circle, The Impact of American Indian Tradition of Western Political Thought and Society*, published in *Indigenous Policy*, Vol XXIV, No 2, Fall 2013.

75. Sachs, Stephen and Johansen, Bruce; Haas, Ein; Donohue, Betty Booth; Grinde, Donald A. Jr. and York, Jonathan, et al. *Honoring the Circle: Ongoing Learning from American Indians on Politics and Society.* Vol 1: *The Impact of American Indians on Western Society Until 1800* (Cardiff, CA: Waterside Productions), Forthcoming, 2020.

76. Stone, William Leete. *Life of William Brant-Thayendanegea: Including the Border Wars of the American Revolution, and Sketches of the Indian Campaigns of Generals Harmar, St. Clair, and Wayne, and Other Matters Connected with the Indian Relations of The United States and Great Britain, From the Peace of 1793 To The Indian Peace of 1725.* Volume 1: Originally published in 1851 (Hardcover book, Palala Press, 2016), p.62.

77. Sachs, Stephen and Johansen, Bruce, Haas, Ein; Donohue, Betty Booth; Grinde, Donald A. Jr. and York, Jonathan, et al. *Honoring the Circle: Ongoing Learning from American Indians on Politics and Society.* Vol 1: *The Impact of American Indians on Western Society Until 1800.* (Cardiff, CA: Waterside Productions), Forthcoming, 2020.

78. Feinberg, Barbara Silberdick. *The Articles of Confederation: The First Constitution of the United States.* Brookfield, Ct.: Twenty-First Century Books, 2002.

79. Seven other presidents were elected after John Hanson—Elias Boudinot (1782–83), Thomas Mifflin (1783–84), Richard Henry Lee (1784-85), John Hancock (1785–86), Nathan Gorman (1786–87), Arthur St. Clair (1787–88), and Cyrus Griffin (1788–89)—all prior to Washington taking office. Hancock also served a term before the Articles of Confederation were ratified.

80. Michael, Peter. *Remembering John Hanson: A Biography of The First President of the Original United States Government* (Amazon. CreateSpace. 2002).

81. Meacham, Jon. *Thomas Jefferson: The Art of Power* (New York: Random House, 2012), pp. 252, 158.

Chapter 4: Preserving the Union for the Long Term: Overcoming Division Through Checks and Balances

82. Chernow, Ron. *Alexander Hamilton* (New York: Penguin, 2005), pp. 222–224.

83. This is not to say that Indian nations never practiced slavery. They were known to take captives from war and make slaves of these people, but this was generally on a temporary basis and there was a process for freeing the slaves to become participants in their society in the future.

84. The idea of a mixed constitution combining elements of monarchy, aristocracy, and democracy goes back to Aristotle, Polybius, and Cicero. Hamilton was almost certainly aware of this.

85. Chernow, Ron. *Alexander Hamilton* (New York: Penguin, 2005), p. 232.

86. Governor Clinton had actually disguised his identity in writing against the Constitution as well, so Hamilton was following suit.

87. Hamilton, Alexander, Madison, James, and Jay, John. *The Federalist Papers* (Mineola, NY: Dover Publications, 2002), Federalist #14, p. 61.

88. Chernow, Ron. *Alexander Hamilton* (New York: Penguin, 2005).

89. Hamilton, Alexander, Madison, James, and Jay, John. *The Federalist Papers*. (Mineola, NY: Dover Publications, 2002) p. 227.

90. Ibid.

91. Hamilton, Alexander, Madison, James, and Jay, John. *The Federalist Papers* (Mineola, NY: Dover Publications, 2002) p. 228.

92. Ibid.

93. Meacham, Jon. *Thomas Jefferson: The Art of Power* (New York: Random House, 2012).

94. https://www.npr.org/2017/05/05/526900818/the-bad-grade-that-changed-the-u-s-constitution.

95. https://www.npr.org/2017/05/05/526900818/the-bad-grade-that-changed-the-u-s-constitution
http://www.nytimes.com/1992/05/08/us/1789-amendment-is-ratified-but-now-the-debate-begins.html.

96. https://www.npr.org/2017/05/05/526900818/the-bad-grade-that-changed-the-u-s-constitution.

97. https://www.npr.org/2017/05/05/526900818/the-bad-grade-that-changed-the-u-s-constitution And Watson has kept on pursuing similar quests since then. In 1995, after realizing that Mississippi never ratified the 13th amendment that abolished slavery, he intervened, and succeeded in getting them to ratify it.

98. Franklin famously said that impeachment would be "favorable to the executive" who had "rendered himself obnoxious," for the only other recourse would be assassination.

99. http://www.oneidaindiannation.com/haudenosaunee-impact-recognized-by-congress/

100. https://www.senate.gov/artandhistory/history/minute/Senate_Censures_President.htm

Part II: Dance of the Opposites

101. Lao Tzu. *Tao Te Ching*. Translators: Gia-Fu Feng and Jane English. New York. Vintage 1997, p.2.

102. Trungpa, Chogyam. *Crazy Wisdom*. Ed. Chodzin,S. Boston. Shambala Publications, 1991 p. 106.

103. Edmund Burke, *A Letter to Sir Hercules Langrishe, Bart., M.P., On the Subject of the Roman Catholics of Ireland, the Propriety of Admitting Them to the Elective Franchise, Consistently with the Principles of the Constitution, as Established at the Revolution* (1792). in *Works of the Right Honourable Edmund Burke* (London: Nimmo 1887), Vol. IV, pp.241–306.

Chapter 5: Dual Aspects of Wholeness

104. Adams Family Papers: An Electronic Archive. https://www.masshist.org/digitaladams/archive/doc?id=L17760331aa Abigail Adams went on to say: "Do not put such unlimited power into the hands of the Husbands. Remember all Men

would be tyrants if they could. If particular care and attention is not paid to the Ladies we are determined to foment a Rebellion, and will not hold ourselves bound by any Laws in which we have no voice, or Representation."

105. Thomas Jefferson to Francis Hopkinson, 1789, available online at: http://etext.virginia. edu/jefferson/quotations/jeff0800.htm

106. Sachs, Stephen and Johansen, Bruce; Haas, Ein; Donohue, Betty Booth; Grinde, Donald A. Jr. and York, Jonathan, et al. *Honoring the Circle: Ongoing Learning from American Indians on Politics and Society.* Vol 1: *The Impact of American Indians on Western Society Until 1800.* (Cardiff, CA: Waterside Productions), Forthcoming, 2020.

107. Ibid.

108. https://www.monticello.org/site/research-and-collections/fraternal-organizations

109. Chernow, Ron. *Alexander Hamilton* (New York: Penguin, 2005).

110. Lepore, Jill. "The Sharpened Quill," The New Yorker, November 6, 2010.

111. I use the term "immediate" loosely, since Paine actually arrived in America desperately ill from the boat ride and took six weeks to recover.

112. Lepore, Jill. "The Sharpened Quill," *The New Yorker*, November 6, 2010.

113. https://www.history.com/this-day-in-history/thomas-paine-publishes-american -crisis. Originally published in Pennsylvania Journal.

114. Levin, Yuval. *The Great Debate: Edmund Burke, Thomas Paine, and the Birth of the Right and Left* (New York: Basic Books, 2014), pp. 5–10.

115. Levin, Yuval. *The Great Debate: Edmund Burke, Thomas Paine, and the Birth of the Right and Left* (New York: Basic Books, 2014), p. 35.

116. Levin, Yuval. *The Great Debate: Edmund Burke, Thomas Paine, and the Birth of the Right and Left* (New York: Basic Books, 2014), p. xix.

117. Burke, Edmund. *Revolutionary Writings.* (Cambridge" Cambridge University Press, 2014).

118. Levin, Yuval. *The Great Debate: Edmund Burke, Thomas Paine, and the Birth of the Right and Left* (New York: Basic Books, 2014).

119. This was the same argument Rousseau made, but Paine did not atttibute Rouseau as his source.

120. Levin, Yuval. *The Great Debate: Edmund Burke, Thomas Paine, and the Birth of the Right and Left* (New York: Basic Books, 2014), p. 50.

121. Levin, Yuval. *The Great Debate: Edmund Burke, Thomas Paine, and the Birth of the Right and Left* (New York: Basic Books, 2014), pp. 72–73.

122. reminiscent of "composthumanism" of Haraway and others.

123. Bateson, Nora. Small Arcs of Larger Circles: Framing Through Other Patterns (Station Offices, Axminster, England: Triarchy Press, 2016), p. 20.

124. Plato. Plato in Twelve Volumes, Vol. 1 translated by Harold North Fowler; Intro- duction by W.R.M. Lamb. (Cambridge, MA: Harvard University Press; London, William Heinemann Ltd., 1966).

125. Levin, Yuval. *The Great Debate: Edmund Burke, Thomas Paine, and the Birth of the Right and Left* (New York: Basic Books, 2014) p. 225.

Chapter 6: The Birth of the Modern Democratic and Republican Parties

126. Donald Trump was gracious upon winning the president election, pledging to heal divisions and "be the president of all the people," thanking Hillary Clinton for her service, and implying that he would not pursue any legal action against her. Since then, however, he directed the Justice Department to renew investigation of Clinton, which, for the second time, amounted to nothing (she was cleared again).

127. Witcover, Jules. *Party of the People: A History of the Democrats* (New York: Random House, 2003), p. 133.

128. Witcover, Jules. *Party of the People: A History of the Democrats*. New York. Random House, 2003, pp. 133–134.

129. The campaign turned nasty when Adams accused Jackson of murdering six members of his own militia; Jackson retaliated by accusing Adams of using public funds to buy a pool table and gamble in the White House; and when Adams accused Jackson's wife (who had been married previously) of adultery, Jackson accused Adams of using prostitutes to gain favor in Russia during his time there as ambassador. The last accusation has an ironic ring in today's news climate.

130. Witcover, Jules. *Party of the People: A History of the Democrats* (New York: Random House, 2003) p. 147.

131. Witcover, Jules. *Party of the People: A History of the Democrats* (New York: Random House, 2003) p. 149.

132. Johnson, Walter. *River of Dark Dreams: Slavery and Empire in the Cotton Kingdom* (Cambridge, MA: Harvard University Press, 2013), p. 26.

133. Johnson, Walter. *River of Dark Dreams: Slavery and Empire in the Cotton Kingdom* (Cambridge, MA: Harvard University Press, 2013, p. 29.

134. Johnson, Walter. *River of Dark Dreams: Slavery and Empire in the Cotton Kingdom* (Cambridge, MA: Harvard University Press, 2013), p. 29.

135. Johnson, Walter. *River of Dark Dreams: Slavery and Empire in the Cotton Kingdom*. Cambridge, MA: Harvard University Press, 2013), p. 29.

136. Venables, Robert. "The Founding Fathers: Choosing to be the Romans." In *Indian Roots of American Democracy*. Editor José Barreiro. (Ithaca: Akwe:Kon Press, Cornell University, 1992) p. 85.

137. Richardson, Heather Cox. *To Make Men Free: A History of the Republican Party* (New York: Basic Books, 2014) p. 7.

138. https://www.mercurynews.com/2019/05/14/california-lawsuits-trump-administration-xavier-becerra-50-times/

139. The highest income tax rate under Lincoln, however, was only 5%.

140. According to the late Grandfather Leon Secatero, at a time when Navajo morale was at its lowest point, they asked a medicine man three times to help them, but each time he refused. Then, finally, he said he would help and to expect a messenger. A lone

coyote then came into the Fort Sumner camp, and circled around the camp. The medicine man said that if the coyote went north or south, they would die at the hands of their enemies. If it went east, they would be permanently stuck away from their territory, but if it went west, they would return home. It went west, and then the US government permitted the Navajo to go home.

141. Personal communication.

Chapter 7: Historical Influences on the Politics of Gender and Race Relations

142. Whitehead, Alfred North. *Science and the Modern World* (New York: NY Free Press, 1925).

143. For further development of this theme, see Gebser, Jean. *The Ever-Present Origin* (Athens: Ohio University Press, 1985) or Parry, Glenn Aparicio. *Original Thinking: A Radical ReVisioning of Time, Humanity, and Nature* (Berkeley, CA: North Atlantic Press, 2015).

144. Wagner, Sally Roesch, Ed. *The Women's Suffrage Movement* (New York: Penguin, 2019), pp. 8–9. During the United States Constitutional Convention, the states were given the authority to determine voting qualifications for their individual state. While almost all of the newly formed states denied women suffrage in the constitutions they created, some states, such as Rhode Island, South and North Carolina, Georgia, Tennessee, and Pennsylvania did not deny women suffrage until after the Civil War. In New Jersey, women and African American men were permitted to vote from 1790 to 1807.

145. Wagner, Sally Roesch. *Sisters of Spirit: Haudenosaunee (Iroquois) Influence on Early American Feminists* (Summertown, Tn., 2001).

146. Wagner, Sally Roesch. *Sisters of Spirit: Haudenosaunee (Iroquois) Influence on Early American Feminists* (Summertown, Tn., 2001), p. 57.

147. The Dream of the Earth is a common phrase among Native Americans and was also adopted by Thomas Berry in his book of the same name. Two good sources for further exploration into the concept are: Forest, Ohky Simine. *Dreaming the Council Ways: True Native Teachings from the Red Lodge*. York Beach. Samuel Weiser, 2000 and Berry, Thomas. *The Dream of the Earth*. San Francisco. Sierra Club Books, 1988.

148. Wagner, Sally Roesch. *Sisters of Spirit: Haudenosaunee (Iroquois) Influence on Early American Feminists* (Summertown, Tn. 2001), p. 34.

149. Stanton, Elizabeth Cady, Anthony. Susan Brownwell, Gage, Matilda Joslyn, and Harper, Ida Husted. History of Women's Suffrage Volume 1. Salem, NH. Ayer Company Publishing. 1985. (Reprinted from a copy in the State Historical Society of Wisconsin Library), p. 70–71. https://www.nps.gov/wori/learn/historyculture/declaration-of-sentiments.htm

150. Stanton, Elizabeth Cady, Brownell, Anthony, Susan B., Gage, Matilda Joslyn, and Harper, Ida Husted. *History of Women's Suffrage* Volume 1. Salem, New Hampshire. Ayer Company Publishers, Inc. Rprint Edition, 1965 (Reprinted from State Historical Society of Wisconsin Library), pp. 456–457.

151. Wagner, Sally Roesch. *Sisters of Spirit: Haudenosaunee (Iroquois) Influence on Early American Feminists* (Summertown, Tn. 2001), pp. 11–12.

152. Gage, Matilda Joslyn. *Woman, Church, & State: The Original Exposé of Male Against the Female Sex* (New York: Humanity Books), p. 84.

153. Sachs, Stephen and Johansen, Bruce, Haas, Ein. Donohue, Betty Booth. Grinde, Donald A. Jr. and York, Jonathan, et al. *Honoring the Circle: Ongoing Learning from American Indians on Politics and Society.* Vol 1: *The Impact of American Indians on Western Society Until 1800* (Cardiff, CA: Waterside Productions, Forthcoming, 2020).

154. Fuller, Margaret. *Woman in the 19th Century.* Reynolds, Larry, Ed. (New York. Norton & Co., 1998) pp. 41–42. Note: Fuller did not exclude unmarried woman who had made a union with God from her highest category of union.

155. De Beauvoir, Simone. *The Second Sex* (New York: Alfred A. Knopf, Inc., 1952).

156. Winifred, Conkling. *Votes for women! : American Suffragists and the Battle for the Ballot* (First ed.) (Chapel Hill, North Carolina), p. 27.

157. https://www.britannica.com/topic/The-North-Star-American-newspaper

158. http://www.loc.gov/teachers/classroommaterials/presentationsandactivities/presentations/timeline/civilwar/freedmen/mott.html
https://en.wikipedia.org/wiki/American_Equal_Rights_Association

159. The state of Wyoming gave women the right to vote a full fifty years before the rest of the nation. This was said to be because Wyoming wanted to induce more women to move there, but other territories tried to do the same, and failed.

Chapter 8: A Country in Conflict: The Civil War Comes Full Circle

160. Goodwin, Doris Kearns. Said during appearance on The 11th Hour MSNBC TV. July 24, 2018. http://www.msnbc.com/transcripts/11th-hour-with-brian-williams/2018-07-24.

161. https://www.conservapedia.com/Fairness_Doctrine.

162. https://www.forbes.com/sites/katevinton/2016/06/01/these15-billionaires-own-americas-news-media-companies/#5c2dcf0d660a.

163. Brooks, David. "*Who Killed the Weekly Standard?*" *New York Times*, December 15, 2018.

164. Taplin, Jonathan. "Rebirth of a Nation: Can State's rights Save Us from a Second Civil War?" (*Harpers*, January 2019).

165. https://www.vox.com/policy-and-politics/2018/11/13/18091646/fbi-hate-crimes-2017. There was a slight decrease in hate crimes from 2017 to 2018, down from 7,175 to 7,120.

166. https://www.vox.com/2018/6/18/17477376/families-belong-together-march-june-30

167. https://en.wikipedia.org/wiki/George_Wallace%27s_1963_Inaugural_Address.

168. Baker, Peter. *The Call of History* (New York: New York Times/Callaway, 2017), p. 11.

169. Goodwin, Doris Kearns. *Team of Rivals: The Political Genius of Abraham Lincoln* (New York: Simon & Schuster, 2005).

170. *New York Times* Editorial, September 30, 2016.

171. The Trump presidency can also be compared to Warren Harding. Harding lowered taxes on the wealthy, had one of the wealthiest Cabinets in American history, was anti-immigrant (particularly toward the Chinese). Harding was also a notorious womanizer. The Harding legacy was similarly tainted by scandal from members of his Cabinet, although not by Harding himself. The most infamous scandal was known as the Teapot Dome Scandal, in which an unprecedented level of corruption was exposed in the federal government. Until Watergate, the Harding administration was considered the most scandal plagued in history. A curious fact is that the Teapot Dome Scandal was responsible for the law that now permits Congress to request and receive tax returns of elected officials from the IRS.

172. Foner, Eric. *Reconstruction: America's Unfinished Revolution* (New York: Harper Collins, 1988), p. 335.

173. https://www.facinghistory.org/reconstruction-era/civil-rights-act-1866

174. Foner, Eric. *Reconstruction: America's Unfinished Revolution*. (New York: Harper Collins, 1988), p. 251.

175. The term "High Crimes and Misdemeanors" is often misunderstood to be equivalent to Felonies and Misdemeanors, but this is a mistaken idea because during the time of the founding fathers, the legal term misdemeanor had not yet been implemented. It is more likely the founding fathers meant something closer to Bad Crimes and Bad Behavior. In Andrew Johnson's case, they were effectively seeking to remove him largely because he had a pugilistic attitude that made him impossible to work with.

176. From CNBC transcript: https://www.cnbc.com/2017/08/15/read-the-transcript-of-donald-trumps-jaw-dropping-press-conference.html

177. https://www.cnn.com/2017/08/15/politics/trump-charlottesville-delay/index.html

178. Taplin, Jonathan. "Rebirth of a Nation: Can State's Rights Save Us from a Second Civil War? *Harpers* January 2019.

Part III: Maximum Diversity

179. O'Dea, James. *Soul Awakening Practice: Prayer, Contemplation, and Action.* London. Watkins Publishing, 2017, p 140.

180. https://www.nobelprize.org/prizes/peace/1990/gorbachev/26100-mikhail-gorbachev-nobel-lecture-1990-2/

181. Sundance Community Journal Vol III, No 1, Winter 79. Based on an address presented before the American Academy of Psychoanalysis, 1977.

Chapter 9: The Apocalypse: The Ending of Our World Order?

182. Gabrielli, Julie. Weaving and Unraveling in Black Dog Times. https://juliegabrielli.com/2016/11/09/weaving-and-unraveling-in-black-dog-times/

183. Meade, Michael. *Why the World Doesn't End. Tales of Renewal in Times of Loss.* Housatonic. Green Fire Press. 2012.

184. To add to the confusion, the term neoliberal is also sometimes called neocon when a conservative is in power, but "neocon" has essentially the same meaning as neoliberal.

185. Keynes, John Maynard. *The General Theory of Employment, Interest, and Money.* Amazon Digital. 2018.

186. Whitehead, Alfred North. *Science and the Modern World* (New York: Macmillan), p. 200.

187. Daly, Herman and Cobb, John. *For the Common Good: Redirecting the Economy toward Community, the Environment, and a Sustainable Future.* (Boston: Beacon Press, 1989).

188. Bateson, Nora. *Small Arcs of Larger Circles: Framing Through Other Patterns* (Station Offices, Axminster, England: Triarchy Press, 2016).
    Bateson said he is dull because "all his mental rocesses are quantitative and his preferences transitive."

189. The Century of the Self Part I. It is also true that Bernays also became the American agent of Sigmund Freud's writings. His uncle's theories were not yet known in America, but Bernays helped make Freud a household name—and not coincidentally—later turned that around to his advantage in promoting himself.

190. Curtis, Adam. *The Century of the Self Part I Video Documentary (Happiness Machines).* Originally broadcast in 2002.

191. Ames, Denise. *Global Economy: Connecting the Roots of a Holistic System.* Albuquerque, Global Awareness Publishing, 2013, pp. 135-175.

192. Schumacher, E. F. *Small is Beautiful: Economics as If People Mattered.* (New York: Harper Perennial, 1989).

193. Ames, Denise. *Global Economy: Connecting the Roots of a Holistic System* (Albuquerque, Global Awareness Publishing, 2013, pp. 145-149.

194. Friedman, Thomas. Foreign Affairs: Big Mac 1. New York Times, December 12, 1996. https://www.nytimes.com/1996/12/08/opinion/foreign-affairs-big-mac-i.html.

Chapter 10: The Turning Point:
The 2016 Election Amid Changes to Society

195. Levitsky, Steven and Ziblatt, Daniel. *How Democracies Die* (New York. Crown Publishing, 2018), p. 40.

196. Tomasky, Michael. *If We Can Keep It: How the Republic Collapsed and How it Might Be Saved.* (New York: W W. Norton & Company, 2019), p. 222.

197. Coppins, McKay. *The Man Who Broke Politics. The Atlantic,* November, 2018.

198. Coppins, McKay. *The Man Who Broke Politics. The Atlantic,* November, 2018.

199. Coppins, McKay. *The Man Who Broke Politics. The Atlantic,* November, 2018.

200. Private communication with Thomas Polgar, a Washington veteran who served under Senator Rudman.

201. Coppins, McKay. *The Man Who Broke Politics. The Atlantic,* November, 2018.

202. Strauss, William and Howe, Neil. *The Fourth Turning: An American Prophecy* (New York: Broadway Books) 1997.

203. Mahatma Gandhi was once asked, "What do you think of Western civilization?" and he replied, "That would be a good idea."

204. Coppins, McKay. *The Man Who Broke Politics. The Atlantic*, November, 2018.

205. According to one of his former aides, Keith Hennessy. https://www.realclearpolitics.com/articles/2013/04/25/george_w_bush_is_smarter _than_you_118125.html

206. https://www.realclearpolitics.com/video/2017/07/05/ny_times_investigates_president _trump_and_the_world_of_pro-wrestling.html.

207. Cohn was gay and died of AIDS-related complications, which is noteworthy only because Cohn had previously pushed Eisenhower into making US policy against admitting gays to the military in the 50s.

208. Tur, Katy. *Unbelievable: My Front Row Seat to the Craziest Campaign in American History* (New York: Dey Street Books (imprint of Harper Collins), 2017.

209. The accuracy of the 2016 presidential exit polls have since been brought into question. According to a later study published by the Pew Research Center, the percentage of white women who voted for Trump was estimated to be 47% compared to 45% for Clinton.

210. Clinton, Hillary. *What Happened*. New York. Simon & Schuster, 2017, p. 111.

211. Astor, Maggie. "How Sexism Plays Out on the Campaign Trail." *NY Times*, February 12, 2019, Front page.

212. DuBois, W. E. B. *The Souls of Black Folk*. (Electronic Text) University of Virginia Library. http://sites.middlebury.edu/soan105tiger/files/2014/08/Du-Bois-The -Souls-of-Black-Folks.pdf

213. Although the 2018 election was the first time that Native American women were elected to Congress, it is not the first time that Native American women have influenced Congressional politics. In addition to the influence of women's councils on the founding fathers, a Comanche woman, LaDonna Harris, then wife of Congressmen Fred Harris, was highly effective in influencing political decision-making. Among other accomplishments, she successfully lobbied Richard Nixon to restore the sacred Blue Lake to the Taos Pueblo Indians.

Chapter 11: The Trickster President:
A Necessary Devolution Before Evolution?

214. Lee, Bandy X, Ed. *The Dangerous Case of Donald Trump: 27 Psychiatrists and Mental Health Experts Assess a President* (New York: Thomas Dunne Books, 2017). In the second edition, there were 37 psychiatrists that contributed.

215. In 1964, the Johnson campaign created probably the most effective political ad ever, coupling a young girl counting the daisy petals she plucked with the ominous countdown to a nuclear explosion; then stating: "The stakes are too high in this election" .... [so] "vote for President Johnson."

216. Pein, Corey. "Magical Thinking," The Baffler, March 4, 2016. https://thebaffler. com/magical-thinking/donald-trump-trickster-god.

217. Hynes, William J, and Doty, William G. *Mythical Trickster Figures* (Tuscaloosa: University of Alabama Press, 1997).

218. This arguably changed when Trump ordered the political assassination of General Soleimani.

219. Pein, Corey. "Magical Thinking," The Baffler, March 4, 2016. https://thebaffler. com/magical-thinking/donald-trump-trickster-god.

220. https://www.tandfonline.com/doi/full/10.1080/19409052.2017.1309780.

221. https://www.google.com/search?client=safari&channel=mac_bm&q=How+many +British+soldiers+died+in+Iraq+and+Afghanistan%3F&sa=X&ved=2ahUKE wihgr3O2rPkAhUVr54KHaVZDL8Qzmd6BAgLEAs&biw=1199&bih=712.

222. Trump did achieve a measure of success in late 2019, since several European countries agreed to up their defense spending. Most of those increases, however, were a result of negotiations done in 2014 during the Obama administration.

223. Only four agencies – the CIA, FBI, NSA, and DNI (Director of National Intelligence) have directly confirmed they came to the conclusion of Russian interference, but the DNI speaks for all 17 US intelligence agencies. Moreover, none of the other intelligence agencies have denied Russian interference.

224. *Wall St. Journal* Editorial. January 4, 2019.

225. https://www.ploughshares.org/world-nuclear-stockpile-report

226. https://www.washingtonpost.com/world/despite-talk-of-a-military-strike -trumps-armada-was-a-long-way-from-korea/2017/04/18/e8ef4237-e26a -4cfc-b5e9-526c3a17bd41_story.html?utm_term=.3e3459f1b2ce.

227. "Who Can Trust Trump's America?" *The Economist*. October, 2019, p. 11.

228. https://www.vox.com/2019/2/18/18229268/pence-europe-viral-clips-speeches -trump-allies.

229. "Read the Whistle-Blower Complaint." *New York Times*, September 26, 2019.

230. "Read the Whistle-Blower Complaint." *New York Times*, September 26, 2019.

231. Baker, Peter. *NY Times*, Dec 10, 2019.

232. https://www.nytimes.com/2020/02/05/us/politics/mitt-romney-impeachment -speech-transcript.html

233. https://www.nytimes.com/2018/05/08/world/middleeast/trump-iran-nuclear -deal.html?action=click&module=RelatedCoverage&pgtype=Article&region=- Footer

234. https://www.nytimes.com/2019/09/21/us/politics/trump-iran-decision.html

235. Slavin, Barbara. "*Qassim Suleimani's Killing Will Unleash Chaos*." New York Times, January 3, 2020. https://www.nytimes.com/2020/01/03/opinion/qassim-suleima- ni-death.html?action=click&module=RelatedLinks&pgtype=Article&fbclid=I- wAR1c8gBwQVcET7F_zcrid3qRQkmLvVcwLW8BitAsnW6zPEqOtS_Po12F9Ts

236. Remnick, David. "The Sober Clarity of the Impeachment Witnesses." *New Yorker*, November 15, 2019.

237. Tomasky, Michael. *If We Can Keep It: How the Republic Collapsed and How It Might Be Saved* (New York: W.W.Norton & Company, 2019), p. xxvii.

Chapter 12: Fascist America or Sacred America?

238. *The Political and Social Doctrine of Fascism*, Jane Soames authorized translation (London: Hogarth Press, 1933), p. 14.

239. The Political and Social Doctrine of Fascism, Jane Soames authorized translation (London: Hogarth Press, 1933), p. 14.

240. https://metaxas-project.com/doube-axe-labrys-pelekys-metaxas-zeus-eon/

241. Albright, Madeline. *Fascism: A Warning* (New York: Harper Collins, 2018) p. 28.

242. Trump refers in a tweet to his great and unmatched wisdom. https://www.boston-globe.com/news/politics/2019/10/07/

243. Levitsky and Ziblatt, *How Democracies Die.* (New York: Crown Publishing, 2018), p. 98.

244. Levitsky and Ziblatt, *How Democracies Die.* Crown Publishing, New York, 2018), pp. 23–24.

245. Levitsky and Ziblatt, *How Democracies Die* (New Yor: Crown Publishing, 2018), pp. 23–24.

246. Regniers, Beatrice Schenk. *The Abraham Lincoln Joke Book* (New York: Scholastic Book Services, 1965), p. 30.

247. Arendt, Hannah. *The Origins of Totalitarianism* (New York: Harcourt Brace, 1973), p. 5.

248. Arendt, Hannah. *The Origins of Totalitarianism* (New York: Harcourt Brace, 1973), p. 4.

249. Kakutani, Michiko. *The Death of Truth: Notes on Falsehood in the Age of Trump* (New York: Tim Duggan Books (Division of Crown Publishing), 2019), p. 80.

250. Kakutani, Michiko. *The Death of Truth: Notes on Falsehood in the Age of Trump* (New York: Tim Duggan Books [Division of Crown Publishing], 2019) p. 96.

251. Saslow, Eli. *Rising Out of Hatred: The Awakening of a Former White Nationalist* (New York: Doubleday, 2018), p. 248.

252. Calamur, Krishnadev, "Short History of America First," *The Atlantic*, Jan 21, 217. https://www.theatlantic.com/politics/archive/2017/01/trump-america-first/514037/

253. Inspector General report: https://www.washingtonpost.com/context/read-the-inspector-general-s-report-on-the-trump-russia-investigation/f97e93ca-d5b4-4d8f-a37f-8b2cdfdcdc88/

Part IV: Return to Wholeness

254. *Biophilia Hypothesis.* Ed, Wilson, E. O. From Chapter 5: "Searching for the Lost Arrow: Physical and Spiritual Ecology in the Hunter's World" by Edward O. Wilson (Washington DC: Island Press), p. 225.

255. From Wendell Berry's endorsement statement for *The Dying of the Trees* (1997) by Charles E. Little.

256. Kinew, Wab. *The Reason You Walk* (Toronto: Penguin Canada, 2015), p. 288.

Chapter 13: Making America Sacred Again: First Steps

257. Bohm, David. *Wholeness and the Implicate Order*. Abington-on-Thames. Routledge Publishing. 2002.

258. https://www.cnn.com/2018/01/22/politics/susan-collins-bipartisan-talks-congress-shutdown-talking-stick/index.html.

259. Haselby, Sam. *The Origins of American Religious Nationalism* (Oxford: Oxford University Press, 2015).

260. There was also a decrease in funding for prosecution of white collar crime (the latter contributing to a rise in political corruption that should not be ignored).

261. According to Dave Zuckerman, a counter-terrorism expert, during the George W. Bush administration, Attorney General Gonzalez put out a memo warning of white supremacist infiltration of law enforcement around the country, but little was done to intercede.

262. Fitzpatrick, Kevin. "One Week After FBI Warnings About White Supremacist Terrorism, Mass Shootings Strike El Paso and Dayton," *Vanity Fair*, August 4, 2019.

263. Williamson, Marianne. *A Politics of Love* (New York: Harper One, 2019).

264. In fairness to the Democrats, the Affordable Care Act initially went through regular order. The bill was assigned to three House committees and two Senate committees; it was subject to over 50 hours of bi-partisan debate and considered over 100 amendments. The final passage, however, was done through the reconciliation process.

265. The Republicans also did not wait for a Congressional Budget Office (CBO) score to be done prior to voting, a highly unusual tactic.

266. Stenner, Karen. "Three Kinds of Conservatism," *Psychological Inquiry*, August 2019.

267. A good resource regarding the rise of green conservativism in Europe is Roger Scruton's *Green Philosophy: How to Think Seriously About the Planet*.

268. Scruton, Roger. *Green Philosophy: How to Think Seriously About the Planet*. London, Atlantic Books, 2013.

Chapter 14: The Dream of Mother Earth: A Turtle Island Renaissance

269. Bateson, Nora. *Small Arcs of Larger Circles*: Framing Through Other Patterns (Axminster, England: Triarchy Press), p. 137.

270. Buffy Saint Marie from the song "No No Keshagesh." Keshagesh means greed in Cree. It was the name of a puppy that would eat its own dinner and then want everyone else's.

271. The Sand Creek massacre occurred just 13 years after the Fort Laramie treaty of 1851, in which the Arapahoe and Cheyenne were granted ownership of the land all the way from the Arkansas River to the Nebraska border. But the gold rush changed all that, and the treaty, like many other treaties, was broken. Columbine did

not occur on that site, but it was the Sand Creek massacre that enabled the settlers to move in. Columbine then became a model of future school shootings. https://www.washingtonpost.com/education/2019/04/18/school-shootings-didnt -start-columbine-heres-why-that-disaster-became-blueprint-other-killers-created -columbine-generation/.

272. For a fuller explanation of how restorative justice is being used today in the US, see Molly Rowan Leach and her organization Restorative Justice on the Rise. https://restorativejusticeontherise.org.

273. Bateson, Nora. *Small Arcs of Larger Circles: Framing Through Other Patterns* (Axminster, England: Triarchy Press, 2016), p. 137.

274. Private communication.

275. For more information on the SEED Language of Spirit dialogues, see www.seednm.org or www.originalthinking.us.

Chapter 15:
Biophilia: Love of Life and Nature in the Face of Climate Change

276. Wilson, E. O. *Biophila: The Human Bond with Other Species* (Cambridge, MA: Harvard University Press, 1984) p. 16.

277. Snyder, Gary. "On Top." Available online: https://www.poetry-chaikhana.com/ blog/2010-11-08/gary-snyder-on-top/

278. Eisenstein, Charles. Climate: A New Story. Berkeley, Ca. North Atlantic, 2018, pp. 43–44.

279. Eisenstein, Charles. *Climate: A New Story* (Berkeley, CA: North Atlantic Books, 2018) p. 20.

280. When I say root causes, I mean this both metaphorically and literally, because healthy roots mitigate soil erosion, one of the chief causes of climate change.

281. This quote, or versions similar to it, is also sometimes attributed to Alanis Obamsawin, a Canadian film maker of Abenaki descent.

282. Snyder, Gary. *The Practice of the Wild* (Berkeley: Counterpoint, 1990), p. 109.

Chapter 16: From Politics to Love:
A Journey from Fragmentation to Wholeness

283. O'Dea, James. *Soul Awakening Practice: Prayer, Contemplation, and Action* (London: Watkins Publishing), 2017, p. 91.

284. Snyder, Gary. *Tomorrow's Song* in *Turtle Island* (New York: New Directions Publishing), p. 77.

285. Thompson, Frank Charles, Ed. The Holy Bible Genesis 1–2. B.B. Kirkbride Bible Co. Indianapolis, 1964. Matthew 7:7–8.

286. Cajete, Gregory. *Native Science: Natural Laws of Interdependence* (Santa Fe: Clear Light Publishers, 2000), p. 117.

287. This was something Dan Moonhawk Alford was fond of saying.

288. From an interview Panache Desai held with Kute Blackson at the 2019 Global Gathering. www.globalgathering2019.com I learned of this interview from Kennedy Braden, who is knowledgeable about Panache Desai's work.

289. Letter from a Birmingham Jail April 16, 1963. https://www.africa.upenn.edu/Articles _Gen/Letter_Birmingham.html

290. King, Dr. Martin Luther. *Strength to Love* (New York: Harper & Row, 1963). p. 37.

291. https://kinginstitute.stanford.edu/king-papers/documents/ive-been-mountain-top-address-delivered-bishop-charles-mason-temple

292. https://www.youtube.com/watch?v=GoKzCff8Zbs

293. Private conversation with Michael Two Bears Andrews, who worked closely with Marcellus Bearheart.

Index

About the Author

Photo by Kyle Zimmerman

GLENN APARICIO PARRY, PHD, of Basque, Aragon Spanish, and Jewish descent, is also the author of the Nautilus award-winning book, *Original Thinking: A Radical Revisioning of Time, Humanity, and Nature* (North Atlantic Books, 2015), and an educator, ecopsychologist, and political philosopher whose passion is to reform thinking and society into a coherent, cohesive, whole. The founder and past president of the SEED Institute, Parry is currently the director of a grass-roots think tank, the *Circle for Original Thinking*. He earned his BA in Psychology from Allegheny College and went on to earn both his MA in East-West Psychology and his PhD in Humanities with a concentration in Transformative Learning from the California Institute of Integral Studies.

Parry organized and participated in the groundbreaking Language of Spirit conferences from 1999–2011 that brought together Native and Western scientists in dialogue. He has appeared in several documentary films, including Journey to Turtle Island by Spanish film maker Miryam Servet and SEEDing Change: A Retrospective of the Language of Spirit

Dialogues, directed by Joyce Anastasia and produced by the Foundation for Global Humanity.

Parry is a member of the Institute of Noetic Sciences and the Theosophical Society as part of a life-long interest in bridging the arts and sciences. His first career was as a rock and roll booking agent in Woodstock, NY. He has lived in northern New Mexico since 1994.

The Circle for Original Thinking is an inclusive, grass-roots think tank. Our mission is to seek out the deep origins of contemporary thought in order to remember and restore heart-centered wisdom for humanity and all our relations on Earth. We accomplish our mission through intercultural dialogue circles, ceremonies, and conferences in partnership with like-minded organizations. We invite your participation and support. Membership is open to all.

For more information about
Dr. Parry and *Circle for Original Thinking*,
visit www.originalthinking.us or write to the author:

Glenn Aparicio Parry
Circle for Original Thinking
12231 Academy Rd NE Suite 307 Albuquerque, NM 87111

ABOUT ECOLOGY PRIME™ PUBLICATIONS

Ecology Prime™ is a pioneering global collaborative platform engaging students, teachers, consumers, and businesses worldwide in environmental studies and the day's ecological dynamics. Linking all cultures regardless of language, it provides an easy-to-access and-use multimedia, communications and social connectivity system that doubles as a source for publishing, eco-exploration, and personal wellness via a network of affiliated destinations around the world.

Ecology Prime™ Publishing was created in collaboration with SelectBooks and Waterside Productions.

http://ecologyprime.com